WORD MAGIC

The Powers and Occult Definitions of Words

Second Edition

By: Pao Chang

Esoteric Knowledge Publishing
2019

This book is dedicated to the living men and women who are not afraid to stand up for their natural rights and speak the truth.

Disclaimer

The author has made every effort to ensure the accuracy of the materials herein. Please take notice that the materials herein have no warranty, either expressed or implied, and are intended for informational and educational purposes only. Please take further notice that the materials herein are not intended as a substitute for legal advice. The materials herein are offered to readers as a group of ideas or concepts with the intention to motivate readers to explore reality and words beyond conventional thinking. The author accepts no responsibility for any and all injuries and damages that arise from using the materials herein.

Table of Contents

Introduction

Words are used by people to communicate every day, yet most people still do not realize how words shape their lives and perception. Did you know that most people speak over 7,000 words per day? As of May 2016, there are about 7.4 billion people living on Earth. If you multiply 7,000 words by 7.4 billion people, you get 51,800,000,000,000 or 51.8 trillion words. This means that at least 51.8 trillion words are spoken every day. Even though people hear and speak words all the time, most of them have little or no clue as to how powerful words are. Words are not just elements of speech or writing because when words are spoken aloud they transform into sound, frequency, and vibration. Words also carry information which plays an important role in communication. Without information we will have a hard time learning things and communicating to one another. Because words carry information, sound, frequency, and vibration, they play a very important role in our lives. Furthermore, they can be used to harness the power of energy.

As mankind, we did not always rely heavily on words to communicate because we used to have a strong telepathic bond with one another. Due to certain tragic events in our past that caused the higher elements of our DNA to, in a sense, mutate and turn off, many words were introduced by the Dark Forces as hypnotic symbols to manipulate and control our minds. One of the sources of the Dark Forces' malevolent behaviors is a cosmic "virus". This virus is not your common virus because it is very intelligent. The main goal of the cosmic virus is to infect all living things in the universe with its selfish and destructive thoughts. Many people's minds are infected with the selfish and destructive thoughts of the cosmic virus, especially people who have strong psychopathic traits. Like any virus, the goal of the cosmic virus is to drain its host of energy until it dies, and therefore its mission is to cause death and destruction throughout the universe. The good news is that this virus can only infect us when we live in a state of ignorance, fear, hatred, and irresponsibility. As we learn to peaceably live with one another and heal our bodies and activate the higher elements of our DNA, our frequency will increase beyond the limit of the cosmic virus, making us immune to it.

Today, many scientists like to refer to the higher elements of our DNA as "junk" DNA because they believe these elements have no function. There is nothing "junk" about the higher elements of our DNA because Nature would never create something that has no role to play in the progression of the universe. Our so-called junk DNA contains the higher and more powerful elements of our DNA. Because of this, it holds some of the keys to unlocking memories of our true history and activating our dormant spiritual powers (e.g., telepathy).

The reason that our junk DNA or dormant DNA does not seem to function is because the frequencies of our bodies are not vibrating in harmony with it, causing it to "turn off". In our current physical condition, turning on all the higher elements of our DNA at the same time would destroy our health. The current state of our bodies cannot handle the high frequency energy that travels through the higher elements of our DNA. To safely activate our dormant DNA without damaging our bodies, we need to slowly increase the frequencies of our bodies to the point where they harmonize with the frequencies of our dormant DNA. Once this happens, our dormant DNA and bodies will communicate and function properly. Because the higher elements of our DNA are, in a sense, turned off, our spiritual powers and higher senses are weakened, making it easier for the Dark Forces to use words to deceive us. All the languages of mankind have been distorted by the Dark Forces, allowing them to use many words as magic spells to manipulate us. However, they can only manipulate us when we do not know how to use words wisely.

When you study the origin and history of words and languages, and investigate their connection to certain secret societies, you should eventually realize that all languages are interconnected on a very deep level. Furthermore, you should eventually know that the secrets of the universe and the true history of mankind are hidden in words. By the end of this book, you will know why all languages of mankind are interconnected and how to decipher words to find their hidden definitions and spiritual meanings, giving you the knowledge to use words to create your reality and manifest heaven on earth. By learning how to decipher words to find their spiritual meanings, you also enhance your ability to innerstand the knowledge of God, making it easier for you to achieve spiritual freedom and eternal life.

Chapter 1
The Power of Words and the Art of Word Magic

Many spiritual teachings have taught mankind that the world is made up of space (expansiveness and infinity), air (mobility), fire (temperature), water (fluidity), and earth (solidity).[1] These five elements are not based on physical qualities but spiritual qualities. Besides these five qualities of spiritual energy, the world is also made of words because we live in a world that relies heavily on words to communicate. When words are spoken aloud, they transform into sound, frequency, and vibration which are some of the fundamental building blocks of matter. The physical world we live in is made of matter; therefore, it is also made of sound, frequency, and vibration. On a deeper level, the material world was brought into existence using the power of spoken words. A spoken word has sound, frequency, and vibration, giving it the power to affect how energy manifests itself into physicality. Hence, the biblical saying, "In the beginning was the Word".

Phonetically, the term **world** sounds similar to the term **whirled** which is the past tense of the term **whirl**, meaning "to turn around, **spin**, or rotate rapidly" (bold emphasis added).[2] Before you were born, you were whirled into existence. The evidence of this is the fact that your physical body is made of atoms. What do atoms do? They **spin**, vibrate, and rotate very rapidly. This may be why the movie *The Matrix* has a character named Neo. In Latin, the word *neo* means "produce by spinning, **spin**, weave" (bold emphasis added).[3] [4] The term "world" also sounds similar to the term "word" and the term "word" sounds similar to the term "whir". One of the origins of the

1

term **whir** is the Old Norse word ***hvirfla***, meaning "to turn".[5] In English, the term **whir** is defined as "to go, fly, revolve, or otherwise move quickly with a humming or buzzing sound".[6] The definitions of the boldface words in this paragraph are all related to the word **spin**. Why the word spin? Because everything in the universe spins to some degree and we live in a galaxy that spins. The world ("whirled") also spins to a certain degree and the people living on it use spoken **words** to create their **worlds** and realities.

The language system, which is a system that uses symbols, signs, and sounds to convey thoughts and emotions, is made of words because words have magic powers and are great for enlightening, disempowering, or deceiving you. One of the reasons that words can easily deceive you is that they can be misinterpreted and misunderstood. Furthermore, each letter of a word can be rearranged to hide the word's deeper meaning. In addition, a word can be given many different definitions to confuse you. Words with many different definitions are often used by judges and attorneys to trick you to temporarily surrender your natural rights which are your God-given rights. This is why it is important that you learn how to decipher words and really pay attention to their definitions.

To innerstand why words have the power to deceive you, you need to know one of the occult definitions of the word language. Keep in mind that one of the origins of the word **language** is the Latin word ***lingua***, meaning "tongue".[7] To find one of the occult definitions of language, you need to separate the word language into three words and study the definitions of these three words, so you know what they mean on a deeper level. When you separate the word language into three different words, it transforms into "lan", "gu", and "age".

Language = Lan / Gu / Age

"Lan" is the feminine Chinese and Vietnamese name for "orchid." The Vietnamese "lân" changes this to the masculine context meaning "unicorn" coming from "Kỳ lân." When "Kỳ lân" is translated from Vietnamese to Latin, we get the word "unicornis." The Kỳ lân was a dragon type creature that was said to only protect the noble ones. It was also known as the "Qulin."

"Gu" is the god of war in the Dahomey mythology. So now we have "Lan," a monster that protects the noble ones and

"Gu," the god of war. "Age" is the "age" or "ages" of the zodiac. Hence, Lan / Gu / Ages are the "monsters of war that protect the noble ones or "golden gods" (Au-dio) throughout the ages."[8]

The language system is an effective tool to help us communicate with one another. However, because of our ignorance of the power of words, the Dark Forces (false **gods**) have used it against us to wage **war** on mankind for many **ages**. They have used the language/lan-gu-age system to divide mankind and prevent us from communicating to people who speak a different language. This made it easier for the minions of the Dark Forces to engineer wars between nations, thereby tricking us to fight one another which in turn prevents us from making the real perpetrators liable and responsible for their crimes against mankind. The Dark Forces are obsessed with wars for the reason that wars cause a lot of death and destruction, thereby generating a large quantity of fear which is a negative energy that the Dark Forces like to consume. On a deeper level, wars are sacrificial rituals for generating negative energy and preventing us from increasing our frequency beyond certain levels, making it harder for us to ascend to higher states of consciousness.

In the English language, many words are carefully designed and put together in a way that allows them to be used to cast spells. The Dark Magicians are well aware of this which is why they like to use the English language to trick us to play their con game to enslave mankind. English is the language that the Dark Forces want to use to control the world. One of the reasons for this is that many English words are great for creating deceptive contracts. In addition, English has become the global language of business. The good news is that there are many powerful words in the English language. When we learn how to use these words wisely, we can stop the Dark Forces from diminishing our freedom and sovereignty. By the end of this book, you will learn many empowering words that you can use to restore and protect your freedom and sovereignty.

The Secret Power of the English Language

To innerstand how powerful the English language is, one of the first things that you need to do is study the etymology of English. The word English is a very interesting word to investigate because hidden inside

3

it are many secrets of the universe. When you decipher the word English deeply enough, you will eventually know that the people who created the English language were inspired by God. To find evidence of this, you need to use certain dictionaries, the Bible, and the art of word magic to help you decipher the word English. According to EtymOnline.com. the word **English** etymologically means:

> "the people of England; the speech of England," noun use of Old English adjective *Englisc* (contrasted to *Denisc, Frencisce*, etc.), "of or pertaining to the **Angles**," from *Engle* (plural) "the **Angles**," the name of one of the Germanic groups that overran the island 5c., supposedly so-called because *Angul*, the land they inhabited on the Jutland coast, was shaped like a fish hook (see angle (n.)). The use of the word in Middle English was reinforced by Anglo-French *Engleis*. Cognates: Dutch *Engelsch*, German *Englisch*, Danish *Engelsk*, French *Anglais* (Old French *Engelsche*), Spanish *Inglés*, Italian *Inglese*. [Bold emphasis added][9]

The word **English** is defined by Dictionary.com using these exact words: "the people of England collectively, especially as distinguished from the Scots, Welsh, and Irish."[10] The same online dictionary also defines it as: "the Germanic language of the British Isles, widespread and standard also in the U.S. and most of the British Commonwealth, historically termed Old English (c450–c1150), Middle English (c1150–c1475), and Modern English (after c1475)."[11]

In the definition of the word English from EtymOnline.com, it shows that the word **English** comes from Old English *Englisc*, meaning "of or pertaining to the **Angles**" and *Engle*, meaning "the **Angles**" (bold emphasis added). The **Angles** were "one of the main Germanic peoples who settled in Great Britain in the post-Roman period. They founded several of the kingdoms of Anglo-Saxon England, and their name is the root of the name England."[12] The Angles were said to speak the language **Angleish**. Today, this language is known as **English**. Keep in mind that the words **Angle**ish and **Angle**s both have the word **angle** attached to them. In geometry, the word **angle** means "the space within two lines or three or more planes diverging from a common point, or within two planes diverging from a common line."[13] It is important to know that the word **angle** is an anagram for the word **angel** which means, "one of a class of spiritual beings; a celestial attendant of God. In medieval angelology, angels constituted the lowest of the nine celestial orders (seraphim, cherubim, thrones, dominations or dominions, virtues, powers, principalities or princedoms, archangels, and angels)."[14]

At the surface, the words angle and angel seem to have no connection except that they are made up of the same five letters. However, when you investigate and decipher them deeply enough, you will see that they have a strong connection to each other. One of their connections can be found when you use the art of anagram to switch the letters "e" and "l" in the word ang**el**, transforming it into the word **angle**, meaning "the amount of rotation needed to bring one line or plane into coincidence with another, generally measured in **radians** or in degrees, minutes, and seconds, as in 12° 10prime; 30″, which is read as 12 degrees, 10 minutes, and 30 seconds" (bold emphasis added).[15] The word **radian** means "a unit of plane angular measurement that is equal to the **angle** at the center of a **circle** subtended by an **arc** whose length equals the radius or approximately 57.3 degrees" (bold emphasis added).[16]

One of the words in the previous paragraph that is important for helping you find the connection between the words "angle" and "angel" is "radian". This word has a strong connection to the word **radiant** which means "a point or object from which rays proceed."[17] Etymologically, the words **radian** and **radiant** are related to the word **radius**. This word is derived from the Latin word *radius*, meaning "staff, stake, rod; spoke of a wheel; **ray of light**, beam of light; radius of a circle" (bold emphasis added).[18] Therefore, the words angel, angle, radian, radiant, and radius are all related to a significant degree. To find more evidence that the words angel and angle are related to a significant degree, you need to study how **radiant** light **radiates** from the Sun (**circle**-like object) and how the Earth's atmosphere affects the trajectory of light. According to Merriam-Webster.com, the word **radiant** means "radiating rays or reflecting beams of light".[19] Keep in mind that the words **radiant** and **radiate** have a strong connection to the word **radian** and the term **ray of light**. Also, keep in mind that an **angel** is often depicted as a **light** being.

When light travels from the Sun to Earth, it has to travel through the Earth's atmosphere before it reaches the surface of the Earth. As light travels through the atmosphere, it **refracts** which is defined as "(of water, air, or glass) make (a **ray of light**) change direction when it enters at an **angle**" (bold emphasis added).[20] This process, which is

5

known as atmospheric refraction, causes light rays to **bend** and change direction. In other words, it causes light rays to **angle** (verb), meaning "to move or **bend** in an **angle**" (bold emphasis added).[21] It is important to know that the words **ang**le and **ang**el both have the prefix **ang-** which etymologically means "to bend".[22]

Based on the information and definitions in the previous few pages, the word "English" has a strong connection to the word "**Angle**ish" which can be anagrammatically written as "**Angel**ish". Is this evidence that English/Angleish is the language of angels? An angel (**angle** of light) is said to be a messenger of God. English is a language that is useful for conveying messages in many different **angles**. The word **angle** can mean "a viewpoint"[23] and is related to the word **perspective**. English, like many languages of mankind, often has many words to describe and define a thing, allowing us to understand it from different viewpoints/perspectives/angles.

The English alphabet that makes up the English language is derived from the Latin alphabet. What most people do not know about the Latin alphabet is that it was created using sacred geometry, sacred numbers, lines, **arcs**, and **angles**. The word **geometry** means "the branch of mathematics that deals with the deduction of the properties, measurement, and relationships of points, lines, **angles**, and figures in space from their defining conditions by means of certain assumed properties of space" (bold emphasis added).[24] In this paragraph, an important word to decipher is **alphabet**; this word comes from the combination of the Greek letters A/α (*alpha*), meaning "the first letter of the Greek alphabet (A, α)" or "the first; beginning";[25] and B/β (*beta*), meaning "the second letter of the Greek alphabet (β, B)".[26] It is interesting to know that in astronomy the word **alpha** means, "used to designate the brightest star in a constellation";[27] as for the word **beta**, it means "a star that is usually the second brightest of a constellation".[28]

The Greek letters *alpha* and *beta* are derived from the Hebrew letters א (*aleph*), which means "ox" or "bull", and ב (*beth*), meaning "house". According to the book *Mysteries of the Alphabet* by Marc-Alain Ouaknin, the Hebrew letter *aleph* means "strength" or "man", and the Hebrew letter *beth* means "house" and is a "metaphor for the womb".[29] The letter *aleph* is strongly associated with the words father, man, and **male**; and the letter *beth* is strongly associated with the words mother, woman, and **female**. Keep in mind that the English letters **A/a** and **B/b** are also derived from the Hebrew letters *aleph* and *beth* respectively. This is why the English letter "B", which is derived from the Hebrew letter "*beth*" (meaning "house" and "womb"), looks like two breasts (B). Did you notice that the initial letter of the word "breasts" is "b"?

On a deeper spiritual level, the letters of the alphabet contain important information about a polaric and divine story. This sacred story is about the Divine Masculine Energy and the Divine Feminine Energy and their journey to achieve balance and harmony. Hidden in the words, letters, and symbols of this divine story are the secrets of the universe and the records of mankind's true history. This divine story is strongly connected to the Alpha and the Omega, meaning "the Beginning and the End". In the Greek alphabet, **Alpha** is written as the letter **A** which is the **beginning** or the **first** letter; and **Omega** is written as the letter **Ω** which is the **end** or the **last** letter. Keep in mind that the New Testament of the Bible was originally written using the Greek alphabet.

> "I am the Alpha and the Omega, the Beginning and the End," says the Lord, "who is and who was and who is to come, the Almighty." (Revelation 1:8, NKJV)

> And He said to me, "It is done! I am the Alpha and the Omega, the Beginning and the End. I will give of the fountain of the water of life freely to him who thirsts. He who overcomes shall inherit all things, and I will be his God and he shall be My son. (Revelation 21:6-7, NKJV)

> "And behold, I am coming quickly, and My reward is with Me, to give to every one according to his work. I am the Alpha and the Omega, the Beginning and the End, the First and the Last." (Revelation 22:12-13, NKJV)

Let us turn our attention back to the word angel. Throughout history, angels are often depicted as beings of **light**. An important fact about light is that it has electromagnetic waves which are waves that express the characteristics of the Divine Masculine Energy and the Divine Feminine Energy. The evidence of this can be seen when the word "electromagnetic" is separated into two words, transforming it into the prefix "electro-" and the word "magnetic". The prefix **electro-** is a word-forming element that etymologically means "electrical, electricity".[30] As for the word **magnetic**, it etymologically and literally means "having the properties of a magnet".[31] **Electricity** represents power and the **Divine Masculine Energy**, and **magnetism** represents the **Divine Feminine Energy**. Electricity and magnetism are, in a way, opposites; however, one cannot exist without the other.

The letters of the alphabet were created to express the infinite expression of the Divine Masculine Energy and the Divine Feminine Energy, allowing polaric ideas, such as positive and negative, male and female, order and chaos, good and evil, etc., to manifest in the material world. This is one of the reasons that letters are grouped into the word alphabet/alpha-beta (**alpha** represents the **masculine** principle and **beta** represents the **feminine** principle), the system of sacred symbols that is used by man to manifest worlds through the power of positive and negative words. Hidden in the alphabet is the secret knowledge of the archangels.

The word **archangel** etymologically means "an angel of the highest order" and is derived from the Greek word *arkhangelos*, meaning "chief angel".[32] *Arkhangelos* is made up of the Greek prefix *arkh-* and the Greek word *angelos*. The Greek word *arkhon*, which means "ruler, commander, chief, captain",[33] is strongly connected to the Greek prefix *arkh-*, meaning "chief, first".[34] When the Greek word *arkhon* is converted into English, it transforms into the English word **archon**. In Gnosticism, an **archon** is "any of a number of world-governing powers that were created with the material world by a subordinate deity called the Demiurge (Creator)."[35] The word "archon" is made up of two words which are "arch" and "on". The word **on** has a strong connection to **power** and **light**. The word archangel also has a strong connection to power and light. Based on the information and definitions in this paragraph, archangels are the modern day versions of archons.

The words **arch**angel and **arch**on both have the word **arc** attached to them. The word **arc** means "any unbroken part of the circumference of a circle or other curved line."[36] It can also mean "the apparent path described above and below the horizon by a celestial body (such as the sun)".[37] The word **arc** comes from the Latin word *arcus*, meaning "a bow, **arch**" (bold emphasis added).[38] These definitions connect the word arc to the words arch, angel, angle, Angleish, and English. In other words, the definitions in the previous few pages show strong evidence that English is one of the languages of angels (angles of light). Remember, the words **ang**el and **ang**le both have the prefix **ang-** which etymologically means "to bend". To create an **arc** from a line you need to **bend** it in many angles; to create an

8

arc from a ray of light you also need to **bend** it in many angles.

An important word in the previous paragraph that is beneficial for you to know its deeper meaning is arch. It is important to know that the word arch can be a noun, verb, adjective, prefix, and suffix. As a suffix, -arch is attached to certain words, such as monarch, oligarch, hierarch, and patriarch. As a prefix, arch- is attached to many words, such as archbishop, archaeology, archetype, architecture, and archangel. The prefix **arch-** is derived from Greek **arkhi-**, meaning "first, chief, primeval".[39] This prefix is similar in meaning to the Greek word **arche** which means "beginning", "origin", or "first cause".[40]

Now in Greek, 'arche' is written with the letters alpha, rho, chi and eta, or as 'ἀρχή'.[4] And this Greek word 'arche' can, just as the English 'arch', be phonetically boiled down to the sound 'rk', which in Greek capitals would be written as 'PX'. 'Arche', the beginning and origin, brought back to its essence, is written as 'PX'. This is of great importance. For when these two letters are combined in one monogram then the well known Christian symbol ☧ results. For Christians this symbol stands not so much for 'arche', but for Christ. In that case the monogram is read as 'XP'. These letters correspond to the basic sound in 'Christ', namely 'kr'. So it is in this so called 'chi-rho' monogram that a relation occurs between 'arche' and 'Christ'.[5] Arche is Christ. But who is Christ? In esoteric thought is the term 'Christ' not so much used to refer to the person Jesus of Nazareth, but more primarily to a principle; the 'Christ principle'. This principle is considered to occur when spirit relates to matter, and is held to be the same as the soul principle. As such is it the intermediating factor between the aforementioned poles (as Jesus Christ is considered to be the intermediating factor between man and God).[6]

So far this chi-rho symbol has been considered grammatically, but it can also be looked upon in a geometrical way. The symbol represents a sound, but in being representative does it have a distinctive shape and form. Now the basic features of the symbol are a more or less oval shape on top and a cross at its base. This considering it may dawn that as a geometrical symbol it has not so much been introduced by the Greeks on base of their grammatical script signs, but that it is derived from the older Egyptian [ankh] symbol. For the meaning of this Egyptian 'ankh', as the symbol is called, is remarkably similar to the chi-rho symbol of the Christians. The meanings attached to the ankh symbol are namely 'life' and 'soul'.[7] In these meanings can clearly Christ be recognized. After all did Jesus Christ himself proclaim to be the life.[8] But the relation of Christ with the ankh goes obviously further, for all will recognize the Christian cross in the ankh. The crucifixion of the son of God on the cross brings forth the Christ, just as the entering of spirit into matter brings forth the Christ or soul principle.[9] The ankh as Christ and as arche is the beginning and the origin, because it is only through the relation of spirit and matter that anything comes to being.[10] Through the union of father-spirit and mother-matter, Christ (being the son and the soul) is the firstborn.[11] And being the firstborn from whence everything else originates, may in this way Christ be well considered to be the origin of all things.[41]

The union of Father (Spirit) and Mother (Matter) bore Christ, the Son of God. This divine story is recorded in the English alphabet. Keep in mind that the English alphabet is derived from the Latin alphabet. To find this divine story in the English alphabet, we need to turn our attention to the number 12. The twelfth (12th) letter of the English/Angleish/Angelish alphabet is L/l. Phonetically, L/l is **El**, the Hebrew word for **God**. According to many religious, esoteric, and occult teachings, **God** is **Light**! L/l is the initial letter of the word light, connecting it to the word angel. An angel is often depicted as a being of **light**. Did you notice that the word ang**el** has the Hebrew word **el** attached to it?

The number 12 is made up of the numbers 1 and 2. In the English alphabet, the first (1st) letter is A/a and the second (2nd) letter is B/b. When these two English letters are translated into Greek, A/a transforms into A/α (*alpha*) and B/b transforms into B/β (*beta*). Remember, the Greek letters **alpha** and **beta** are derived from the Hebrew letters א (*aleph*) and ב (*beth*) respectively. The letters *alpha* and *aleph* are strongly associated with the words father, man, and male. As for the letters *beta* and *beth*, they are strongly associated with the words mother, woman, and female. In other words, the letter *alpha* represents the **masculine principle** and the letter *beta* represents the **feminine principle**. Together, they transform into the Greek word "alphabeta" which is written in English as "alphabet". The English/Angleish/Angelish alphabet/alphabeta is a writing system made up of sacred letters. In certain esoteric and occult teachings, these sacred letters are known as gods.

Another letter that is important for helping us see the divine story of the birth of Christ in the English alphabet is C/c. This letter is the third (3rd) letter of the English alphabet and is the product of 1 + 2 or the product of the union of A/a (masculine principle) and B/b (feminine principle). The letter C/c is born from the **womb** which is represented by the letter **B/b**. Remember, the letter **B/b** is derived from the Hebrew letter *beth* which means "house" and is a "metaphor for the **womb**" (bold emphasis added).[42] Therefore, the letter C/c is the product, child, or son of the letters A/a and B/b. The word **c**hild even has the letter "c" as its first letter. The word **C**hrist also has the letter "C" as its first letter. A/1/Father + B/2/Mother + C/3/Son = the **Holy Trinity**, meaning "the Father, the Son, and the Holy Spirit existing as one God."[43] Keep in mind that the letter C/c is called *gimmel* in Hebrew and Phoenician.

> After the primal strength (the *aleph*) and the place made for it (the *beth*), this strength must be given the possibility of expressing itself, going out, deploying itself, going beyond itself, opening up to the outside, crossing the expanses of the desert in order to discover new lands, leaving the autarky of the house, breaking the ties of the family home, the womb, finding one's own way.... This important plan may be put into action through the third letter of the alphabet, the *gimmel*.[44]

Based on the information and definitions in the previous few pages, the letter C/c esoterically represents Christ. According to the Bible, Christ was born in Bethlehem. The word **Bethlehem** is made up of two Hebrew words which are *beth* and *lehem*, meaning "house" and "bread" respectively.[45] [46] Therefore, the word **Bethlehem** means "house of bread". The **house** of bread esoterically represents the **womb** that nourishes Jesus before he becomes the Christ, and the **bread** represents **Jesus**. Hence, the Bible verse John 6:51 (KJV):

I am the living bread which came down from heaven: if

any man eat of this bread, he shall live for ever: and the bread that I will give is my flesh, which I will give for the life of the world.

The information in this subchapter shows the connection between the words arc, arch, angle, angel, archangel, light, alphabet, English, and Christ. In certain esoteric teachings, Christ or Jesus Christ is used to represent the soul principle. The word "soul" is phonetically "sol". In Latin, **sol** means "the sun".[47] The word "sun" is phonetically "son". This is one of the reasons that Jesus is sometimes called the "Son of God" which is phonetically "Sun of God". The word **son** etymologically means "descendant";[48] therefore, the "Son of God" can be translated as the "Descendant of God". The word descendant can be separated into the word "descend" and the suffix "-ant". The word **descend** comes from the Latin word **descendere**, meaning "come down, descend, sink".[49] Jesus Christ is the Descendant of God; hence, the Bible verse John 6:41 (NKJV), "... I am the bread which came down from heaven." As for the suffix **-ant**, it generally means "characterized by or serving in the capacity of".[50] Keep in mind that a descendant can be a man or a woman.

The Power of Words

To have a deeper innerstanding of how powerful words are, we need to investigate the term word so we know what it means on an esoteric and spiritual level. Before we explore its esoteric and spiritual meaning, it is important that we study its common definitions and investigate other words related to it. One of the definitions of the term **word** is, "A sound or a combination of sounds, or its representation in writing or printing, that symbolizes and communicates a meaning and may consist of a single morpheme or of a combination of morphemes."[51] The term **word** also means, "A single distinct meaningful element of speech or writing, used with others (or sometimes alone) to form a sentence and typically shown with a space on either side when written or printed."[52] In simple terms, a word is a sound or a symbol that conveys information. Keep in mind that when the "w" in the term "word" is capitalized, it is sometimes used to represent Jesus.

In the beginning was the Word, and the Word was with

God, and the Word was God. He was in the beginning with God. All things were made through Him, and without Him nothing was made that was made. In Him was life, and the life was the light of men. (John 1:1-4, NKJV)

The Word was in the beginning because the **Word** was the **Spiritual Seed**, the Source of Life. To find evidence that "words" are "seeds", we need to turn our attention to the Bible verse Luke 8:11 (NKJV): "Now the parable is this: The seed is the word of God." A **seed** (word) is the **nucleus** of a thing and therefore is the **beginning** or source of that thing. Hence the biblical saying, "In the beginning was the Word". Within the Word (Spiritual Seed) is the source of vibration. In physics, the word **vibration** means, "An oscillation of the parts of a fluid or an elastic solid whose equilibrium has been disturbed or of an electromagnetic wave."[53] Vibration allows the creation of sacred geometry, one of the foundations of the universe. It also allows the creation of movement or **action**. Therefore, "vibration" can be written as "verbration".

The word **verb** in "**verb**ration" (vibration) comes from the Latin word ***verbum*** which means "word" in English.[54] **Verb** is defined as, "any member of a class of words that function as the main elements of predicates, that typically **express action**, state, or a relation between two things, and that may be inflected for tense, aspect, voice, mood, and to show agreement with their subject or object" (bold emphasis added).[55] It is important to remember that **verbs** express **actions**. All actions require **verb**ration/vibration and therefore without verbration/vibration there are no actions. The power of verbration/vibration allows the creation of motion and light. "Then God said, "Let there be light"; and there was light" (Genesis 1:3, NKJV). **Light** is also known as **photon** which is defined as "a quantum of electromagnetic radiation, usually considered as an elementary particle that is its own antiparticle and that has zero rest mass and charge and a spin of one."[56] In physics, a photon is usually indicated by the symbol γ (*gamma*). The uppercase of γ (*gamma*) is this Greek symbol Γ.

The Greek symbol ***gamma*** has a strong connection to the English word **grammar**. *Gamma* (the third letter of the Greek alphabet) is derived from the Phoenician letter *gimel* (*gimmel*). This letter *gimel* is the origin of the English letters C/c and G/g. Keep in mind that the first letter of the English word **g**rammar is G/g. The letter G is also the first letter of the word **G**od. In Freemasonry, the letter G stands for God; however, it also stands for geometry.[57] Many esoteric, occult, and religious teachings have said that God is Light. Remember, **light** is also known as **photon** and the symbol for photon is γ (*gamma*). This Greek symbol (*gamma*) is one of the origins of the English letter G/g, the initial letter of the word God.

> The Pythagoreans reverenced numbers as sacred; geometry was to them the sacred science. It initial letter, Gamma, a square, was especially revered. The Gamma looks like a square used by builders; it was the symbol of the actual, four-sided, or geometrical square, the first whole number square, and therefore, the representative of deity, the four-letter word, the tetragrammaton. Symbols are easily converted the one into the other and back again. If the Gamma, which appeared like a workman's square, was a symbol of the geometrical square, which in turn was a symbol of Deity, then, by a simple reconversion looked like Gamma, which in one position looked like the square of the workman, soon came to symbolize the tetragrammaton or four-letter word.[58]

A term that has a strong connection to the word **photon** is **gamma ray** which is defined as, "a **photon** of penetrating electromagnetic radiation (gamma radiation) emitted from an atomic nucleus" (bold emphasis added).[59] Because the definition of the term "gamma ray" has the clause "a photon of penetrating electromagnetic radiation", it shows evidence that there is a connection between the term **gamma ray** and the Greek letter γ (*gamma*), the symbol for **photon**. It is important to know that all the boldface words in this paragraph and the previous few paragraphs are directly or indirectly connected to the English word **grammar** which means, "the study of the way the sentences of a language are constructed; morphology and syntax."[60] In simple terms, grammar is the study of how words are put together in order to make sentences to express thought. Keep the information in this paragraph in mind as you read the rest of this chapter.

What Is Word Magic?

In the occult world, certain words are used along with rituals and sacred geometries to direct and control energy to create certain desired effects. This process of using words, rituals, and sacred geometries to control and direct energy is known as magic or magick. Keep in mind that I am not talking about the magic tricks you see on television or magic shows. However, many magic tricks do use real magic. Most people will laugh at the idea of magic being real; but if they knew what magic really is and how magic is used to control them, they would not be laughing. The world is dominated by magic, which is why **governments**, **banks**, and **religious institutions** are some of the biggest practitioners of magic spells. Until you train your eyes to see how magic is used to control you, you will never know how the world really works.

The Controllers who pull the strings of many politicians are well aware of how magic works. Many of them practice the art of magic, which is why they are sometimes referred to as the Dark Magicians. The problem is that they like to use magic for power and evil purposes, instead of using it to unite mankind and change the world for the better. It is important to know that one of the most powerful things in the universe is energy. When you learn how to control and direct energy, you can become one of the most powerful people on Earth. The unlimited power of energy is the reason that the Dark Magicians are so obsessed with the process of controlling energy. The key to controlling energy is magic which is the art of using sacred sound, sacred geometry, and natural forces to direct and control energy to produce certain desired effects.

The word magic is derived from Old French *magique*, Latin *magicus*, and Greek *magikos*. One of the earliest definitions of **magic** is "art of influencing or predicting events and producing marvels using hidden natural forces".[61] Today, the word **magic** means "the art of producing a desired effect or result through the use of incantation or various other techniques that presumably assure human control of supernatural agencies or the forces of nature."[62] Magic has a strong connection to magnetic energy and electrical energy. Did you notice that the word **magnetic** has the word **magic** in it? When you take out "net" in the word "mag**net**ic", you are left with the word "magic". The art of magic is often practiced along with certain words and sacred geometries. The words that are often used in magic rituals are the words that produce powerful sound tones when spoken aloud. These sound tones have powerful vibrational patterns that can be used to direct and control energy, and harness its power. Sound is able to direct energy for the reason that it carries frequency patterns that attract energy to flow in a controllable manner. Furthermore, sound is one of the natural forces that is used by Nature to create crystalline structures and sacred geometries which are some of the building blocks of matter. If you want to know and see how sound controls and directs energy to produce sacred geometries, study cymatics and watch these two fascinating short videos on YouTube titled *Cymatics: Sacred Geometry Formed by Sound* and *Cymatics: Science Vs. Music*.

Because you now know what magic is, let us turn our attention to what words are so you can learn what the term "word magic" means. A **word** is defined in the previous subchapter "The Power of Words" as, "A sound or a combination of sounds, or its representation in writing or printing, that symbolizes and communicates a meaning and may consist of a single morpheme or of a combination of morphemes."[63] When you put the terms "word" and "magic" together, you get the term **word magic** which means "the communication art of using sacred sounds and symbols, and hidden forces to direct and control energy to produce certain desired effects or marvels." All words have magic properties. However, certain words have more magic properties for the reason that they carry more energy and intention. This is why during magic rituals certain specific words are used. Word magic can be used for good or evil purposes. The bad news is that the Dark Forces and their minions have a strong control over the language system of Earth and therefore are able to effectively use word magic to control us. The good news is that when we figure out how word magic works and become **aware** of how it is being used to control us, the magic power of words cannot affect us as much.

Why Words Are More Powerful Than Swords

Words are powerful because they carry energy, sound, and frequency which are some of the building blocks of matter. In addition, they carry information that can be used as knowledge to create or destroy things. When this knowledge is experienced into wisdom, it becomes very powerful and can be used to expand and strengthen a man's consciousness and spiritual power. This is why applied knowledge is power! Did you notice that the term **words** is an anagram for the term **sword**? Move the letter "s" in the term "words" to the left of the "w" and you get the term "sword". Words are like swords because they can be used to harm and "cut" you. In a way, words are more powerful than swords because they can harm or heal you at the deepest levels of your being.

To spiritually innerstand why words are more powerful than swords, we need to further decipher the Bible verse John 1:1. In John 1:1 of the King James Bible, it says, "In the beginning was the Word, and the Word was with God, and the Word was God." Esoterically, this verse is talking about the laws, principles, forces, and knowledge of the universe which can be expressed through **words** to create **worlds**. A very important information about the King James Bible and other versions of the Bible is that many of their verses are written in **allegories**. Because of this, if you believe that the verses only have literal meanings, you prevent yourself from acquiring the empowering knowledge hidden in the allegories. Furthermore, all versions of the Bible contain esoteric and exoteric knowledge. The esoteric knowledge of the Bible often has the most empowering spiritual knowledge. Another important information about the King James Bible is that its New Testament was translated from Greek to English. Therefore, the biblical saying "In the beginning was the Word" is referring to the **Source** that manifested the universe. Do you need evidence of this? Read further and I will show you the evidence.

The English term **word** can mean a few different things, but when it is translated to Greek it means "logos". The word **logos** is defined as, "the **source** that controls the universe, the written word or inspiration of God, or a logic and rational argument" (bold emphasis added).[64] In ancient Greek philosophy, the word **logos** means "... the controlling principle in the universe".[65] The Greek word for logos is λόγος. Many people pronounce it as "low goes"; however, many linguists pronounce it as "lah gahs" or "law gahs". According to NewWorldEncyclopedia.org, **logos** "is often translated into English as "Word," but can also mean thought, speech, meaning, reason, proportions, principle, standard, or logic, among other things. In religious contexts, it can indicate the divine Word, wisdom, or truth."[66] Britannica.com defines **logos** as, "... the divine reason implicit in the cosmos, **ordering** it and giving it form and meaning" (bold emphasis added).[67] Did you notice that the first syllable of logos, which is "lah", sounds like "law"? The **Laws** of Nature are the natural **laws** that give **order** to the universe. Hence, the word logos which is pronounced as "**law** gahs". In other words, the **Word/Logos** is the **lawgiver**. "For the LORD is our judge, the LORD is our lawgiver, the LORD is our king; he will save us" (Isaiah 33:22, KJV).

Today, the concept of logos can be found in every religion, such as Christianity. To find the concept of logos in Christianity, all you need to do is read certain verses of the Bible. In the King James Bible, there is a clause in the verse John 1:1 that says, "In the beginning was the Word". The deeper meaning of the term **word** is **logos** which is "the **source** that controls the universe". In other words, "In the beginning was the **Logos** or **Source**". The Source of what? The Source of the symbols and the alphanumeric codes of reality. These symbols and alphanumeric codes were first created by God and He wrote them into the fabric of space. Some of the letters of the alphanumeric codes can be found in DNA. Today, scientists often refer to them as genetic letters. The symbols, letters, and numbers of God have the power to create words, codes, and formulas which can be used to express the Laws of Nature. These Divine Laws give order to the universe, making it possible for life to exist on Earth.

Another word that is beneficial for you to know its deeper meaning is universe. The word "universe" is composed of two words which are "uni" and "verse". The prefix **uni-** is derived from the Latin prefix **uni-**, meaning "one".[68] As for the word **verse**, it etymologically means "line or section of a psalm or canticle" or "line of poetry".[69] Based on these definitions, the word **universe** means "one line of poetry".[70] A line of poetry has **words** that usually have allegorical and metaphorical meanings. To connect the dots, the hidden knowledge within the word universe tells us that the universe is an abstract-like reality field made of poetic and magical words/logos/laws/forces. In other words, we live in a magical and poetic "play" known as the universe, and therefore God is the main author and we are the co-authors. Quantum physicists have done experiments showing that the universe is indeed an abstract-like or dream-like reality field composed of energy and forces.

To spiritually innerstand why words are more powerful than swords, we need to turn our attention back to the word light and investigate it further. Based on the information in the subchapter "The Power of Words" we already know that the word "light" is strongly connected to the word "photon". Remember that in physics a **photon** is usually indicated by the symbol γ which is the lower case letter of the Greek letter Γ (*gamma*).[71] Some etymologists believe that the Greek letter *gamma* is where the word **grammar** is derived from. In English, **grammar** means "the study of the classes of words, their inflections, and their functions and relations in the sentence".[72]

Grammar is the art of inventing symbols and combining them to express thought; logic is the art of thinking; and rhetoric is the art of communicating thought from one mind to another; the adaptation of language to circumstance.[73]

Another origin of the word **grammar** is the Old French word *gramaire*. As described on EtymOnline.com:

late 14c., "Latin grammar, rules of Latin," from Old French *gramaire* "grammar; learning," especially Latin and philology, also "(magic) incantation, spells, mumbojumbo" (12c., Modern French *grammaire*), an "irregular semi-popular adoption" [OED] of Latin *grammatica* "grammar, philology," perhaps via an unrecorded Medieval Latin form *grammaria*. ... [Bold emphasis added][74]

The Old French word *"gramaire"* has a strong connection to the English word "grimoire". In fact, **grimoire** etymologically means "incantation; grammar"[75] and therefore is strongly connected to the Old French word *"gramaire"* and the English word "grammar". Dictionary.com defines **grimoire** using these exact words: "a manual of **magic** or witchcraft used by witches and sorcerers" (bold emphasis added).[76] The definitions of certain boldface words in this subchapter reveal that grammar, or the way words are used, has a strong connection to magic. They also reveal that words have the potential to control energy. Keep in mind that light is a form of energy.

In the Bible verse Genesis 1:3 (KJV), it says, "And God said, Let there be light: and there was light."[77] In this verse, the Bible tells you that God used **words/logos/sound** to manifest **light**. Keep in mind that the word "light" has a strong connection to the terms "word", "grammar", "logos", and "universe". The word **logos** is defined as, "in classical Greek philosophy, reason regarded as constituting the controlling principle of the universe and as being manifested by speech".[78] The ancient Greek people believed that the power of the logos was expressed through words and used to create mystical things (e.g., sacred geometry). Have you ever wondered why the **symbols** of corporations are called **logos**? It has to do with magic and sacred geometry! The evidence that the power (sound) of the logos/word has the power to create mystical things, such as sacred geometry, can be seen in cymatics. Here is a quote from the New King James Bible, Hebrews 4:12, that talks about how powerful words are:

> For the word of God is living and powerful, and sharper than any two-edged sword, piercing even to the division of soul and spirit, and of joints and marrow, and is a discerner of the thoughts and intents of the heart.

By now you should know how powerful words are. What most people do not know about words is that they can be used to hide information in plain sight. The process of using words to hide information in plain sight is often used by the Dark Forces to hide their true intentions. One of the reasons that they do this is to prevent them from violating your free will. A medium that the Dark Forces like to use to tell you what they are doing to you in plain sight is movie. Many movies have images and words with occult meanings embedded in them to deceive you to temporarily give up your natural rights through silence. **By being silent, you choose not to exercise your natural rights**. The good news is that you cannot truly give up your natural rights for the reason that they will always be there, just like the Laws of Nature.

For example, when you watch a movie about human trafficking or wars and do not say something to express your disapproval of it, you, in a way, agree through silence; therefore, the Dark Forces can use your silence as an excuse to continue trafficking people or waging wars. This is how the Dark Forces and the Dark Magicians can get away with most of their evil deeds. Ignorance is no "excuse" and silence implies "consent". To be more accurate, being silent is known as "implied consent". In the Information Age (Computer Age), there is little or no excuse for not knowing these things, especially when you live in a country that has easy access to the Internet. Because being silent is a form of consent, it is important to be aware of what the Dark Forces are doing so you can say no and preserve your consent. Ignoring the Dark Forces is not going to help you preserve your consent. When enough of us say no and preserve our consent, the Dark Forces and their minions would have to back off and leave us alone. If they were to not leave us alone and keep harassing or harming us, they would violate our free will and would have to face the consequences of their actions. All thoughts, intentions, and actions are known by God and there is no escaping the consequences of violating His Laws.

There are millions and possibly billions of people on Earth who think that they can achieve spiritual freedom or stop the crimes against mankind by ignoring what the Dark Forces and their New World Order are doing. These people are living in a delusional state of mind and are actually making it much easier for the Dark Forces to enslave mankind. If you want to prevent the Dark Forces from enslaving mankind, you need to become aware of what they are doing so you can say no to their actions and agendas. Remember, silence implies consent.

How to Decipher Words to Find Their Deeper Meanings

To find the deeper meanings of words, you need to look beyond their common definitions. To be more specific, you need to look below their surface, dissect their layers, and meticulously study them from many different angles. This means that you may need to use an etymological dictionary to study their origins and rearrange their letters using the art of anagram. Besides the previous techniques, you may also need to use the art of homophone to assist you to find words that sound similar to the words you are investigating. A **homophone** is "a word pronounced the same as another but differing in meaning, whether spelled the same way or not, as *heir* and *air*."[79] Once you find a word's origin, dissect its layers, and meticulously study it from many different angles, the true intent and meaning of the word often magically become noticeable inside your mind. So, the next time you investigate a word, do not only study it at face value but also its origins, prefix, and suffix. Furthermore, pay attention to other words that sound similar to it.

A word that you may want to know its deeper meanings is baptism. When you meticulously look at the word baptism and study its definitions to see what other words are related to it, you should eventually come to the conclusion that **external** baptism is a magic ritual! When someone is baptized from the outside, he is considered to have entered into a "covenant" with the "lord". As a noun, the word **covenant** comes from the Latin word **convenire**, meaning "come together, unite; be suitable, agree".[80] As a verb, it etymologically means "to enter into a formal agreement or contract".[81] The word **covenant** (noun) also means "an agreement, usually formal, between two or more persons to do or not do something specified" or "a solemn agreement between the members of a church to act together in harmony with the precepts of the gospel."[82] When the word "covenant" is separated into two words, it transforms into the word "coven" and the suffix "-ant". The word **coven** means "an assembly of witches, especially a group of thirteen."[83] Etymologically, it means "a

21

meeting, gathering, assembly".[84] The definition of **-ant** is "causing or performing an action or existing in a certain condition; the agent that performs an action".[85] It can also mean "serving in the capacity of".[86] In Turkish, the word **ant** means "oath".[87] As for the word **lord**, it means "a person who has authority, control, or power over others; a master, chief, or ruler."[88] Here is one of Dictionary.com's definitions of **-ant**:

> a suffix forming adjectives and nouns from verbs, occurring originally in French and Latin loanwords (pleasant; constant; servant) and productive in English on this model; -ant, has the general sense "characterized by or **serving in the capacity of**" that named by the stem (ascendant; pretendant), especially in the formation of nouns denoting human agents in legal actions or other formal procedures (tenant; defendant; applicant; contestant). [Bold emphasis added][89]

Before we end our investigation of the word **baptism**, we need to study one of its definitions which is, "a ceremonial immersion in water, or application of water, as an initiatory **rite** or sacrament of the Christian church" (bold emphasis added).[90] A word in the previous sentence that we need to investigate further is **rite**, meaning "a formal or ceremonial act or procedure prescribed or customary in religious or other solemn use".[91] It is important to know that the word "rite" has a strong connection to the word "ritual". In fact, the word **ritual** comes directly from the Latin word **_ritualis_**, meaning "relating to (religious) rites" (bold emphasis added).[92] Rites are often used to initiate someone into a group, organization, or society. Rites are popular among secretive societies, such as the Jesuits and the Freemasons. Phonetically, **rite** is **write** which means "to trace or form (characters, **letters**, **words**, etc.) on the surface of some material, as with a pen, pencil, or other instrument or means; inscribe" (bold emphasis added).[93] It is important to know that "words" are made up of "letters" which are "sigils". The word **sigil** means, "An inscribed or painted symbol considered to have **magical power**" (bold emphasis added).[94] This is why the forming of words from letters is called **spell**ing. In other words, when you **spell**/write words, you are playing with magic **spell**s. Keep in mind that magic can be used for good or evil purposes.

Based on most of the definitions so far in this subchapter, the deeper meaning of the word **baptism** is "an **agreement** (contract) with a **coven** controlled by **witches** or **lords**." Therefore, when people are baptized, they have agreed to serve in the capacity of a coven or make an agreement with a coven, which is controlled by lords or witches. The question people should ask is, "is the one performing the baptism a member of a coven of the true Lord or is he a member of a coven of witches who worship false gods?" The witches who have infiltrated many churches on Earth are the Dark Magicians! These magicians have masters that are known as demons. Their demonic masters are the "lords" that people make contracts with when they agree to be baptized by the minions of the Dark Magicians. This is why it is important to know who is really in charge of a church before agreeing to be baptized by a member of that church.

The process of external baptism promises the body, mind, and soul of a man, woman, or child to a coven of a church, which can be controlled by a coven of the true Lord or a coven of witches who worship false gods. If you go to church, you may want to really think about that before participating in baptism. **True baptism occurs in the body, not outside of it.** Because of this, external baptism will not empower people to achieve spiritual freedom. Churches that practice external baptism are misleading their members because external baptism cannot save their members from original sin. To rise above original sin requires a transformation from within, meaning that "... unless one is born of water and the Spirit, he cannot enter the kingdom of God."[95] What these churches do not teach people is that the **true church** of God is **man's body**, whether male or female. The Bible even says that "you are the temple of God".[96]

> And He is the head of the body, the church, who is the beginning, the firstborn from the dead, that in all things He may have the preeminence. (Colossians 1:18, NKJV)

> Do you not know that you are the temple of God and that the Spirit of God dwells in you? If anyone defiles the temple of God, God will destroy him. For the temple of God is holy, which temple you are. (1 Corinthians 3:16-17, NKJV)

Today, almost all churches and religious institutions do not teach you how to achieve spiritual freedom. What they are good at doing is teaching you how to worship an external savior. When you worship an external savior, it disempowers you by weakening your spiritual powers. Furthermore, you are basically telling God that He did not give you the necessary spiritual powers to empower you to achieve spiritual freedom. This is an insult to God. When you contemplate the information thereof, you should realize that most religious institutions are great at teaching you disempowering beliefs. God, the Creator of the heavens and the earth, gave you His most precious gifts with almost no strings attached. Some of these gifts (spiritual powers) are your natural rights, and the power of thought, consciousness, love, imagination, creativity, and awareness, which are the same spiritual powers that God used to create the heavens and the earth. These spiritual powers have infinite potential, and therefore YOU also have infinite potential.

Whenever you worship an external savior, rely on a religious institution to save you, or refuse to stand up for your natural rights, you are, in a sense, throwing God's spiritual gifts in the trash, thereby disrespecting yourself and at the same time disrespecting God. In other words, you insult God every time you worship an external savior. If you were God, would you want to help a bunch of irresponsible people who keep insulting you? The **external savior program** is a psychological operation and **magic spell** that is used by the Dark Forces to enslave your body, mind, and soul, turning you into a cowardly slave to be used as a biological battery. The sooner you realize this, the sooner you can rise above their artificial matrix and free your body, mind, and soul. You already have all the necessary spiritual powers to achieve spiritual freedom, so it would be wise to accept responsibility for your spiritual growth and learn how to exercise your spiritual powers. One of the keys to exercising your spiritual powers is to learn how to use words wisely. With the right words, you can command the Forces of God to enforce justice and put your will into action.

Chapter 2
Word Magic, the Birthing
Process, and Commerce

To gain a deeper innerstanding of how word magic is used to control your energy, you need to know how words are used in commerce and the birthing process to deceive and manipulate your mind. In order for the minions of the Dark Magicians to effectively manipulate you and the rest of mankind on a global level, they need you and the rest of mankind to play the financial game called commerce. The best time to make you play this financial game is the day when your mother gave "birth" to you. Many words that are used for describing the birthing process are strongly related to commerce. For this reason, you need to know some information about merchants and the sea business, or you will have a hard time seeing the connection between the birthing process and commerce.

Before there were airplanes, automobiles, and trains, when people wanted to send products to people in other countries, they often sent them on a ship. Using ships to send products to other countries became so important that many laws were created to protect merchants and their products. The two laws that dominated the sea business were admiralty law (the law of the sea) and maritime law. Both of these laws originally heard cases involving commerce on the seas. Eventually, they spread beyond the seas and are now used in most court systems throughout the world. Today, almost all courts in the United States of America, Canada, the United Kingdom, and most Western and Eastern countries operate under admiralty law and maritime law. When countries operate under admiralty and maritime laws, it means that their courts are under the jurisdiction of **military** law and **commercial law**; therefore, when people go to court, they are often treated as **properties** and **war criminals**. This is why when people mention their constitutional rights in admiralty or maritime courts, the judge may tell them to sit down and shut up! It is hard to get justice in a court that operates under admiralty law or maritime law.

Let us turn our attention back to ships and merchants so I can explain to you how word magic is used to control your body, mind, and spirit. When a ship reaches its destination, the captain **orders** his crew to prepare the ship for docking. After the ship docks, the crew can start to unload the cargoes and products off the ship. A **ship** is also a **vessel**; therefore, after a ship docks onto a shore it can be called a **berthed vessel**. The word **berthed** is phonetically similar to, if not phonetically the same as, the word **birthed**. These two words are spelled differently, but they sound very similar. This is one of the ways that word magic is used to deceive you.

Before the crew can unload all the cargoes and products off the ship (berthed vessel) and onto the dock, they have to first show a certificate of manifest to the dock operator or whomever is in charge of the dock. A certificate of manifest is a document that has information about a product (e.g., the registration number, the country of origin, the manufacturer, etc.). A **certificate of manifest** is, in a way, a **birth certificate**. On your birth certificate, there is a registration number, country of origin, and manufacturer. Metaphorically speaking, the manufacturers that created you (the product) are your parents. However, in reference to the birth certificate, the manufacturer is the State. The process of using **ship**s to deliver products is where the word **ship**ping comes from. Did you notice that the word shipping has the word ship in it? Another word that has the word ship in it is citizen**ship**. When you separate the word "citizenship" into two words, it transforms into the term "citizen ship", meaning "citizen of a ship". If you are a citizen of a ship, it means that you are under the jurisdiction of admiralty law and maritime law. These two laws are not common laws or constitutional laws; instead, they are commercial laws.

When a ship is in the process of being docked, it is being guided to berth. The word **berth** is defined as, "A space for a vessel to dock or anchor".[1] Based on this information, when a product is unloaded from a ship and onto a dock, it just went through the **berthing** process which is the process of **delivering** the product from the vessel/ship onto the **dock**. This is why when a woman is in the process of giving

26

birth she is said to be **delivering** a baby. Keep in mind that **berth** is phonetically **birth**. The birthing process of a baby is related to the process of delivering a product on a ship. Every woman has a body. Another word for body is vessel. A vessel can also be called a ship. The words body, vessel, and ship can all mean the same thing and be used to represent a woman's body. This is why a ship is often referred to as "she" and the main ship is often called the "mother ship".

To connect the dots, the process of a woman giving birth to a baby can be defined as "the process of **delivering** or **berthing** a product of a ship." Metaphorically speaking, the product is the baby and the ship is the woman's body. When you contemplate all the information about commerce and the sea business in this chapter and relate it to the process of birthing a baby, you should see a strong connection between the **berthing** process of a ship and the **birthing** process of a baby. By spelling the words "berth" and "birth" slightly different and making them sound the same, the Dark Forces and their minions (the Dark Magicians) can trick you to agree to be a product of a ship, so they can have jurisdiction over you. They know that they cannot have jurisdiction over the real you (the living, breathing man or woman made of flesh and blood), which is why they need you to **consent** to be an artificial person (e.g., name, corporation, and citizen). Keep in mind that an artificial person has no natural rights. By consenting to be an artificial person, it allows them to convert "you" into a "product" and make money by selling "you" on the stock market. It is all about using the power of words and semantics to trick you to temporarily give up your sovereignty and natural rights.

When you were in your mother's womb, you were surrounded in **amniotic fluid** which was made of mostly **water.** In other words, you were living in a **sea of water.** Because you were living in water, according to admiralty law (the law of the **sea**), you could be ruled by this law. Admiralty law is also known as the law of money. What is another word for money? Currency! Phonetically, the word "currency" sounds similar to the term "current **sea**". Hence, the law known as the law of the sea (admiralty law). In your mother's womb, the biological thing that connected you to your mother was the umbilical cord. This cord was connected to your **navel**. Metaphorically speaking, you were connected to the "mother ship". The word **umbilical** is derived from the Medieval Latin word **umbilicalis**, meaning "of the navel".[2] The word **navel** sounds similar to the word **naval**, meaning "of or relating to **ships** of all kinds" or "belonging to, pertaining to, or connected with a **navy**" (bold emphasis added).[3] The **navy** is the military of the

sea. They did not name that area of your body the navel by accident. By now you should start to see how all these words are somehow directly or indirectly related to the sea. A very important information you need to know about the word **sea** is that it has a strong connection to the word **energy**. By the end of Chapter 5, you will know why these two words are strongly related.

The Connection Between Babies, Batteries, and Prisoners

On average, a fetus lives in the womb of its mother for a little more than 9 months before the fetus is ready to be born. When you were a fetus, you were living in water (amniotic fluid). Shortly after 9 months, you were born from your mother's body/vessel/ship through her birth canal. The term "birth canal" sounds very similar, if not identical, to the term "berth canal". A canal is an artificial waterway that is used by the captain of a ship or large boat to berth his vessel. Hence, the term **berth/birth canal**.

Before you were born in the hospital, you had to travel through your mother's birth canal. After you came out of your mother's birth canal, you were grabbed by the doctor. The word "doctor" is pronounced similar to "dock-ore". The word **dock** is defined as, "A platform extending from a shore over water, used to secure, protect, and provide access to a **boat** or **ship**; a pier" (bold emphasis added).[4] As for the word **ore**, it is defined as "a metal-bearing mineral or rock, or a native metal, that can be mined at a profit."[5] The word **ore** sounds very similar to the word **oar** which is "a long shaft with a broad blade at one end, used as a lever for rowing or otherwise propelling or steering a **boat**" (bold emphasis added).[6] What you need to know about these words is that they somehow indirectly or directly relate to a ship, the sea, and the birthing process.

Another word that you need to know its deeper meanings is hospital. One of the origins of the word **hospital** is the Old French word *hospital*, meaning "**hostel**, shelter, lodging" (bold emphasis added).[7] In English, the word **hostel** sounds almost exactly like the word **hostile**. The word **hostile** means "not friendly, warm, or generous; not **hospitable**" (bold emphasis added).[8] When you do not know how to exercise your natural rights and claim your baby as your property, a hospital may not be a friendly place to give "birth" to your baby because the hidden role of the doctor/dock-ore is to "deliver" your baby and turn your baby into a "product" of a ship/vessel to be sold in commerce using the birth certificate as the certificate of manifest.

The information on the birth certificate is based on the information on the certificate of live birth, which becomes a valid certificate after the parents and the doctor/dock-ore sign their signatures on it. Once the certificate of live birth is signed by all the parties, the information on it becomes a fact, recording an event. On the other hand, the birth certificate (may be it should be called "berth" certificate) is created a few days after the baby is born and is used to register a product of a ship or corporation; it is similar to a certificate of manifest. If your parents used your birth certificate, on your behalf, as evidence of your identity, they made a huge mistake; your birth certificate is **not** supposed to be used for identification purposes. In other words, after you were born, your parents unknowingly turn you into a "product" of a ship. If your parents are citizens of the United States, your "ship" is the United States which is a corporation.

Have you ever wondered why newborn babies are kept in the maternity **ward** of a hospital? The reason that they are kept in the maternity ward is because their parents have signed their rights away to the State, turning them into "citizens", "products", and "prisoners" of a **ship**. Hence, the status "citizen**ship**" which secretly means "citizen of a ship". The term **ward**, which is found in the term maternity **ward**, is defined as "a section in a prison".[9] In prison, wards are used for caging prisoners. They are also known as prison **cells**. Why the word cells? Because prisoners are being used as "batteries". The word **cell** is defined as "a device for converting chemical energy into electrical energy, usually consisting of a container with two electrodes immersed in an electrolyte".[10] To connect the dots, babies are put in maternity wards to prepare them to become biological batteries. Prisoners are caged in prison cells for the same reason. By the end of this book, you will know what I mean when I say that people are being used as biological batteries. Keep in mind that the process of using people as biological batteries can be used for good or evil purposes. One of the problems concerning this matter is that most governments, hospitals, and corporations are taking advantage of people's labor and not respecting their rights.

An important information that is beneficial for you to know about the word **hospital** is that it has a strong connection to the secret society called the Knights **Hospital**ler, which is one of the factions of the Knights Templar, the private army for the Vatican. One of the symbols of the Knights Templar is the Red Cross. The Red Cross symbol can be found on the flag of the United Kingdom and inside of hospitals. The American Red Cross, the British Red Cross, and the International Committee of the Red Cross use this same symbol to represent their organizations. All secret societies have symbols that they use to communicate. They operate somewhat like street gangs but are much more organized and powerful. Like street gangs, secret societies like to mark their territories with signs and symbols to let certain people know that they control those territories. But unlike street gangs that only control a few blocks or a small town, secret societies control countries! All the Red Cross organizations are controlled by the Knights Templar and the Vatican. The United Kingdom is controlled by them too. Please be aware that not every member of a secret society is a control addict. Furthermore, many secret societies do not support the enslavement of mankind. Today, most secret societies are not secret anymore; therefore, these secret societies should be called secretive societies.

Let us turn our attention back to the word doctor/dock-ore. By now, you should know that one of the hidden roles of the doctor/dock-ore is to deliver babies and turn them into "products" of a ship/vessel to be sold in commerce using the birth certificate as the certificate of manifest. Keep in mind that one of the main reasons that babies are mistaken as products of a ship/vessel is because parents make the mistake of using birth certificates as identity documents. Metaphorically speaking, the word **ore** in the word doctor/dock-**ore** is you (the baby). You represent the **ore** because you are the "battery" that is being used as **energy** to power the artificial matrix. So, when you were delivered from the body/vessel/ship onto the dock, you (the **ore**) was delivered onto the **dock**. Hence, the word doctor/**dock-ore**. This is why the person who delivers babies in a hospital is called doctor. The doctor's/doc's ("dock's") role is to deliver the baby/ore or "dock" the "ore" onto the shore, so it can be sold and used as energy.[11]

The word **ore** sounds similar to the first syllable of the word **au**ra. Aura is an energy field that is part of the bio-electromagnetic field of the physical body. When you separate the word "aura" into two words, you get the term "au ra". The word **au** is derived from the Latin word **aurum**, meaning "gold".[12] This is why in chemistry the symbol for gold is Au. The word "ra" is sometimes used as the name of an ancient god called **Ra** (pronounced "**ray**"). In Egyptian mythology, Ra was the **sun**-god that was often depicted as a man with a hawk head. When you put the words "sun" and "ra" together, you get the word "sunra" or "sunray" which is connected to the sun-god Ra.

Every ship or "body ship" is brought into port and docked, so the doctor can deliver (de-**liver**) the body ship because it is a new "liver" being produced or a new baby being "de-livered" by the doctor as "docked ore", the ore that is now docked and ready to be sold and used as energy.[13] The Dark Forces view each of us like an ore because we are the "ores" that are being **mined** for **gold** (**Au**) through the process of mind control. The word **mind** sounds almost the same as the word **mined**, giving us a clue as to why the Anunnaki came to Earth.[14] Whether the story about the Anunnaki is a myth or not a myth is a matter of further debate; however, all myths often have important morals, spiritual truths, and knowledge hidden inside them. One of the hidden knowledge may be related to thought-forms (creatures of the mind) mining the "gold" in our minds because to control our minds is to control the golden fluid in our bodies and the golden energy in our auras, which can be used to extend their lifespans or power the sun-god Ra. Keep in mind that "gold" and "sun" can be found in the word "aura" which is made up of the words "au" (gold) and "ra" (sun-god Ra). In Greek mythology, the golden fluid was called **ichor**, a precious fluid believed to be found in the blood of certain alien gods, allowing them to live for thousands of years. It is my innerstanding that ichor is found in very small amounts in the physical body. In addition, it has a strong connection to the holy oil produced in the brain. This "holy oil" is sometimes referred to as "Christ". Etymologically, the word **Christ** means "the anointed".[15] The word anoint has a strong connection to oil.

By now you should have a basic innerstanding of what the Dark Forces are doing to mankind. This negative agenda to enslave mankind and use people as biological batteries is what I like to refer to as the Earth Matrix Drama. It is important for you to know that the Earth Matrix Drama is ultimately a spiritual drama for your **soul** and **energy** so you better start paying attention. By the end of Chapter 5, you will know why the Dark Forces need to feed on the energy of mankind to survive. The good news is that we have the power to take control of this drama and turn it into a peaceful drama, as long as we are responsible and courageous, and know how to exercise our natural rights.

Let us turn our attention back to the birthing process, so I can teach you how the Dark Forces are using the birth certificate to enslave your soul and body. Please be aware that the birth certificate can be used for good or evil. In the United States, shortly after you were born, a record was created with certain personal information about you. This record is known as your **certificate of live birth**, which is **not** the same as your **birth certificate**. Please be aware that when I say "your birth certificate", I do not mean that you **legally** own it. In fact, your birth certificate is **legally** owned by the State. Shortly after your parents signed your certificate of live birth, the certificate was sent to the U.S. government. After the U.S. government used it to finish doing whatever they needed to do to your certificate of live birth, they sent your parents a new version of your certificate of live birth. This new version is known as your **birth certificate**. Your new birth certificate is **not** the original certificate of live birth because it is associated with a dead and fictional character that looks like you. In other words, it is basically a **death certificate**.

The term "**birth** certificate" sounds the same as the term "**berth** certificate". When two words or terms sound the same but are spelled differently, they are known as homophones. Phonetically, there is no difference between the terms "birth certificate" and "berth certificate". In word magic, homophones are important because they can be used to hide important information in plain sight. By studying a homophone of "birth", such as "berth", you can acquire important information and clues to help you innerstand what a birth certificate really is. Remember, the word **berth** means, "A space for a vessel to dock or anchor". It is important to know that the improper use of the birth certificate can cause a lot of harm to you. For example, all birth certificates that are issued by the U.S. government are not supposed to be used for identification purposes. When people use them as identifications, they unknowingly agree to allow the U.S. government to turn them into "products" of a ship/vessel to be sold in commerce. They also unknowingly agree to be registered products of the United States (Inc.). This is why birth certificates can be used to issue stocks to be traded on the stock market. Therefore, the occult (hidden/secret) meaning of a **birth certificate** is "a stock certificate of a corporation" or "a certificate of manifest of a product berthed from a commercial ship or vessel."

Have you ever wondered why they like to use the word parents to define your mother and father? The word "parents" sound similar to the term "pair rents" which means "pair that rents".[16] When your parents (pair rents) used your birth/berth certificate to create your identity, they unknowingly attached you to a dead identity (id-entity) of the State, thereby making the mistake of allowing the U.S. government to legally own you and make you a "product" of the United States (Inc.). What this means is that your body and everything you buy or produce under the name on your birth certificate are legally the properties of the State. However, your parents (pair **rents**) are allowed to keep or **rent** you as long as they pay taxes and take decent care of the new product/baby/you.

The name on your birth certificate is a **legal name** and therefore represents an **artificial person** (legal fiction/legal person) that exists on paper. In other words, it is a name of a "dead" thing. This legal name is often written in all capital letters and is **not** the name given to you by your mother and father. Instead, it is a derivative name created by an agent of the government to make it easier for you to do business with the agencies and franchises of the government. However, the government likes to use your legal name as a tool to control you, so it is wise to learn how to use your legal name wisely. To use it wisely, you first need to know some important information about your legal name and given name. The name given to you by your mother and father is known as your "given name"; it is a genuine appellation and is separate from, but can be joined to, your family name. It is important to remember that you and your given name, and any derivative name thereof, are **not** one and the same. A name is a symbol of a thing and therefore is not the thing itself. It is also important to remember that living men and women have autographs, not signatures. A **signature** is used by a **corporate officer** or a **person** to do business with a **corporation**. Because your birth certificate is marked with a legal name, it is a certificate that represents the birth of a **dead thing** and therefore is a **death certificate**. The legal name is sometimes referred to as the strawman.

This is what the lawyers, bankers, and politicians have used to enslave you. It is a crime known as "personage". By arbitrarily creating an Estate trust named after you and claiming to own this thing they created, they have falsely claimed to own you and your assets and to literally buy and sell "you" on stock exchanges, ship "you" out of ports, and tax "you" for doing things you've never done. After all, there is no law against enslaving an ESTATE trust, is there? Or arresting a slave? Or charging a tax on importing revenue to Puerto Rico?[17]

Remember, your birth **certificate** is a "stock **certificate**" of a corporation. Because of this, it works similar to a stock of a company. When you buy a stock of a company, you have an interest in that company. They did not call it a "birth **certificate**" for no reason. Like any stock certificate that is associated with a trust and has your legal name on it, you are the beneficial owner of the trust. Keep in mind that the beneficial owner is not the same as the legal owner, the person who holds the beneficial interest in the property on trust for the beneficial owner. However, the beneficial owner has the right to receive interest generated by the trust.

> A beneficial interest is the right to receive benefits on assets held by another party. The beneficial interest is often related to matters concerning trusts accounts. For example, most beneficial interest arrangements are in the form of trust accounts, where an individual, the beneficiary, has a vested interest in the trust's assets. The beneficiary receives income from the trust's holdings but does not own the account.[18]

To connect the dots, your birth certificate is **evidence** of your **beneficial interest** in a corporation (e.g., the United States). When you improperly use your birth certificate by using it as personal identification, you unknowingly agree to be the person (strawman) associated with the legal name on your birth certificate. This person is the debtor of your birth certificate. As the debtor, you legally owe money to the corporation (e.g., the United States) that created your birth certificate. To correct this mistake, you have to notify the right government agent and let him know that you are the beneficial owner and not the debtor of the trust associated with your birth certificate. Before taking any action, meticulously study how a trust works and learn how to correct false presumptions of the government. Three informative websites that teach you how to correct false presumptions are AnnaVonReitz.com, Freedom-School.com, and YouAreLaw.org. Another informative website is EsotericKnowledge.me, a private online space for living men and women to learn about word magic, God's Law, legalese, freedom, sovereignty, genuine spirituality, and esoteric knowledge.

If you have studied the information on the websites thereof, you should know that when the U.S. government refers to the United States, most of the time they are talking about the corporation called the United States (incorporated) or the United States of America (incorporated). Most of the time, they write the **legal** name "United States" in **all capital letters** and nearly 100 percent of the time they write it without the "Inc.", so they can trick you to agree to be an "employee" of the UNITED STATES, INC. As for the name of the actual country, according to Dixon v. United States (Case No. 3,934), it is written as "The United States of America" (**un**incorporated). The letter "T" in the word "The" in the name thereof is capitalized because it is part of the name. In legalese, the United States (incorporated) or the United States of America (**in**corporated) is NOT the same as the country known as "**The** United States of America" (**un**incorporated). Knowing this fact is essential for innerstanding this chicanery and how the British Monarchy and the New World Order (NWO) have successfully enslaved the American people without their knowledge.

The United States (incorporated), also doing business as the United States of America (incorporated), is a **registered** and **chartered corporation** that resides in Washington D.C., a city-state that is FOREIGN with respect to the 50 states. Why do you think the United States has a president and a vice president? Corporate law requires a corporation, such as the United States, to have a president and a vice president. It is RIGHT IN YOUR FACE and hidden in plain sight! The acronym D.C. stands for the "District of Columbia", which is a district that has a radius of about 10 miles. This district houses the United States (incorporated). So, when the U.S. government talks about the United States, it often refers to a registered and chartered corporation located in the District of Columbia, a **foreign district** that does not really have anything to do with American Citizens and Nationals. In other words, it is NOT really talking about the country. Be aware that United States citizens or citizens of the United States are not the same as American Citizens or American Nationals. Washington D.C. is a foreign district for the reason that it is NOT part of The United States of America (unincorporated), just like Vatican City is not part of Italy. According to the book *Matrix of Power: Secrets of World Control*, Washington D.C. or the District of Columbia was founded by a powerful masonic secret society called the Colombians.[19] This district was named after the goddess of liberty, also known as **Columbia**. Hence, the name District of **Columbia**.

Because you now know that there are a few different versions of The United States of America and that the incorporated versions are the ones that the U.S. government likes to use the most, let us dig deeper into the birthing process so you can learn how the Dark Forces and their minions use word play and word magic to trick you to temporarily give up your natural rights. Before the invention of computers, when babies were born hospitals published their birth

35

information in the newspaper. Nowadays, because of computers, the Internet, and certain laws, they rarely publish birth information in the newspaper. Instead, they send birth information to the government and then its agents publish it on certain government sponsored websites. Some examples of these websites are vital records websites.

In the United States, shortly after a baby is born, the doctor extracts blood from the bottom of the baby's foot. This process is often called the Heel-Stick Test. The bottom of the foot is known as the **sole** of the foot. Keep in mind that the word **sole** sounds very similar to the word **soul**. This blood test is said to check for a variety of genetic disorders and health conditions. However, is there more to it than meets the eye? According to some researchers, if you were born in a hospital, they may also take tissue and blood samples from your mother's placenta. Shortly after extracting blood from the sole of your foot, the blood is sent to the government so its agents can sequence your DNA to determine your genetic blueprint. Your genetic blueprint is like your fingerprint because no one has that same genetic blueprint. Because of this, your DNA is the physical proof of evidence that the government can use to identify you. This makes your DNA important for creating your personal file and identification.

According to some researchers, shortly after a baby is born, his father and mother are supposed to **record** his actual birth at a local land recording office and claim that he is their baby. Unlike the father and mother, the government's job is to **register** the baby's person which is the person associated with the legal name on the birth certificate. Please keep in mind that to **record** something is to transfer it into the **land** jurisdiction and to **register** something is to transfer it into the **sea** jurisdiction. If your father and mother do not record your actual birth after a certain amount of time (usually 7 years), the government has the **legal** right to pronounce you as **legally dead**. The problem with this process is that it is based on presumptions, and therefore the government is not being very honest. Please be aware that when the government says that you are legally dead, it does not always mean that you (the living man or woman) are dead. In law, you can be alive and still be called legally dead.

The legal system operates in a jurisdiction that deals with **fictional** things. This is why the "laws" of the legal system are called **acts** and **statutes**, just like the **acts** and **statues** in a play. Because of this, many of its acts are unlawful. Keep in mind that just because something is unlawful does not mean that it is illegal. Under admiralty law, if you are missing for 7 years, you can be declared legally dead.

This is why people lost at sea are declared legally dead after 7 years. It is important to know that most political and court systems throughout the world today operate under admiralty and maritime laws. Both of these commercial laws deal with commerce on the **sea**. So, when the government is operating under commercial laws and says that you are **legally dead**, on a deeper level, it means that you are **dead at sea**. The government says this because it presumes that you are a citizen of a ship (citizenship), also known as a **sea**man. Furthermore, you are made of mostly water and you were born from a sack of water (the amniotic sac).

Because you are considered **legally** dead, the government can take control of your **legal** name, allowing the government to legally claim your estate. This process is similar to when people die and their estates are transferred to the people included in their wills. This is why the government can **legally** seize your properties and children when you violate their acts and statutes. However, when you rebut their presumptions and let them know that you are not dead, it makes it much harder for the government to confiscate your properties. When you send a letter or writ to the government to notify its agents that you are not dead at sea but is alive and well, you are **correcting your status** and removing yourself from their jurisdiction, which is an imaginary territory that exists in a dead and fictional world. After you correct your status, the government now has to acknowledge you as a living man instead of a dead person/legal person. Please be aware that when I use the word **man** in this book, most of the time I am talking about both gender (male and female).

It is important to know that a dead person, which is known in law as a legal person or legal fiction, has **no natural rights**; it only has artificial rights and privileges. An example of a legal person/legal fiction is a United States citizen or a citizen of the United States. Because United States citizens are legal persons with only artificial rights and privileges, according to the legal system, they have no natural rights. This is why when you (United States citizen) go to court and shout out to the judge about your natural rights or constitutional rights, the judge will often look at you like you are a fool and may tell you to sit down and be quiet. If you refuse to be quiet, he may charge you with contempt of court.

Because the legal person (e.g., United States citizen) is a dead thing, the government has jurisdiction over it. On the other hand, the living and breathing man is not dead and therefore has natural rights, which are **unalienable** rights given to the living man by God. The word **unalienable** means "incapable of being aliened, that is, sold and transferred."[20] According to *A Dictionary of Law* (1889), the word **unalienable right** means "... one which cannot be surrendered to government or society, because no equivalent can be received for it, and one which neither the government nor society can take away, because they can give no equivalent. Of such is the right of conscience." In other words, your natural rights (unalienable rights) are **superior** to all "laws" made by the government and cannot be sold; therefore, the government does not have jurisdiction over you, the living man. However, when you harm another man or violate his natural rights, he has the right to use the government to enforce justice on you.

Why the Word Government Means Ruler of the Mind

If you did not skip the first chapter of this book, by now you should have seen the word government dozens of times. The word government will be used many more times in this book, so it would be wise for you to know the deeper meaning of this word. One of the common and overt definitions of the word **government** is "the form or system of rule by which a state, community, etc., is governed".[21] Here is one of the legal definitions of the word **government**:

> The system of polity in a state; that form of fundamental rules and principles by which a nation or state is governed, or by which individual members of a body politic are to regulate their social actions; a constitution, either written or unwritten, by which the rights and duties of citizens and public officers are prescribed and defined, as a monarchical government, a republican government, etc.[22]

The word **government** is a noun and is derived from the Old French word *governement*, meaning "control, direction, administration".[23] To find some of the occult definitions of the word government, you need to separate it into two words, transforming the word "government" into the word "govern" and the suffix "-ment". One of the origins of the word **govern** is the Latin word *gubernare*, meaning "to direct, rule, guide, govern".[24] The suffix **-ment** is derived from the Latin suffix *-mentum*.[25] This suffix may be related to the Latin word *mentum* which comes from the PIE root *men-, meaning "to think" or "to project".[26] [27] The Latin word **mens**, which means "mind",[28] also comes from the PIE root ***men-**.[29] Words that are derived from the PIE root *men- are related to qualities and states of **mind** or thought. Based on the occult definitions in this paragraph, the word **government** secretly means "to guide the mind", "to rule the mind", or "to govern the mind". Because the word government is a noun, it can be defined as "guide of the mind", "ruler of the mind", or "governor of the mind". Throughout history, governments throughout the world have always used mind control techniques, such as subliminal messages and propaganda, to condition us how to think. The purpose of this is to control how we think, so they can rule and govern our minds.

One of the most popular and effective mind control techniques that the government likes to use to rule our minds is mnemonic. The definition of the adjective **mnemonic** is "assisting or intended to assist the memory."[30] As for the definition of the noun **mnemonic**, it is "something intended to assist the memory, as a verse or formula."[31] The word **mnemonic** comes from the Greek word **mnēmonikos**, meaning "of or pertaining to memory".[32] Based on these definitions, mnemonic is something that is related to the memory. Mnemonic is used in many different media, such as video games, TV commercials, cell phone apps, computers, and movies. The techniques used in mnemonic can be used for good or evil purposes. The problem is that most mnemonics of today are used to program our minds in negative ways and control how we think. One of the most popular technologies for broad**cast**ing mnemonics is television (TV), a popular medium for **cast**ing magic spells on viewers. Have you ever wondered why **TV shows** are sometimes called **TV programs**? They are called TV **programs** because they are being used to **program** your mind with mnemonics and subliminal messages. They did not call them TV programs for no reason. Mnemonics are effective for manipulating your mind because they use the power of sigils, sacred geometry, sound, and light to create magic effects to control your thought patterns. Because of their effectiveness, many corporations are replacing conventional subliminal messages with mnemonics in their advertising campaigns.

A very important information that is beneficial for you to know about the government is that it is a corporation. According to *Black's Law Dictionary* (6th edition), a **corporation** is, "An artificial person or legal entity created by or under the authority of the laws of a state." Because the government is a corporation (artificial person), it is a

39

fictitious entity that has no natural rights and power. Its main source of power comes from "feeding" on the energy of the people. In other words, the people's energy is the main source of power for the government. Because the government needs the people's energy to have power, it has no power without the support of the people. Sadly, most people have been brainwashed to think that the government has power over them. Whenever the government becomes tyrannical, all we need to do is remove our support and it will collapse on its own. This is how we can stop tyrannical governments without violent revolutions. Another misconception that most people have about the government is the idea that the agents of the government have authority over them. Remember, the main source of power for the government is the energy of the people. Without the people, the government has no real power, and therefore its agents also have no power to do anything.

I will say this again for the third time so it sinks deeper into your mind. **The main source of power for the government is the energy of the people**. This is because the government is a creature of their minds and is manifested through the power of their collective thoughts. In other words, the government is a thought-form created by their collective mind. Hence the saying, "the government is a reflection of the people". Because the government is a reflection of the people, when the government becomes irresponsible, it is because of the people's irresponsible thoughts and actions. The government gets its power from the people; therefore, it is the people's responsibility to make sure that the government is honorably and responsibly serving the people. If you want the government to be responsible and honorable, you have to first be responsible and honorable.

One of the forces of the government is the police force. The government agents that make up the police force are sometimes called cops. Today, many cops are not trained to protect and serve the people. Instead, they are trained to serve and protect the Dark Magicians and the corporations that they control. The Dark Magicians often think of cops as the lowest pawns of the government. The word **cop** is derived from the Latin word *capere* which means "to take".[33] Some etymologists believe it is derived from the Middle French word *caper*, meaning "seize, to take".[34] As a noun, Dictionary.com defines **cop** as "a police officer" or "a person who seeks to regulate a specified behavior, activity, practice, etc."[35] As a verb, it defines **cop** as "to catch; nab" or "to steal; filch" or "to buy (narcotics)".[36] To innerstand why the word cop is used to describe the lowest pawns of the government, you need to find and study the hidden meanings of the word cop. Furthermore, you need to know the difference between the words **lawful** and **legal**. The difference between these two words will be explained in more detail in the next chapter. For now, the important information that you need to know about the words lawful and legal is that lawful is more about natural rights (God-given rights) and legal is more about rights given to you by man or the government.

Because the word lawful is related to natural rights, anything that is lawful is above anything that is legal. For example, when cops pull you over for speeding and give you a speeding ticket, they are operating under **legal status** and not **lawful status**. In other words, they are unlawfully giving you a ticket. The reason that it is unlawful for cops to give you a speeding ticket is because it violates your natural right to travel. However, if you have a driver's license and/or your vehicle is registered to the government, cops can pull you over for speeding without having to worry too much about violating your natural rights. Your driver's license or license plate is evidence that you have a "contract" with the government, and therefore it puts you under the jurisdiction of the government and its agents. However, most, if not almost all, contracts of the government do not meet the requirements of a contract and therefore are not really contracts. Your right to travel is protected by Natural Law (a body of Spiritual Laws). It is a natural right inherently given to you by God. Because of this, no man, government agent, or government agency can **lawfully** tell you to stop traveling or how to travel without your **consent**, unless you harm another man, woman, or child while traveling. If they were to force you to stop traveling without your consent, they would be in direct violation of God's Law (Natural Law).

To overcome the problem of violating your natural right to travel, certain government leaders invented the driver's license which is a license that can be used to trick you to give them your consent. When you sign your name on the driver license application, you agree to allow the government and its agents to have jurisdiction over you **when you drive a vehicle**. This is why cops are trained to always ask you for your driver's license. As soon as you give them your driver's license, they have the **legal** right to give you a ticket, unless you did not violate any traffic "law".

Once you know that cops are in violation of your natural rights whenever they force you to do anything without your consent, you should know that the hidden meaning of the word **cop** is a government agent whose main role is to **catch** people and **steal** their

41

money using unlawful citations. The more citations cops give out, the more money their employer (the government) can collect. Do you remember what I said earlier about the definition of the word cop? As a verb, **cop** is defined as "to **catch**; nab" or "to **steal**; filch" or "to buy (narcotics)" (bold emphasis added).[37] This definition of the word cop describes some of the acts that many cops are doing to people these days. Please be aware that most cops have good intentions and risk their lives to keep the peace so we should respect them, as long as they are not acting above the law. The process of using unlawful citations to steal people's money is not only practiced by cops; many government agents (e.g., IRS agents), whether they realize it or not, are also using unlawful citations to steal people's money to finance the greed of corporations (e.g., banks and governments).

By now you should realize that the government is an artificial person. Because the government is an artificial person, also known as a corporation, it cannot directly deal with living people. To overcome this problem, the legal name was created to act like a conduit between living people and corporations, especially commercial corporations. Like the government, the legal name is an artificial person; it is the name on the birth certificate, driver's license, etc. When people do not know how to properly use the legal name, it can be used to control their minds. To rule people's minds and control them, the Dark Magicians have been using certain factions of the government to trick them to consent to play the Legal Name Game. The factions of the government that the Dark Magicians control are collectively known as the Secret Government or the Shadow Government. By participating in the Legal Name Game without knowing the rules, people unknowingly agree to be corporations (artificial persons). This allows corporations, such as banks and governments, to do business with them and have jurisdiction over them. Furthermore, the Legal Name Game makes it easier for the Dark Magicians and the Secret Government to enslave people in the artificial matrix of the Dark Forces. Do you innerstand now why the word **government** means "to rule the mind" or "ruler of the mind?"

The good news is that men and women can become the true rulers of the government by learning how to exercise their natural rights and be responsible sovereigns. In other words, we have the power to become the true "**governors** of our **minds**" which esoterically means "governments". Remember, the word **government** secretly means "ruler of the mind" or "governor of the mind". Once you become the ruler of the government by proving that you are responsible and knowledgeable like a sovereign, the government becomes your servant; therefore, you have tamed the beast and it is no longer your master. This means that you no longer serve two masters. "No man can serve two masters: for either he will hate the one, and love the other; or else he will hold to the one, and despise the other. Ye cannot serve God and mammon."[38] There is a spiritual side to the Earth Matrix Drama, so if you do not know who you truly are and how to exercise your natural rights, you will have a very hard time freeing yourself from the artificial matrix of the Dark Forces. To effectively free yourself from the artificial matrix, you need to learn how to exercise the power of Natural Law. An important Natural Law that you need to learn how to wisely exercise is the Law of Free Will.

Chapter 3
The Legal Name Game

The Legal Name Game is one of the greatest con games that the Dark Forces like to use to enslave your soul. The Dark Magicians, which are the minions of the Dark Forces, like to use the legal name to trick you to temporarily surrender your natural rights to them. Once you do this, everything that you have purchased or owned under the legal name **legally** belongs to their Secret Government. In other words, your children, cars, house, land, and everything that you have purchased or owned using your legal name legally belong to their Secret Government. The good news is that the Dark Magicians did not setup the Legal Name Game in a lawful way and therefore have no **lawful** standing. If you want to learn how to defend your rights effectively, you need to know the difference between the words **legal** and **lawful**.

It is crucial to define the difference between legal and lawful. The generic Constitution references genuine law. The present civil authorities and their courts use the word legal. Is there a difference in the meanings? The following is quoted from A Dictionary of Law 1893:

Lawful. In accordance with the law of the land; according to the law; permitted, sanctioned, or justified by law. "Lawful" properly implies a thing conformable to or enjoined by law; "Legal", a thing in the form or after the manner of law or binding by law. A writ or warrant issuing from any court, under color of law, is a "legal" process however defective. See legal. [Bold emphasis added]

44

Legal. Latin *legalis*. *Pertaining to the understanding, the exposition, the administration, the science and the practice of law: as, the legal profession, legal advice; legal blanks, newspaper. Implied or imputed in law. Opposed to actual*

"Legal" looks more to the letter [form/appearance], and "Lawful" to the spirit [substance/content], of the law. "Legal" is more appropriate for conformity to positive rules of law; "Lawful" for accord with ethical principle. "Legal" imports rather that the forms [appearances] of law are observed, that the proceeding is correct in method, that rules prescribed have been obeyed; "Lawful" that the act is rightful in substance, that moral quality is secured. "Legal" is the antithesis of equitable, and the equivalent of constructive. 2 Abbott's Law Dic. 24. [Bold emphasis added][1]

In simple terms, something that is lawful is superior to something that is legal. If something is legal, it does not necessary mean that it is lawful. For example, killing someone intentionally is unlawful but can be legal. Lawful is more related to ethics, natural rights, and God's Law. Legal deals with the **color of law** and rights given by man or the government. The phrase "color of law" means the "**appearance** of law", and therefore the word legal has nothing to do with true law. Do you need evidence of this? *Black's Law Dictionary* (5th edition) defines the word **color** using these exact words: "An appearance, semblance, or *simulacrum*, as distinguished from that which is real. A *prima facie* or apparent right. Hence, a deceptive appearance; a plausible, assumed exterior, concealing a lack of reality; a disguise or pretext." Therefore, the phrase "color of law" means the "appearance of law". The words lawful and legal are not that hard to innerstand when you know that the word lawful is more related to Natural Law, also known as God's Law, and is used to communicate things of substance. As for the word legal, it is more related to laws created by man and is used to communicate things of form. In simple terms, something that is **lawful** is of **substance** so it is real, and something that is **legal** is of **form** so it appears to be real.

Some law researchers have said that the 1893 Dictionary of Arts and Sciences, and general literature / The R. S. Peale 9th Encyclopedia Britannica defines the word **legal** as "the undoing of

45

God's Law". In the legal system, many legal terms are used to trick you to agree to be a legal person or legal fiction which is an artificial person, also known as a corporation. A corporation (artificial person) is a dead entity that has no natural rights. By tricking you to consent to be a legal person/legal fiction, the Dark Magicians and their agents can legally claim that you have no natural rights, unless you rebut their claim. In other words, the legal system can be used to trick you to temporarily give up your natural rights which are the inherent rights given to you by God. The process of tricking you to give up your natural rights is the "undoing" of God's Law. This is the deeper meaning of why the word legal means "the undoing of God's Law". Please remember and be aware that when I say "God", I am talking about the Creator who created the heavens, the earth, and mankind.

What Is the Legal Name?

The legal name is not the name given to you by your mother and father; instead, it is a derivative name of your given name and family name. This legal name or derivative name was created by the government to make it easier for you to do business with its agencies. A word that has a strong connection to the legal name is signature. It is important to innerstand that signatures are used by persons to do business with corporations. Because of this, a signature is used by a man or a woman who is acting in the capacity of a person, allowing him or her to do business with the Dead. As a living man or woman, you do not have a signature; instead, you have an autograph. To be more specific, your legal name is the corporate name that the government uses to attach you to a dead and fictional character, so the government can identify you and do business with you. Because of this, if you want to successfully free yourself from the control of the Dark Forces, you have to stop thinking that the legal name is who you are. Furthermore, learn how to use the legal name wisely.

Names and legal names are not real people made of flesh and blood. Instead, they are abstract things that only exist in your imagination. In legal terms, names are the designations of artificial persons or legal fictions, also known as corporations. Because corporations are artificial persons, they can be pretty much anything that is not real. For example, religious institutions, banks, names, and governments are all corporations for the reason that they are fictitious entities that only exist in your mind. Remember this important fact:

46

your name or legal name is NOT who you really are because you are the nameless spiritual being living in a physical body made of flesh and blood. It is essential that you get this truth through your head or you will have a very hard time freeing yourself from the Earth Matrix Drama. Once you become aware that the legal name is not who you really are, you should feel the magic spell of the legal name slowly losing its effect, causing you to wake up and become more aware of who you really are.

Some spiritual teachers have said that the legal name is the "mark of the beast". In my opinion, the mark of the beast has different levels of meaning and is associated with a mark of spiritual slavery. The legal name can be used to spiritually enslave you and therefore has a strong connection to the mark of the beast. One of the ways that the legal name can be used to spiritually enslave you is through the art of signing your name on contracts. A word that has a strong connection to the legal name or the mark of the beast is signature. The word **signature** is defined as "a person's name, or a **mark** representing it, as signed personally or by deputy, as in subscribing a letter or other document" or "any unique, distinguishing aspect, feature, or **mark**" (bold emphasis added).[2] Every time you sign your name/signature on a commercial contract, you agree to play the game of commerce which is a game of "battery". If you are not careful and do not know the rules of the game, your legal name and signature can be used to enslave your body, mind, and soul. In other words, it can be used to mark you with a mark of spiritual slavery.

In the legal system, when a name is written in all lowercase letters (e.g., john quincy adams), it represents a natural person. On the other hand, when a name is written in all capital letters (e.g., JOHN QUINCY ADAMS), it represents a dead and artificial person, also known as a corporation. When a name is written properly (e.g., John Quincy Adams), it represents a lawful person. It is important to know that in legalese the word **person** can mean many things, such as a corporation, a partnership, a legal fiction, an artificial person, or a natural person. Keep in mind that the legal system mostly operates under Roman law, such as civil law. Nearly 99 percent of the time when you receive a letter or a document from a bank, a court, or a government agency, the name on the letter or the document is written in all CAPITAL LETTERS. This all caps name tells lawyers, attorneys, and judges that it is a legal name of a corporation or a dead man's estate. According to some law researchers, when a name is written in all capital letters and the letters are italicized (e.g., *JOHN QUINCY*

ADAMS), it represents a ship; furthermore, when a name is written in all capital letters with a middle initial (e.g., JOHN Q. ADAMS), it represents a public transmitting utility.

There are dozens of different potential meanings that can be arbitrarily assigned to anyone's name and used to "represent" radically different entities. In a verbal conversation we can talk all day long about someone or something named "John Quincy Adams" and which john quincy adams or what kind of JOHN QUINCY ADAMS will never be known, except from the context of the conversation — but on paper the use of such a system instantly defines what or whom is being talked about — if you know the system.[3]

Shortly after you were born, your parents/pair-rents gave you a name. They gave you or "ewe" a name because you are going to be a good little sheep for the Dark Magicians.[4] Did you know that the word **ewe** is defined as "a female sheep" and is pronounced similar to the word **you**?[5] The Dark Magicians like to call you/ewe a sheep or sheeple, because sheep are some of the most gullible animals on the planet and they are great at following orders. The word **sheeple** is defined as, "People compared to sheep in being docile, foolish, or easily led."[6] It is derived from the combination of the two words **sheep** and **people**. Why did your parents/pair-rents give you/ewe a name? Because the word "name" sounds like "neighhhm" which is a sound that horses like to make. Besides calling you a sheep, the Dark Magicians also like to call you a horse because **horse** is phonetically **whores**. If you think this is just a coincidence, you have no idea how deep the horse connection goes. Read further and I will show you why it is not a coincidence. Keep in mind that a horse can be used to represent positive or negative characteristics of people.

When couples have relationship problems and are constantly arguing, they are sometimes described as **nag**ging each other. A **nag** is "an old, inferior, or worthless **horse**" (bold emphasis added).[7] If they argue and nag at each other for too long, their voices may eventually sound **hoarse**.[8] When spoken aloud, the word "hoarse" sounds similar to the word "horse". Maybe the relationship is not **stable** because the **groom** did not **pony** up enough courage to get a good job, or maybe he could not afford a baby **crib**.[9] The word **crib** is simply an English synonym for **pony**. As for the word **groom**, it is defined as "a man or boy in charge of **horses** or the **stable**" (bold emphasis added).[10] The word **stable** means "a building for the lodging and feeding of **horses**, cattle, etc." (bold emphasis added).[11] In horse racing, the word **stable** means "an establishment where **racehorses** are kept and trained" (bold emphasis added).[12] When you really think about it, people are being trained and groomed by the Dark Forces and their minions to become the horses/whores of Babylon, the ancient capital city of Babylonia.[13] Today, many teachings and philosophies of certain secretive societies can be traced back to Babylon. The word **Babylon** is derived from the Greek version of Akkadian ***Bab-ilani***, meaning "the gate of the **gods**" (bold emphasis added).[14] Be aware that they are not talking about God; instead, they are talking about the **ancient gods**. Keep in mind that most, if not all, ancient gods are the personifications of important principles within us.

Let us turn our attention back to the horse connection. One of the major reasons that a couple argues is because they do not know how to manage their time. Etymologically, the word **manage** is derived from the Italian word ***maneggiare*** which means "to handle", especially "to control a **horse**" (bold emphasis added).[15][16] A word that has a strong connection to the word **manage** is **manager**, meaning "a person who has control or direction of an institution, business, etc., or of a part, division, or phase of it."[17] Based on the definitions in this paragraph, a **manager** is "a person who manages or controls **horses**." Metaphorically speaking, the horses are the workers or employees. Keep in mind that the words "manage" and "manager" may be related to the word "manger" because they all are directly or indirectly connected to horses. The word **manger** means "a box or trough in a stable or barn from which **horses** or cattle eat" (bold emphasis added).[18]

Another term that is related to **horse** is **ponytail**. Sometimes a man does not like it when his woman puts her hair in a ponytail. This may sound silly but some men do get angry at their women for putting their hair in a ponytail too many times. Furthermore, women who do not have nice **bangs** can be turn-offs for some men. Bangs usually do not cause too many issues in relationships, so they should not be the main problem. Oh, I know! Maybe the man does not like to **bang** his woman anymore. When the word **pony** is translated from German to English, it means "bang", "**bangs**", or "fringe".[19] In English, the word **pony** is defined as "a **horse** of any small type or breed" (bold emphasis added).[20] Do you still think the **horse/whores** connection

49

is just a coincidence? We have barely scratched the surface of this subject.

The Legal Name and Commerce

In commerce, when you see a name written in all capital letters, it is a corporate name or a legal name. The legal name plays a significant role in your life because it is used by the government as a conduit or a liaison, so it can do business with you (the living man). This is why whenever the government, the bank, or any corporation sends you a document with your legal name on it, 99 percent of the time it is written in all capital letters. The process that allows the government to **legally** claim you as a corporate entity involves the creation of a fictional character and tricking you to consent to be that fictional character, which is the artificial person associated with your legal name. This legal name was created shortly after you were born and was recorded on a bond. This bond that represents the date of your artificial person's birth is publicly known as your birth certificate. The word **bond** is legally defined as "a contract by specialty to pay a certain sum of money; being a deed or instrument under seal, by which the maker or obligor promises, and thereto binds himself, his heirs, executors, and administrators, to pay a designated sum of money to another; usually with a clause to the effect that upon performance of a certain condition (as to pay another and smaller sum) the obligation shall be void."[21]

To connect the dots, the birth certificate bond is a financial contract that can be used to enslave your body, mind, and soul by turning you into **collateral** to backup the debt of the government. However, when the birth certificate is used properly, it can be used to discharge corporate debt. Anyone who has improperly used a birth certificate by accepting it as an identification has been physically and spiritually enslaved by the Dark Forces. Sadly, most people are unaware of this artifice. Because of this, they have little chance of freeing themselves from the birth certificate bond. This certificate is a **magic contract**; therefore, it not only bonds you on the physical level but also on the spiritual level. Have you ever wondered why birth certificates have seals on them? These seals are sigils. The word **sigil** is derived from the Latin word **sigilla**, meaning "seal".[22] Keep in mind that each letter of the alphabet is also a sigil. The word **sigil** is defined as "a sign, **word**, or device held to have occult power in astrology or **magic**" (bold emphasis added).[23] The letters of words were created using sacred geometry and occult science to harness the power of thought and magic; therefore, words are sigils.

Let us turn our attention back to the legal name. A few days after you were born, the government gave you a legal name that looked similar to the name given to you by your mother and father. Your legal name, which is used by the government to do business with you (the body of **water** or **liquid**), is written in all capital letters because it is a piece of **liquidated capital** or "cap-it-all".[24] In other words, your legal name has been securitized and turned into a financial instrument that is bonded to your body. This gives value to any financial instrument with your legal name on it, allowing it to be sold in commerce. Hence, the term liquidated capital. To liquidate something is to sell it for money or sell it to pay off a debt. Keep in mind that you, the natural man or the natural woman, were born in your mother's womb which was mostly made of water (liquid). You are also made of mostly water. Because you are made of mostly **liquid** and have been **securitized**, you are considered **liquidated capital**. The word **capital** comes from the Latin word **capitalis**, meaning "of the head", hence "capital, chief, first" (bold emphasis added).[25] It also comes from another Latin word **caput** which translates to English as "head".[26]

When you really study the occult definitions in the previous few paragraphs, you should come to the conclusion that the process of turning you into capital money or liquidated capital is their way of saying that you have a "bounty on your head". Your birth certificate is the **bond** with your legal name written on it in all **capital** letters; therefore, it is the financial document (security/**capital**) or insurance certificate that has the value of the **bounty** on your **head**. This is why your birth certificate can be used to issue bonds to trade on the stock market. The good news is that when you properly use your birth certificate, you, as the beneficial owner, are first to receive the beneficial interest of your birth certificate.

In most, if not almost all, Western and Eastern countries, shortly after babies are born, governments put a bounty on their heads because they think of them as potential enemies. According to Judge Dale, author of *The Great American Adventure: The Secrets of America*, if you reside in the United States, the act that makes "you" an enemy of the U.S. government is the Trading with the Enemy Act. Even if the corporate U.S. government considers you (United States citizen) as an enemy of the State, it actually has no jurisdiction over you, the man (male and female) living in a physical body made of flesh and blood. However, when you agree to **act** in the **capacity** of a United States citizen, then the U.S. government has jurisdiction over you.

The good news is that the U.S. government only has jurisdiction over you when you are **acting** in the **capacity** of a United States citizen or a citizen of the United States. For example, within the United State of America, if you have a driver's license, the only time when the police can legally pull you over for violating traffic laws is when you drive a vehicle registered to the State, strictly speaking. When you do this, they **presume** that you are **acting** in the **capacity** of a government agent or employee. In other words, the U.S. government only has **legal** jurisdiction over you when you are using your driver's license, or any government issued ID, to **perform acts of government**. However, it does not have **lawful** jurisdiction. The reason that the U.S. government has legal jurisdiction over United States citizens or citizens of the United States is that they are considered artificial persons (corporations) and therefore have no natural rights. Furthermore, citizens of the United States are considered "employees" of the United States (incorporated) and therefore are bound to the acts and statutes of this corporation. If you want evidence that the United State is a corporation, look at subsections 15 and 15(A) in *Title 28 U.S. Code § 3002* and you should see this sentence, " 'United States' means— (A) a Federal corporation".

The act that set in motion the creation of the United States (Inc.), which is often mistaken for **T**he United States of America, was the *District of Columbia Organic Act of 1871*. Unlike the country **T**he United States of America, which operates under a **republican** form of government, the United States is a municipal **republic** and the United States of America is a territorial **democracy**. Keep in mind that the United States of America (controlled by the British Monarchy) and the United States (controlled by the Holy See) are not the same as **T**he United States of America (controlled by the American People). These are three separate business entities which is why there are three constitutions: (1) "The Constitution **for** the **u**nited States of America" (Federal Constitution), (2) "The Constitution **of** the United States of America" (Territorial Constitution), and (3) "The Constitution of the United States" (Municipal Constitution). The first constitution is a business contract between the American Government and the Federal Government; the second constitution is a business contract between the American Government and the British

Monarchy; and the third constitution is a business contract between the American Government and the Holy See.

In the previous paragraph, an important word that you need to know its deeper meaning is democracy. In a society where the people are ignorant and irresponsible, democracy is one of the worst forms of government. The word **democracy** (demo-cracy) comes from the Greek words *demos* which means "common people", and *kratos* which means "rule, strength".[27] A group of common people can also be called a **mob**. One of the origins of the suffix **-cracy** is the Latin word *cratia*, meaning "power, might; rule, sway; power over; a power, authority".[28] Based on these definitions, democracy can mean "mob rule". In a democracy, the voting power of the majority overrules the rights of the minority. For example, if a man, acting as one of the people, were on trial for not believing in God and 51 percent of the people in the room were to vote that he should be hung, that man would be hung for not believing in God. In a state operating under a certain common law, such as American common law, his free will and natural rights would be protected. Do you innerstand now why democracy means mob rule? This is why in a society where the people are **ignorant** and **irresponsible** democracy is one of the worst forms of government.

Today, most citizens throughout the world are ignorant and irresponsible, which is why it is easy for the Dark Magicians and their Secret Government to enslave them under the rule of democracy. Do you innerstand now why the Secret Government is always talking about spreading democracy throughout the world? When citizens are ignorant and irresponsible, **democracy** often leads to **communism**. One of the main differences between these two political systems is that in a democracy the people have the **privilege** to vote. However, their votes do not matter as much as they think because the voting system is rigged. Keep in mind that a privilege is not a natural right and therefore can be taken away by the government.

How the Voting System Is Used to Drain Your Energy

This spring (2016), many Americans will be watching the 2016 Presidential Debate, so they can make an "informed" decision to vote for the candidate that they believe is the best to lead their country. What most Americans do not realize is that the presidential debate is a "play", and therefore all presidential candidates are basically actors auditioning for an acting job of a **corporation** called the United States. **May the best actor win!** After being hired, the new president is assigned to more acting lessons, so he or she can become one of the best professional actors that money can buy. The Dark Magicians like presidents who are professional actors, especially the ones that are professional liars, because they can easily fool the American people to support the United States (incorporated) and help expand its franchise throughout the world. The word **franchise** means "the right or license granted by a company to an individual or group to market its products or services in a specific territory."[29] But did you know that the word **franchise** can also mean "the right to vote"?[30] Every time you vote in their private corporate elections, you agree, whether you realize it or not, to be a franchise of their corporation (United States, Inc.). As a franchise, you are under the jurisdiction of commercial laws, such as admiralty law and the Uniform Commercial Code (UCC).

Like any corporate employee, when a presidential candidate wins an election and is sworn into office, he or she becomes an employee of a corporation. The main difference is that he or she gets to play the role of the CEO of the United States, a **Federal corporation**. Do you remember what I said earlier about *Title 28 U.S. Code § 3002*? Under *Title 28 U.S. Code § 3002* subsections 15 and 15(A), " 'United States' means— (A) a **Federal corporation**" (bold emphasis added). It is right in their so-called laws which are not really laws but are "acts" and "statutes". A play also has "acts"; furthermore, it often has "statues" as props. Hence, the play called the presidential debate. This debate is a play because it has presidential candidates/**actors** standing behind a podium like **statues** as they are worshiped like **idols** by naive citizens. The word **idol** is defined as "an image or other material object representing a **deity** to which religious worship is addressed" (bold emphasis added).[31] Today, the U.S. government is the new god or deity for Americans and their new religion is democracy.

As an employee of the United States (incorporated), the President has to follow the rules, codes, acts, and statutes of the United States (incorporated) or the President can be fired. Unlike a traditional employee, the President can only be fired by his or her **board of directors**, also known as the **Congress**. By now you should start to see how the offices of the United States are structured like a corporation, which is why the United States has a president and a vice president, and a few secretary offices. One of its departments is even called U.S. Department of Human Resources. Because the United States is a corporation, it also has **shareholders**. Some of these shareholders practice the art of dark magic and therefore are sometimes called the Dark Magicians. Some people like to refer to them as the Elite or the Cabal. Because the United States has shareholders, one of its top priorities is to make sure that its shareholders are happy. One of the most profitable businesses for the United States (incorporated) is war. Many wars have been engineered or partially planned by the Dark Magicians of the Secret Government to make money and spread tyranny throughout the world.

An important information that you need to know about the United States (incorporated) is that it has, to a large extent, seized the flag of The United States of America, which is the **war** flag with the 50 stars and 13 stripes made up of the colors red and white. Because of this, it is under the control of the corporation known as the United States (incorporated), usually written in all capital letters (UNITED STATES) in legal documents. The good news is that they did not seize the flag lawfully and therefore have no lawful standing. Another important information that you need to know about the war flag with the 50 stars and 13 stripes is that when its border has a gold fringe, it represents the U.S. military flag of war. This flag deals with martial law, territorial law, admiralty law, and maritime law. When you see the gold fringe U.S. flag in a government building (e.g., courtroom), it means that common law rights and the Constitution are suspended or void, and therefore the building is operating under military and commercial laws.

The U.S. military flag of war, which is the U.S. flag with the gold fringe on its border, was traditionally flown over U.S. military buildings only during wartime. Today, this flag is seen in nearly every court in the United States and in the offices of U.S. politicians! To make matters worse, almost all American courts operating under American common law have been replaced by foreign courts operating under military and commercial laws. In other words, Americans are living under a less severe form of **martial law**. In simple terms, Americans have been conquered from within because of their ignorance and irresponsibility. If you have the flag with the 50 stars and 13 stripes in your home or yard, you may want to remove it. This flag does not really represent freedom because it is a flag of **war**. If you were to display it, you would be expressing that you are at war. Because of this, you can be labeled as an enemy combatant, preventing you from being eligible for the Law of Peace. This flag is controlled by the United States, an incorporated entity controlled by the New World Order (NWO). However, this does not mean that Americans cannot regain control of it. To do this, Americans need to wake up and repopulate their lawful courts and government offices.

Because the flag with the 50 stars and red and white stripes is a flag of **war**, if you are the type of man or woman who likes to protest against the wars of the U.S. government, do not bring that flag with you to the protest. If you were to bring it with you and wave it around like it represents freedom, you would be making a fool of yourself. It is like going to a protest against the Nazi while at the same time wearing a pro-Nazi shirt and carrying a Nazi flag. An important information that is beneficial for you to know about protests is that they do not create significant and empowering changes, so it is best to avoid them. When you protest, you are basically telling the government that you want change, but you want the government to do it for you. In other words, you are thinking and acting like an incompetent baby who is not responsible enough to be truly free from the control of the government.

Once you know that U.S. presidential candidates are actors auditioning for a corporate job of the United States (incorporated), you should know why it is pointless to vote for these candidates, unless you want to be their subject. The truth is, as a United States citizen, you do not have the "right" to vote. In legal terms, your right to vote as a United States citizen is actually a privilege because to be a "United States citizen" means that you are a "legal person" or an "artificial person", also known as a "corporation". According to *Black's Law Dictionary* (6th edition), a **corporation** is "an **artificial person** or **legal entity** created by or under the authority of the laws of a state" (bold emphasis added). An **artificial person/legal person** is considered a **dead entity** because it does not exist in the real world. Because a corporation is an artificial person, it has no natural rights, such as the right to vote, the right to speak, and the right to make choices. So, when U.S. politicians tell you that you have the right to vote as a United States citizen, they are already lying to you. Keep in mind that **voting** is NOT the same as **electing**.

To innerstand what voting is on a deeper level, you need to investigate the word vote and its definitions. Furthermore, you need to investigate its etymology. As a noun, **vote** is derived from the Latin word ***votum***, meaning "a vow, wish, **promise** to a **god**, solemn pledge, dedication" (bold emphasis added).[32] It has a strong connection to the Latin word ***votus***, past participle of ***vovere***,

56

meaning "to promise, dedicate".[33] As a verb, **vote** etymologically means "give a vote to" or "to **vow**" (bold emphasis added).[34] Every time you vote for U.S. politicians to represent you in office, you consent to be governed by many anti-constitutional politicians. Many U.S. politicians do not really care about you for the reason that they work for the Dark Magicians and their Secret Government. All U.S. politicians working in Washington D.C. have sworn a solemn oath to the New World Order, and therefore their allegiance is to the British Monarchy and the Holy See, not to the American people. However, without the American people to pay for their government services, their empires will lose a great deal of power. Because of this, when the American people wake up and realize that their rights and freedom have been usurped under the color of law, the British Monarchy and the Holy See will have to "drain the swamp" or face the consequence of losing the American people as their customers. Let us continue investigating the word vote. *Black's Law Dictionary* (5th edition) defines the word **vote** using these exact words:

> **Suffrage**; the expression of one's will, preference, or choice, formally manifested by a member of a legislative or deliberative body, or of a constituency or a body of **qualified electors**, in regard to the decision to be made by the body as a whole upon any proposed measure or proceeding or in passing laws, rules or regulations, or the selection of an officer or representative. And the aggregate of the expressions of will or choice, thus manifested by individuals, is called the "vote of the body." Commonwealth v. Baker, 237 Ky. 380, 35 S.W.2d 548, 549; Sawyer Stores v. Mitchell, 103 Mont. 148, 62 P.2d 342, 348. [Bold emphasis added]

Dictionary.com defines the word **vote** as, "a formal expression of opinion or choice, either positive or negative, made by an individual or body of individuals" or "the means by which such expression is made, as a ballot, ticket, etc."[35] CollinsDictionary.com defines the word **vote** as, "A vote is a choice made by a particular person or group in a meeting or an election."[36] To innerstand the word vote on a deeper level, you need to investigate two important terms in the previous definition which are "suffrage" and "qualified electors". The term **suffrage** is defined by *Black's Law Dictionary* (6th edition) using these exact words: "A **vote**; the act of voting; the right or privilege of casting a vote at public elections. The last is the meaning of the term in such phrases as "the extension of the suffrage," "universal suffrage," etc." (bold emphasis added). Merriam-Webster.com defines the word **suffrage** as "the right of voting: **franchise**" (bold emphasis added); also "the exercise of such right".[37] A word in the previous definition that you need to investigate is franchise. The word **franchise** means "the right or license granted by a company to an individual or group to market its products or services in a specific territory."[38] Do you remember what I said earlier that "the word **franchise** can also mean 'the right to vote' " and that "every time you vote in their private corporate elections, you agree, whether you realize it or not, to be a franchise of their corporation (United States, Inc.)"?

To connect the dots, the moment you become a citizen of a "country" (please be aware that nearly all countries on Earth have been incorporated and therefore are registered and commercial corporations), you also agree to be a franchise of the "country" thereof. For example, in The United States of America (unincorporated), most Americans have been tricked into believing and accepting that they are citizens of the United States (incorporated). Because of this, they are its **franchises** which is why they can **vote**. Remember, the word **franchise** means "the right to vote". This concept of allowing franchises to vote is similar to the franchise system of fast food restaurants, such as McDonald's franchise system. In the franchise system of McDonald's, each franchise has a right to vote before McDonald's decides to change certain rules.

Because citizens of the United States are franchises of the United States (incorporated), they have the "privilege of casting a vote at public elections". They are also subject to the acts and statutes of their parent corporation (United States (Inc.)). The term **parent corporation** means "a company that owns other companies where the other companies are a subsidiary of the parent company."[39] In other words, **citizens**/franchises are **subjects** of their parent corporation. An important word that is strongly connected to the word **franchise** is **enfranchise**, meaning "to grant a **franchise** to; admit to **citizenship**, especially to the right of **voting**" (bold emphasis added).[40] In other words, before you can be a citizen/franchise and given "the right of voting" (suffrage), you need to first be enfranchised, allowing the government to legally grant you citizenship status. Keep in mind that the act of turning people into franchises is not limited to the United States. Because you now know what the term suffrage means, let us investigate the term qualified electors. Here is an excerpt from *The Errant Sovereign's Handbook* by Augustus Blackstone that does a great job of deciphering the term **qualified electors**:

The government, through Congress, **represents** *the will of the majority*. **Who** are *the majority*? **Voters**, right? Voters are **qualified electors**. That implies rather plainly that there are *electors* who are **not** *qualified*. So what is this "qualified" business about? We know that to register to vote there are age, citizenship and residency **restrictions**. Is there anything else to be considered? Perhaps we should examine the word "qualify." As a verb, its root meaning is to **limit**, to **reduce** from a general to a specific form. The word "limit", as a verb, essentially means to **restrict**. "Reduce" means to lessen, to **diminish** the quantity or **quality** of something. Since the object of the limitation or reduction is the *elector*, we must then ask, **what** is being diminished or restricted? What is the elector losing or giving up to obtain a *qualified status*? What does an elector still have that a *qualified* elector no longer has? To ascertain we will have to determine what an elector is, what an elector does or is capable of doing, and what an elector has or may have as a matter of course.

As a verb, the root meaning of *elector* is to *choose*. An elector is one who chooses or has the capacity to choose **at will**. In Law, **that** is a power and a right possessed by a **sovereign**. So it would seem that the elector must limit or diminish some aspect of his individual **sovereignty** in order to obtain a *qualified* status.

Because you now have a better understanding of the terms "suffrage" and "qualified electors", let us further investigate the word vote. Do you remember what I said earlier that "the word **vote** is derived from the Latin word *votum*, meaning "a vow, wish, **promise** to a **god**, solemn pledge, dedication"? The lowercase form of the word **god** is defined as, "one of several deities, especially a male deity, presiding over some portion of worldly affairs" or "an image of a deity; an idol."[41] The word **idol** means "an image or other material object representing a deity to which religious worship is addressed" or "an image of a deity other than God."⁴² Because the word vote etymologically means "promise to a god" or "solemn pledge", when you vote, you are making a promise to a god which is the government. In other words, the **government** is the **god** of **voters**. Why do you think the word vote etymologically means "promise to a god"? To find evidence that the government is the god of voters, you need to study certain definitions of the word government. According to *A Dictionary of Law* (1889), the word **governmen**t means:

> Government is formed by depriving all persons of a portion of their natural rights. The rights they enjoy under government are not conferred by it, but are those of which they have not been deprived. It is only by a deprivation of all persons of a portion of their rights that it is possible to form and maintain government. ...

> **Government** is an **abstract entity**. It **speaks** and **acts through agents**; these hold offices under law, constitutional or statutory, with prescribed duties and limited authority. [Bold emphasis added]

One of the terms in the previous paragraph that you need to investigate is "abstract entity". In this term, the word "abstract" is used as an adjective. The adjective form of the word **abstract** means, "Existing in thought or as an idea but not having a physical or concrete existence."⁴³ In other words, the government is an imaginary thing that exists in the collective mind of the people. In the world of occult magic, an abstract entity (government) is known as an **egregore** which is a "thought-form" or "collective group mind". It is important to innerstand that an egregore is a psychic entity. This type of entity relies on people's psychic energy to charge it with energy, strengthening its power and allowing it to continue to exist and function properly. In other words, an egregore functions like a psychic battery so it needs people to support it with their currency or it will eventually become weak and powerless, just like a dead battery. This is why the government needs your support and currency (money). A very important information about egregores is that the act of **worshiping** them can transform them into false **gods**.

There is nothing immoral about supporting an honorable government that respects your rights and freedom; however, **worshiping** it is not wise because it will eventually lead to the enslavement of your mind and body. When you worship a government, you accept, whether you realize it or not, that it is your master, transforming it into a false god. Worshiping any government is a violation of God's Law because it is **idolatry**, meaning "the religious worship of idols."[44] Remember, the word **idol** means "an image or other material object representing a deity to which religious worship is addressed" or "an image of a deity other than God." Today, most people have forgotten who the true God is which is why they go to man-made buildings, such as churches and temples, to worship images and material objects representing deities (idols). Furthermore, they trust and obey the government more than God, and then they wonder why God does not answer their prayers and protect them. If you want God to answer your prayers and give you protection, one of the first things that you have to do is stop worshiping idols. You also have to trust God and obey His Ten Commandments.

> You shall not make for yourself a carved image—any likeness of anything that is in heaven above, or that is in the earth beneath, or that is in the water under the earth; you shall not bow down to them nor serve them. For I, the LORD your God, am a jealous God, visiting the iniquity of the fathers upon the children to the third and fourth generations of those who hate Me, but showing mercy to thousands, to those who love Me and keep My commandments. (Exodus 20:4-6, NKJV)

Let us turn our attention back to the voting system of the United States. Voting in the United States is a political chicanery because your vote does not matter that much and the voting system is rigged somewhat like a casino. Until they drain the swamp of corrupt government agents and stop vote rigging, the voting system should not be trusted. It is important to know that when you, as an American, vote for a U.S. president, you are not voting for a president of a country but are voting for a president of a FOREIGN corporation known as the United States (incorporated), also doing business as the United States of America (incorporated). Another important information to know about the voting system of the United States is that many presidential candidates are selected by the Dark Magicians and they control many politicians of the Republican and Democratic parties. The idea that citizens have choices when it comes to electing U.S. presidential candidates is an illusion. The fact that presidential candidates are first selected before they are voted into office is evidence that the ones doing the selecting are in control of which presidential candidates are available for citizens to vote for. The good news is that people are waking up and seeing through the deception, causing the ones doing the selecting to change the voting system into a better system.

As an American, when you **vote** for U.S. politicians instead of **electing** them, you basically commit a treacherous act against the country called The United States of America, which is made up of separate states operating as a nation on the land jurisdiction. The United States, when doing business as the United States of America, operates under the international jurisdiction of the sea; this jurisdiction is based on admiralty law (law of the sea). Admiralty law deals with commerce and therefore is sometimes known as the law of money. If you really want to know what you are doing when you vote, you need to study the occult definitions of the word vote. On a deeper level, the act of voting is a religious ritual that can be used to drain your energy and enslave your body, mind, and soul. Do you need evidence of this? Read further and I will show you the evidence.

The word **vote** is defined as "a formal expression of opinion or choice, either positive or negative, made by an individual or body of individuals" or "the means by which such expression is made, as a ballot, ticket, etc."[45] These two definitions only show you the overt meanings of the word vote. To find its occult meanings, you need to use the art of homophone to help you find other words phonetically related to the word vote. Phonetically, the word **vote** sounds nearly identical to the word **volt**. Where do voters go **vote/volt** at? They go to a voting booth or a polling/**poll**-ing booth. The word **poll** sounds similar to the word **pole** which is defined as "either of the two regions or parts of an electric battery, magnet, or the like, that exhibits electrical or magnetic polarity."[46] In other words, a pole is the electric battery pole of positive (+) or negative (-). This is why when you go **vote** you go to the **polls/poles** so you can place your **vote/volt** on the candidate who you want to see put in **charge**.[47] Once the votes/volts are counted, the politician or "**pole**-itician" who receives the most votes/volts will be elected into the position of **power**. Maybe this is why it is called power politics. Every time you vote, you CONSENT to give your **electrical energy** to the government so its agents can use it to power their corporations, also known as corpses (dead bodies).

It is important to innerstand that **voting** is NOT the same as

electing. As a verb, the word **vote** etymologically means "give a vote to" or "to vow".[48] As for the verb **elect**, it etymologically means "to pick out, **choose**" (bold emphasis added).[49] When you investigate the previous definitions, you should come to the conclusion that the word **elect** has a strong connection to **sovereignty** and the word **vote** has a strong connection to **slavery**. The former connection can be seen when you investigate the words elector and sovereign. An elector and sovereign both have the power to **choose**. In man, that is the power of free will. The compound noun **free will** means, "The ability or discretion to choose; free choice".[50] Many words that start with "el" have a strong connection to sovereignty. For example, the words elect, elector, and elite all start with "el". The word **elite** comes from the Latin word *eligere*, meaning "choose".[51] The words **elect** and **elector** are also derived from the same Latin word. An important fact to know about the word "el" is that it means "god".[52] The word **god** has a strong connection to **sovereignty**.

Based on the information in the previous paragraph, the word **vote** etymologically means "to vow". When you make a **vow**, you agree to make a **solemn promise**. The moment you make a solemn promise (vote/vow) to someone, you give up some of your power to choose. On the other hand, when you elect someone, you exercise your power to choose. This is why voting does not really make a difference when it comes to true freedom and sovereignty, which is why they allow and encourage you to vote. When you really think about it, the words **vote** and **elect** are **opposites**. Once you innerstand this on a deeper level, you should know that **electing** is for **sovereigns** and **voting** is for **subjects**. Keep in mind that "subjects" can be defined as "slaves". Do you want to be a sovereign or a subject/slave? All registered voters of the United States (a registered corporation) are subjects (franchises) of the United States and therefore are not sovereigns. If you are a registered voter of the United States and want to be a sovereign, you have to revoke your voter registration and then do not participate in anymore corporate elections of the United States.

When you contemplate all the information in this subchapter, you should realize that the presidential election of today is a game that is often used to con you to agree to be a "battery", so corporations can drain your life force energy to power their dead matrix and franchises. This is why before they can summon you to go to court they need to **charge** you first, just like charging a battery before its energy is drained to power electronic devices. The good news is that when more men and women know how to be peaceable sovereigns and exercise

63

their God-given rights, they can create a world where the living (men and women) and the dead (governments and corporations) can all thrive in peace. Peace can only happen when the living and the dead work together in a harmonious way and respect each other's jurisdiction.

Let us turn our attention back to the legal name and the birth certificate and investigate them further, so we can finish this chapter (The Legal Name Game) before it gets too shocking and mind-boggling for some people to read. By now you should know that your legal name is a name of a legal person (legal fiction) which is why nearly 99 percent of the time it is written in all capital letters on legal documents. It is important to know that even when your legal name is not written in all capital letters it could still represent a legal person or corporation. Once you innerstand this process, you should know that your legal name is written in all capital letters because it has been incorporated and securitized so it can be used in commerce.

Another reason that your legal name is often written in all capital letters on legal documents (e.g., birth certificate) is because capital letters are more effective for creating magic spells! Your birth certificate is not just a record of birth; it is also a legal document sealed with magic. This is why there are sigils (seals) on your birth certificate. Your parents' **signatures** are also **sigils/seals**. Because of this, the birth certificate that they have signed on your behalf can spiritually seal you to it. When you separate the word "signature" into two words, it transforms into "sig nature". The abbreviation **sig.** is defined as "write; **mark**; label" (bold emphasis added).[53] It is derived from the Latin word **signā**. In English, this Latin word is written as **signa**, meaning "**mark**; write; label" (bold emphasis added).[54] As for the word **nature**, one of its origins is the Latin word **natura** which literally means "**birth**".[55] It can also mean "course of things; natural character, constitution, quality; the universe".[56] In other words, a **signature** is a "birth mark". Based on the definitions in this paragraph, when your parents signed their signatures on the birth certificate with your name on it, they **marked** you at **birth** with **sigils** and therefore spiritually and magically **bonded** you to the birth certificate. This can be beneficial or unbeneficial to you, depending on how the birth certificate is used.

When your birth certificate is used properly, it works like a stock certificate. In other words, your birth certificate is **evidence** of your **beneficial interest** in a corporate trust. Like any stock certificate that is associated with a trust and has your legal name on it, you are the beneficial owner of the trust, giving you the right to receive interest generated by the trust. However, when your parents used your birth certificate, on your behalf, as evidence of your identity, they unknowingly attached you to a dead identity (legal fiction) of the State, making you the debtor and thereby preventing you from receiving interest generated by the trust. By doing this, they allowed the State to claim you as its legal property. Sadly, your parents most likely did not know this for the reason that they lacked the knowledge to innerstand the power of word magic, trust, signature, and the legal name. The **signature** and **legal name** can be used to spiritually enslave you. This is why it is very important to use them wisely, so they cannot be used to mark you with the **mark of the beast**.

Chapter 4
The Secrets of the Systems of Education and Religion

There is a secretive and dark side to the education system. If you are not aware of it by now, you have already been enslaved by it to a significant degree. The good news is that there are ways to free yourself from the dark side of the education system. By the end of this book, you will know how to not only free yourself from it, but also free your mind and soul from the dead matrix of the Dark Forces. In the United States of America, most children start school around the age of 4 or 5. The first class of elementary (primary) school that is used to school children to be good little sheep is kindergarten. The word "kindergarten" is derived from two German words which are *"kinder"* and *"garten"*. When these two German words are translated to English, **kinder** means "children" and **garten** means "garden".[1] Therefore, **kindergarten** means "garden of children". In English, the word **garden** means "a plot of ground, usually near a house, where flowers, shrubs, vegetables, fruits, or herbs are cultivated."[2]

Now, ask yourself this question and think about it for a minute. Why is it that the first class of elementary school is called kindergarten (garden of children)? To innerstand why we need to turn our attention to the story of Adam and Eve and the Garden of Eden, and investigate the occult meanings behind this story. According to the Bible, shortly after God created the heavens and the earth, He also created a garden and a man named Adam. This man was given dominion over the plants and animals in the garden which was called the Garden of Eden. Shortly after creating Adam, God used one of Adam's rib to create a woman named Eve to be Adam's companion.

Before I reveal some controversial information about Adam and Eve and the Garden of Eden, I need to show you the Bible verse Genesis 1:26 (NKJV). This verse is important for helping you innerstand some of the occult meanings of the story of Adam and Eve.

> Then God said, "Let Us make man in Our image, according to Our likeness; let them have dominion over the fish of the sea, over the birds of the air, and over the cattle, over all the earth and over every creeping thing that creeps on the earth."

Did you notice that the first seven words that God said was, "Let Us make man in Our image"? This verse is talking about more than one god. When the Bible talks about God, it is not always talking about God as One Supreme Being. In Genesis 1:26, the Bible may be talking about the Holy Trinity (the Father, the Son, and the Holy Spirit). It has been mentioned by some biblical scholars that the early version of the Bible verse Genesis 1:26 was changed from "Then **Elohim** said, 'Let Us make man in Our image' " to "Then **God** said, 'Let Us make man in Our image.' " The word **Elohim** is a plural noun and is a Hebrew word that is used to express God's most powerful character; therefore, **Elohim** means "Supreme One", "Mighty One", or "Strong One". In Hebrew, the singular noun for "God" is **Eloh**.[3] **Elohim** "is the first name for God given in the Tanakh".[4] Here is an excerpt from Hebrew-Streams.org that does a great job of explaining why God is plural in Genesis 1:26:

> Biblical usage suggests that Elohim reflects a "plural of honor" or "plural of fulness." The plural ending gives greater honor to God. It's like capitalizing the word, instead of printing "god." ... though Hebrew has no capital and small letters.

> The Hebrews believed theirs was the only deity who embodied all definitions of the title God, Deity, Supreme Power. So they amplified the noun. Elohim doesn't mean "Gods" but something like "the Greatest God of all."[5]

According to the Bible, there are many gods besides *Elohim*. Some researchers of ancient civilizations referred to some of those gods as alien gods and believed that they visited Earth thousands of years ago. One of the alien races that they believed visited Earth was the Anunnaki. It is said that during ancient times some of those alien races were worshiped as gods. Even today, many secretive societies still worship alien gods. Is it true that intelligent extraterrestrial beings have visited Earth? Based on my research, I can confidently say that there are some truths to this claim; however, be aware that there is a lot of false information in the public domain about extraterrestrial beings.

From the perspective of Earth, extraterrestrial beings are beings that are foreign to her body. This becomes obvious when you separate the word extraterrestrial into two words (extra terrestrial) and study their definitions. Etymologically, the word-forming element **extra** means "outside; beyond the scope of; in addition to what is usual or expected".[6] As for the word **terrestrial**, it etymologically means "of or pertaining to the earth".[7] Based on these definitions, **extraterrestrial** means "outside of earth" or "beyond the scope of earth". In other words, an extraterrestrial being is any being that is beyond the scope of earth; therefore, astral beings, thought-forms (creatures of the mind), and alien gods can be called extraterrestrial beings. These extraterrestrial beings can affect the minds of men and women, causing changes in their DNA and bodies.

The alien gods were said to come from the stars. One of those stars is called Sirius. The word **Sirius** is related to the Latin word *siri* which translates to English as "Sirius, **greater dog-star**" (bold emphasis added).[8] Some ufologists believed that the **Grays** came from the Sirius star system, while others believed that they came from Zeta Reticuli. The Latin word for **gray** is *canus*.[9] This Latin word sounds very similar to the Latin word *canis*, meaning "dog" or "**dog star**" (bold emphasis added).[10] The Latin word *canis* is related to the constellation **Canis Major** which means "the greater dog". Canis Major represents the bigger dog following the constellation Orion which is known as the mythical hunter. Certain ancient civilizations believed that the **stars** were the physical manifestation of the different states of **God**. Hence, the term "star god" or "sun god". When you spell the word **god** backwards, you get the word **dog**. Put the word "dog" in front of the word "star" and you get the term "dog star". The information in this paragraph reveals that the word **god** has a strong connection to the words **dog** and **Sirius**, the star system where many of the ancient alien gods are said to come from. Keep in mind that the external universe is a reflection of the internal universe.

In other words, it is a reflection of the mind. Because of this, the ancient alien gods are thought-forms that exist within the mind.

If you have read my articles on ancient and biblical myths, you should know that the Bible is a religious book full of metaphors, allegories, codes, symbols, esoteric anagrams, and parables; therefore, if you do not learn how to decipher the Bible, you will not be able to access many of the empowering truths hidden in the metaphors, allegories, parables, and words of the Bible. This is why the sentences in the Bible are called **verses**. The word **verse** is defined as, "A single metrical line in a poetic composition; one line of **poetry**" (bold emphasis added).[11] An important information that is beneficial for you to know about a poem is that it often has **metaphors**. If the information in this paragraph is hard for you to accept, look at the Bible verses Matthew 13:34-35 (NIV) and you will find evidence that the Bible has parables.

> Jesus spoke all these things to the crowd in parables; he did not say anything to them without using a parable. So was fulfilled what was spoken through the prophet:
>
> "I will open my mouth in parables, I will utter things hidden since the creation of the world."[12]

Because you now know that the Bible is a religious book full of parables, let us turn our attention back to Adam and Eve and the Garden of Eden. When the Bible refers to Adam, it is not always referring to a man made of flesh and blood. In Genesis of the Bible, the character **Adam** has a strong connection to the **atom** (atomic particle). The Hebrew word for Adam is אָדָם (*adam*), meaning "man" in English. The name **Adam** etymologically means, "Biblical name of the first man, progenitor of the human race, from Hebrew *adam* "man," literally "(the one formed from the) ground" (Hebrew *adamah* "ground")".[13] According to the Bible, God formed man or אָדָם (*adam*) of the dust of the ground. "And the LORD God formed man of the dust of the ground, and breathed into his nostrils the breath of life; and man became a living soul" (Genesis 2:7, KJV). The first man was called **Adam** because he was made of dust. What is dust made of? **Atoms**! Adam is phonetically atom.

Another word that sound similar to "Adam" is "atman". In Hinduism, the word **atman** means "the principle of life", or "the

69

individual self, known after enlightenment to be identical with Brahman" or "(initial capital letter) the World Soul, from which all individual souls derive, and to which they return as the supreme goal of existence."[14] Based on this definition, atman has a strong connection to atom. **Atman** means "the principle of life" and **atom** is known as "the building block of life". Atman and atom are necessary for the creation of Adam. Without atoms, DNA and **genes** cannot exist. The word "genes" has a strong connection to the "Book of **Genes**is". The word **genesis** is derived from the Greek word *genesis*, meaning "origin, creation, generation".[15] The word "genesis" has a strong connection to the word "genius" and the root "gene". Etymologically, the word **genius** means "tutelary or moral spirit" or "guardian deity or spirit which watches over each person from birth; spirit, incarnation; wit, talent".[16] As for the root **gene**, it means "give birth, beget."[17] The Book of Genesis uses parables and metaphors to secretly tell you about the separation and the union of the atoms to create man, DNA, and genes; hence, the title "Genesis" which can be spelled as "Genes-Is", "Genes-Isis" or "Genes of Isis".

Esoterically, genes are made up of letters. Today, scientists refer to these letters as genetic letters. "Four letters make up the genetic alphabet: A, T, G, and C. In one sense, a gene is nothing more than a sequence of those letters, like TTGAAGCATA..., which has a certain biological meaning or function."[18] When genetic letters are spelled into genetic codes, which are genetic **words**, they allow genes to translate energy into proteins which in turn **become flesh**. The discovery of genetic codes reveals that life is created through **letters** which are what **words** are made of. Furthermore, it shows strong evidence that a divine creator used letters, words, and symbols to program life into physical existence. Hence the Bible verse John 1:14 (NKJV), "And the Word became flesh and dwelt among us, and we beheld His glory, the glory as of the only begotten of the Father, full of grace and truth." Genetic letters and codes are pieces of evidence that God exists.

In certain occult teachings, **Adam** represents the sun-god **Atum** and **Eve** represents the **Moon**. Throughout mankind's history, the Sun has always been associated with the Divine Masculine Energy and the Moon and the Earth have always represented the Divine Feminine Energy. On a very deep level, the biblical story of Adam and Eve is nothing more than a story of the two creative forces of polarity and why those two forces are constantly fighting and making love with each other, similar to what a couple does in an intimate relationship.

This process of fighting (expanding) and making love (contracting) allows the manifestation of negative and positive experiences. The knowledge and experience gained from those experiences teach the two creative forces of polarity to achieve a state of balance and harmony. Once you innerstand the occult (secret/hidden) meanings of the story of Adam and Eve, you will know that it is a story of the two creative forces of polarity and their magical journey to achieve a state of balance and harmony. Hence, the story of Adam and Eve, the Sun and the Moon, the sperm and the egg, the conscious and the subconscious, the light ("good") and the darkness ("evil"), the positive and the negative, the Divine Masculine Energy and the Divine Feminine Energy, the Christ and the anti-Christ, etc.

During ancient times, there were some secret societies and civilizations that worshiped the Moon. Back then, the name **Sin** was used to call the **Moon**. To be more specific, Sin was the name of an ancient moon-goddess. However, according to certain ancient myths, Sin was a moon-god. The Moon represents the Divine Feminine Energy and has a strong connection to the female body. Because of this, using a moon-goddess to represent the Moon makes more sense. Today, we live in a world ruled by secretive societies controlled by mostly men. These male-dominated secretive societies have conditioned most of us to worship the Divine Masculine Principle which is represented by the Sun, Jesus, and Lucifer. To prevent us from worshiping the Divine Feminine Principle, which is represented by the Moon, they tell us that we can only be saved by worshiping the **external** Sun/Jesus and accept him as our savior. This is misleading because the true savior is **within** us. For us to achieve spiritual freedom and rise above duality, we have to balance the Divine Masculine and Divine Feminine Energies within us. The truth is that the Divine Masculine Energy cannot exist in a balanced and conscious state without the Divine Feminine Energy. If the Divine Feminine Energy were to suddenly cease to exist, the Divine Masculine Energy would become so out of balance that it would also cease to exist.

The main reason that a large percentage of the world is in a state of turmoil or chaos is because we live in a reality where the Divine Masculine Energy has become so strong and distorted that it has endangered the integrity of the harmonious interaction between the Divine Feminine and Divine Masculine Energies. The result of this distortion has manifested potentially destructive things to Mother Nature, such as wars, nuclear weapons, transhumanism, artificial intelligence, genetically modified organisms, false religions, and tyrannical governments. Transhumanism is nothing more than the **distorted version** of the Divine Masculine Energy wanting to prove to God that it can bear life without the physical body and achieve immortality without spirituality. It is left-brain dominant scientists' sick way of wanting to prove to God that men can bear life without women (womb-men). The word **transhumanism** means "... the idea that the capability of the human species can be enhanced using technology. It is the idea that by adding non-biological components to a biological system, the human body, future societies will get quantifiable results in human ability and potential."[19] The path of transhumanism will not lead to eternal life; instead, it will eventually lead to the near destruction of mankind. Men and women need to learn how to balance their Divine Masculine and Divine Feminine Energies so they can live in harmony with one another, or they will most likely destroy themselves and their home called Earth.

It is essential to know that every man, woman, or child has both the Divine Masculine and Divine Feminine Energies inside him or her. However, women have more attributes of the Divine Feminine Energy and men have more attributes of the Divine Masculine Energy. The action of men waging a war against the Divine Feminine Energy is pointless because they are only waging a war against themselves. This also applies to women waging a war against the Divine Masculine Energy. In the Bible, the Divine Masculine Energy is represented by Adam and the Divine Feminine Energy is represented by Eve. It is important to know that the religious story of Adam and Eve and other stories of the Bible often have more than one meaning. In other words, the stories of the Bible often have many layers of hidden messages. This prevents most people, especially the ones who have not expanded their consciousness to a state that allows them to spiritually discern information, from acquiring the really important knowledge in the Bible. Because the stories of the Bible often have more than one meaning, the name **Adam** can also mean **red man**.

The name "Adam" (Hebrew: אָדָם) was linked with the triliteral root אָדַם ('ADM), meaning "red", or the red earth-clod. It is related to the words: adom (red), admoni (ruddy), and dam (blood). This is where we get the name Edom, meaning the red man, and also Odem, meaning the sardius, ruby, or red jewel.

The meaning of atom is, "such particles as a source of nuclear energy: "the power of the atom". The atom is a basic unit of matter, that consists of a dense central nucleus surrounded by a cloud of negatively charged electrons.

In a previous article, The Science of 666, I had explained that the number 666 relates to the carbon atom and man. Carbon-12 is one of the 5 elements that make up the human DNA, being composed of 6 protons, 6 electrons and 6 neutrons, which equates to 666. Carbon-12 is the most abundant of the two stable isotopes of the element carbon, accounting for 98.89% of carbon.[20]

Here is another way to decipher the hidden codes behind the biblical story of Adam and Eve. This method uses the art of cryptography to decipher the codes of the Bible, revealing another occult meaning of the story of Adam and Eve.

Acroamatic ciphers, as you know, are cryptograms about various Letters of a "sacred Alphabet". In the acroamatic cipher,

"The creation myths of the world are acroamatic cryptograms, and the deities of the various pantheons are only cryptic characters which, if properly understood, become the constituents of a divine alphabet. The initiated few comprehend the true nature of this alphabet, but the uninitiated many worship the letters of it as gods."

Thus in Adam and Eve, the proper acroamatic transposition is to take the Letter M and divide it into its constituent components, as thus:

M = I V I

This represents a "D-IVI-SION", which means "double (di) vision". Here we deal again in "duality", or "male/female". In the case of M = IVI, we reorder the IVI to reveal VII, or

73

the word SEVEN. The VII is then ciphered further as

V = VE = EVE

II = PI = ADM = 1413 = 3.141

EVE then is the number 666, and thus the Letter M divides into VII and then further into SEVEN and then further into

SN = 3.14

EVE = 666,

and so forth.

The Letter M, therefore, is the primary cryptic letter (acroamatic cipher) to the Adm and Eve story, which further illuminates the core numbers of "Pi" and "666", each central to the Illuminatus philosophy.[21]

Another occult meaning of the biblical story of Adam and Eve and the Garden of Eden is related to genetic engineering. In this version, the Garden of Eden is the garden where the alien gods created life using genetic engineering techniques. According to the book titled *The Cosmic Code* by Zecharia Sitchin, one of the alien races called the Anunnaki came to Earth roughly 445,000 years ago. According to certain researchers of Zecharia Sitchin's work, the Anunnaki was one of the first alien races to tinker with the DNA of the ancient humans. They also believed that the Anunnaki combined some of their DNA with some of the human test subjects' DNA and were able to successfully create a new human hybrid race. Some researchers believed that the new human hybrid race eventually evolved to the humans of today.

The idea that alien gods played a role in creating modern humans may sound crazy. However, over the past few decades, some geneticists have suggested that the human DNA has foreign DNA that may not be from Earth. Even if this is true, it does not mean that the Anunnaki were the original creators of mankind. Some researchers of alien gods suggested that humans were also used as a food source.

This makes me wonder if the Garden of **Eden** is the Garden of **Eatin'**.[22] Is there evidence proving that humans were and are still being used as a food source? I have not found irrefutable proof that humans have been used as food, so I do not know for sure if it is true. However, I have found some very interesting evidence that points toward that direction and I do know that people are being used as biological batteries to power corporations. After you read Chapter 5, you will most likely support the idea that people are being used as biological batteries.

An important information that is beneficial for you to know about the Dark Forces is that they like to tell you what they are doing to you or are planning to do to you in certain movies and TV shows. They also like to use video games, music videos, and other popular media to tell you their future plans for mankind. Some evidence of this can be seen in the movie *Jupiter Ascending*. In this movie, there is a scene where Titus shows Jupiter a room full of thousands of vials filled with youth serums. By drinking the youth serums, it allows Titus and his race to live for thousands of years. What is shocking about the serums is that each of them was made from harvesting nearly 100 dead people. Could this be the ichor (golden fluid) that the Greeks used to talk about? This golden fluid could be one of the main reasons that the Dark Forces have been promoting the idea that alien gods will come save mankind or the Rapture event will take certain people back to God.

The word **rapture** is connected to the Latin word *raptus* which means "a carrying off, abduction, snatching away; rape".[23] Therefore, the etymological meaning of the word **rapture** is "snatching away", "rape", or "abduction". Christians who are planning to participate in a rapture event may want to investigate the word rapture more deeply. The Rapture is a program or more specifically a savior program that is designed to keep people living in a state of victim mentality, so the Dark Forces can weaken their spiritual powers, allowing the Dark Forces to exploit their bodies, minds, and spirits. The good news is that they are forbidden to rapture people, unless they have their CONSENT. If the Dark Forces are after people's golden fluids, which contain their energies of youth, then the ascension process that mankind is currently going through would be the best time to trick people to agree to be harvested from the garden of Earth. They have to trick people because they need their consent. If they were to take people by force, they would violate the Law of Free Will. To overcome the problem of violating people's free will, the Dark Forces like to use contracts to trick them to give up some of the power of their free will. The good news is that most of their contracts are not valid contracts. This means that you can nullify their contracts, as long as you know how contract law works. A website that teaches you how to nullify contracts using the power of contract law is YouAreLaw.org.

If the physical body can produce more ichor (golden fluid) during ascension cycles, it would make sense for the Dark Forces to use contracts to control people during these cycles. This will make it easier for them to trick people to agree to go with them, so they can harvest their ichor or more specifically their spiritual energy. Maybe this is why **ascension** is sometimes called **the harvest**, as stated in the book titled *The Ra Material*. A word that may give us a clue to support the harvesting of people during ascension is fetus. Phonetically, the word "fetus" sounds similar to the term "feed us". After the fetus is born, he or she is called a baby. When the word "baby" is spoken aloud, it sounds like "bay bee" which can be written as "baybee". The word **bay** is defined as "a body of water partially enclosed by land but with a wide mouth, affording access to the sea".[24] Because you are made of water, you are like the bay. As for the word **bee**, it is a name for identifying flying insects that are known for producing **honey**. Based on the previous two definitions, the word **baby** (baybee) means "a body of water that produces honey". Combine water and honey and you get the golden fluid that the alien gods need for longevity. More babies mean more golden fluid or "honey" for the alien gods. Why do you think a couple in a relationship calls each other honey or baby? Because every man, woman, and baby has golden fluid or "honey" inside him or her.

To connect the dots, when you are old enough to go to kindergarten (garden of children), you (the baby/baybee) are put into a building designed for housing a **colony**. This building is used to school you to be an obedient worker so when you grow up to be an adult you are ready to work like a honeybee. One of the largest colonies on Earth is the United States of America which is the new colony of the Queen of England. The Queen is sometimes called "Queen Bee". Even the unmarked lorries that are used for transporting the Queen's personal belongings are known as the "Queen Bees". This is why, before the creation and union of the States, the United States of America was known as the 13 Colonies. A colony can be defined as a large group of bees that lives in a **hive**. So, who are the workers (bees) of the Queen of England? United States citizens!

In legal terms, the word **colony** means "a union of citizens or subjects who have left their country to people another, and **remain subject** to the mother country" (bold emphasis added).[25] As for the word **hive**, it is defined as "a shelter constructed for housing a colony of honeybees; beehive."[26] Based on the definitions and information in the previous few pages, the public school system is a colony for schooling children to be good little honeybees so when the time comes their golden fluid or "honey" can be used as energy. This is not necessarily an "evil" thing. However, when people become irresponsible and do not know how to exercise their natural rights, the Dark Forces can use certain corporations to control them and steal their honey, turning them into slaves to be used as batteries. In other words, it is your responsibility to learn how to exercise your natural rights and control the negative force inside of you so it does not get out of control. When you allow your negative force to get out of control, it strengthens the power of the Dark Forces.

In kindergarten, one of the first things they teach you is the alphabet which is made up of letters created by using the art of sacred geometry. These letters are ideograms which are written symbols that represent ideas. An important information that is beneficial for you to know about all written symbols is that they are created into existence from the egg (the dot) and the serpent (the line). The egg and the serpent are important symbols in esoteric and occult teachings. After they teach you how to write the letters of the alphabet, they also teach you how to spell words correctly. One of the hidden agendas of teaching you the alphabet and how to **spell** words correctly is to prepare you for the day that you can cast magic **spell**s through the act of **spell**ing! Another reason that they teach you how to spell words correctly is to train and condition you to make sure that each letter (geometry) of words is arranged the same way every time you write words, strengthening their magic powers. Did you notice that the term "magic **spell**" and the word "**spell**ing" have the word **spell** in them? This did not happen by accident. It is right in your face and hidden in plain sight! The hidden intent of spelling is to cast magic spells. Do you remember those spelling **bee** contests in middle school? The spelling programs of the education system are schooling children or babies (bay**bees**) to be good **spellers**. Hence the term **spelling bee**.

An important word in the previous paragraph that you need to decipher is spell. The word **spell** is derived from the Old English word **spell**, meaning "story, saying, tale, history, narrative, fable; discourse, command".[27] This definition alone already tells you that the word spell has a strong connection to mythical, magical, and historical stories.

77

Some examples of these stories are Aladdin, Alice in Wonderland, Beauty and the Beast, Cinderella, Peter Pan, Santa Claus, and the Great Flood. Keep in mind that these stories are often full of hidden knowledge that teaches you important lessons in life. Furthermore, they usually have very subtle but powerful magic spells. When you innerstand their magic spells and use them wisely, they can empower you. On the other hand, when their magic spells are used unwisely, they can curse you.

> The conception of spells appears to have arisen from the idea that there is some natural and intimate connection between words and the things signified by them. Thus if one repeats the name of a supernatural being the effect will be analogous to that produced by the being itself. It is assumed that all things are in a "sympathetic" connection and act and react upon one another; things that have once been in contact continue to act on each other even after the contact has been removed. People in ancient Egypt believed that certain secret names of gods, demi-gods, and demons unknown to human beings might be discovered and used against them by the discoverer.[28]

One of the most popular books that is largely composed of mythical, magical, and historical stories is the Bible. Most, if not all, the stories of the Bible are full of myths, legends, parables, riddles, and magic **spells**. When these biblical stories are deciphered into knowledge and the knowledge is used wisely, they can empower people to achieve spiritual freedom and enlightenment. On the other hand, when they are read literally without discernment and their myths, legends, parables, and riddles are not deciphered properly, they can curse people and prevent them from achieving spiritual freedom and enlightenment. The Bible is a holy and magic book which is why some of the books of the Bible are called Gospels (e.g., the Gospel of John). The word **gospel** is derived from the Old English word **godspel** (*god* means "good" and *spel* means "story, message") which literally means "good spell".[29] Therefore, the word "Gospels" can be translated as "God spells" or "spells of God".

Let us turn our attention back to the word **spell**. As a verb, Dictionary.com defines it as, "to name, write, or otherwise give the letters, in order, of (a word, syllable, etc.)". As a noun, it defines the word spell as, "a word, phrase, or form of words supposed to have magic power; charm; incantation" or "a state or period of enchantment".³⁰ Based on the information and definitions in this paragraph and the previous few paragraphs, the word spell has a strong connection to magic and spelling. For you to innerstand this connection on a deeper level, you need to explore the concept of spells. *The Columbia Encyclopedia* (second edition, 1950) describes the concept of spell using these exact words:

> word, formula, or INCANTATION believed to produce a magical effect. Belief in the spell is based on the idea that by "naming" a vague power one can focus the power on a desired end, consequently there is an intimate connection between the word and the thing denoted by it. It is similar to the belief that the name of a man is identical with his self. The spell could be used for evil or good ends, if evil, it was a technique of sorcery. Many authorities believe that the "word" was the precursor of prayer. The spell was a Teutonic form of exercising occult power and was sometimes used to summon the spirits of departed heroes to give prophetic utterances. Once cast, the spell was supposed to remain in force until broken by a counterspell or exorcism.

For you to innerstand spells more deeply, you need to explore the art of magic. Remember, **magic** is defined as "the art of producing a desired effect or result through the use of incantation or various other techniques that presumably assure human control of supernatural agencies or the forces of nature."³¹ It can also mean "art of influencing or predicting events and producing marvels using hidden natural forces".³² Keep in mind that magic is an art that uses occult (hidden/secret) knowledge to access certain spiritual powers to control energy to cause change according to the will. Based on these concepts and definitions of magic, the act of using the mind to manifest thoughts into reality is a form of magic. However, this act falls into the category of esoteric (internal) magic. Most people who practice magic often like to use magic tools outside of them to help them cast magic spells. This is known as exoteric (external) magic.

A popular magic tool that magic practitioners like to use to help them cast magic spells is a **sigil**, meaning "a sign, word, or device held to have occult power in astrology or magic".³³ What most people do not know about sigils is that they are all around them. For example, the **logos** of corporations that people see on buildings and in TV commercials are, in many ways, **sigils**. When designed correctly, sigils can be used to summon spirits and cast magic spells. This is why corporate logos can be used to influence people's minds. The people controlling the big corporations of the world are well aware of the power of logos/sigils, which is why many of them hire experts in astrology and other magic arts to design their corporate logos. It is important to remember that the letters of the alphabet are also sigils. Each of these letters/sigils represents a will of God. Esoterically, letters are the building codes of matter. For example, in genes there are four letters (A, T, G, C) that are used by the body to create genetic codes to translate energy into amino acids and proteins which in turn become flesh.

The magic art that allows the body to transform letters into amino acids, proteins, flesh, cells, organs, and other parts of the body is known as the art of alchemy. The word **alchemy** is defined as, "a form of chemistry and speculative philosophy practiced in the Middle Ages and the Renaissance and concerned principally with discovering methods for transmuting baser metals into gold and with finding a universal solvent and an elixir of life."[34] What most people do not innerstand about alchemy is that the physical body is one of the most impressive alchemical systems in the universe, which is why it has the magic power to transmute "letters" into the "elixir of life". This elixir is the holy oil that is produced in the brain. It is also known as the holy chrism; however, the chrism that is used by priests to perform certain rituals is not the true holy oil (elixir of life). The Greek letters that are used to represent the sacred oil are XPI. These three letters are also used to represent Christ.

The letters of the alphabet are very powerful sigils. This is why letters/sigils and words are used in magic rituals by all practitioners of magic. When letters are spelled into words, they tell a magical story. Every time you spell words using letters/sigils, you often subconsciously tell a story. In other words, you **command** the letters/sigils to cast spells. This is the occult (secret) meaning of spelling. Hence, the etymological definition of the word **spell**: "story, saying, tale, history, narrative, fable; discourse, **command**" (bold emphasis added). The art of spelling is a magic art of storytelling. Because of this, when you learn how to decipher letters and words you can access the secret stories and spells hidden in the letters and words.

By now you should know how powerful the art of spelling is. This magic art plays a very important role in your life; without knowing how to spell, you will have a very hard time thriving and surviving in today's society. Because spelling plays such an important role in your life, it is one of the first things that they teach you in kindergarten. However, before you can spell properly, you need to learn how to write the letters of the alphabet. After learning the alphabet, you are taught how to spell by combining letters to make words. This process is used to train you to be a good speller or spellcaster, so the magic power of letters and words can be used to transfer or cast your thoughts into the external world, causing your reality to change according to your will.

During the process of teaching you how to spell, they also teach you how to correctly say the letters of the alphabet using specific sounds. This process is important for creating the right sound for each letter of the alphabet, which is essential for casting magic spells. The sound of each letter of the alphabet has powerful magic power, allowing it to organize matter into sacred geometry. Keep in mind that many letters are symbols representing ancient gods. When you combine the letters of the alphabet into words and speak the words aloud, you are not just uttering words but are also casting your thoughts, emotions, intentions, and vibrations into Earth's magnetic field or magic field, which is the energy field that manifests the reality of Earth. If you are not careful and say certain words together, you can cast a negative spell without even knowing it.

Most people do not know how magic works because they lack the knowledge to innerstand sigils, energy mechanics, sacred sound, and sacred geometry. Because of this, they have no idea what they are doing when they yell harsh words at one another using **swear** words or **curse** words. As a verb, the word **curse** means "to wish for something evil or unpleasant to happen to someone or something, as by asking a magical power"; as a noun, it means "something evil or unpleasant that happens to someone or something, by or as if by a magical power".[35] In other words, curse words can be used to cast dark magic spells. They did not call them curse words for no reason. Why do you think that most parents tell their children to stop **cursing** when they **swear** too much? Most parents tell their children to stop cursing because they intuitively know that it can cause harm to other people. When you shout curse words at people, you actually cast dark magic spells on them. It is important to be aware that the Law of Attraction, which is always working and does not judge between good and evil, will reflect certain aspects of those dark magic spells back

81

unto you. In other words, there are consequences for saying curse words. This is why you should be careful of the words you use when you yell at people. Are you starting to see how the language system and words are strongly related to magic and energy?

After learning how to spell and say words correctly, they teach you how to cast those spellings/spell-ings into sentences and phrases without teaching you about the magic effects of spelling. The purpose of this is to prevent you from knowing the true power of words, making it easier for corporations to control your mind using words and magic spells. Their magic spells cannot control 100 percent of your mind, but they do affect your mind more than you may realize. Magic spells work similar to subliminal messages which are hypnotic suggestions that can be used to manipulate your subconscious to a large degree. Subliminal messages are a form of magic spells!

By now you should know the deeper meaning of what I said in Chapter 1: "In the English language, many words are carefully designed and put together in a way that allows them to be used to cast spells. The Dark Magicians are well aware of this which is why they like to use the English language to trick us to play their con game to enslave mankind." It is important to know that English is not the only language that can be used to cast spells; all languages have the power to cast spells. The magic power of words is the main reason that words are so effective for deceiving and enslaving you. However, the right words can empower your spirit and free your mind. Do you innerstand now why words are more powerful than swords?

There are certain words that have the power to manifest powerful magic spells that can be used to control your mind to a significant degree. The good news is that there are effective ways to protect your mind from being hypnotized by their magic spells. Words can be used to create magic spells to control your mind, but when you become **aware** of their powers and know how they are used to control you, they cannot affect your mind as much. For example, when certain magicians perform magic tricks, they can fool you to believe that their tricks are real. But when you figure out how their tricks are done, they can no longer fool you because you know that their tricks are illusions. In other words, you have become **aware** of how their tricks work, and therefore they cannot deceive you anymore. Other ways to protect your mind from magic spells are by overcoming your fears and increasing your frequency. These things can be achieved through the right knowledge and experience. The way magic tricks work is similar to how the Dark Magicians are using magic spells to control your mind. Once you become aware of how their magic spells work, the magic effects of their spells greatly diminish. Your awareness is one of the most powerful spiritual powers that you have. Learn how to use it wisely and the Dark Magicians will not be able to control and deceive you using the art of word play and magic. Keep in mind that words can be used for "good" or "evil" purposes and therefore can be used to free or enslave your mind.

Let us turn our attention back to the question about why the first class of elementary (primary) school is called kindergarten (garden of children). To find the answer to this question, we need to go back to Chapter 1. In this chapter, there is a paragraph that says: "The Word was in the beginning because the **Word** was the **Spiritual Seed**, the Source of Life. To find evidence that "words" are "seeds", we need to turn our attention to the Bible verse Luke 8:11 (NKJV): "Now the parable is this: The seed is the word of God." A **seed** (word) is the **nucleus** of a thing and therefore is the **beginning** or source of that thing." Kindergarten (garden of children) is the first class of elementary school because it teaches children how to use words (seeds). During the process of learning how to use words to communicate, spiritual seeds (words) are planted in children's minds. This process programs children to think, behave, and act in certain ways. The **minds** of children are like **gardens** that are rich in nutrients, and mostly free of weeds and plants, making them great for planting spiritual seeds (words). This is one of the reasons that the word kindergarten secretly means "garden of children".

When you deeply contemplate the information in this chapter, you should see a strong connection between the Garden of Eden and kindergarten. In the Garden of Eden, there is a tree that gives Adam and Eve the knowledge to know good and evil. Kindergarten teaches children the alphabet, giving them the knowledge to know good and evil. The evidence of this can be found in the word alphabet. In Chapter 1, I said that the "letters of the alphabet were created to express the infinite expression of the Divine Masculine Energy and the Divine Feminine Energy, allowing polaric ideas, such as positive and negative, male and female, order and chaos, good and evil, etc., to manifest in the material world." I also said that "the word alphabet/alpha-beta (**alpha** represents the **masculine** principle and **beta** represents the **feminine** principle)" is "the system of sacred symbols that is used to manifest worlds through the power of positive and negative words." In other words, **alpha** represents **Adam** and **beta** represents **Eve**. In a way, kindergarten is a garden of Eden.

Chapter 5
How the Legal System and Commerce Drain Your Energy

In the legal system, when you go to court for a trial, you are not really going to "court" but are going to a "game arena" where they are planning to con you using word play, legal words, and word tricks. Where do you go to when you want to play basketball, volleyball, or tennis with your friends? You go to a basketball **court**, volleyball **court**, or tennis **court**. Therefore, a court is where you go to when you want to play a game. They did not name the place where you go to **trial** a courtroom by accident. A word in this paragraph that is important to investigate is trial. Phonetically, the word "trial" sounds like the word "tryout". The word **tryout** means "a **trial** or **test** to ascertain fitness for some purpose" (bold emphasis added). When in court, the plaintiff and the defendant are at a trial/tryout/test to see which person is better at using words to convince the judge to choose him as the winner of the game. This is why the **judge** is sometimes referred to as the **administrator**. The judge is there to administer or manage the rules of the game in the court/game arena, which is why the judge sits behind the raised wooden desk called the bench. The word **bench** is defined as "a seat occupied by an official, especially a judge" or "the seat on which the players of a team sit during a **game** while not playing" (bold emphasis added).[1] Another role of the judge is to act as a **banker** because he or she is the administrator of a **commercial** court. It is about commerce and not really about justice.

One of the words that judges and attorneys like to use to trick you to temporarily give up some of your natural rights in court is contract. The word **contract** is derived from the Old French word **contract** and Latin word **contractus**, meaning "a drawing together, a shrinking; a contract, an agreement".[2] A contract is a very powerful document for the reason that it can be used to trick you to temporarily give up some of the power of your free will. It can also be used to bind you to certain terms and conditions, limiting your choices and demanding you to do something to satisfy those terms and conditions. Most people know that a contract is an agreement between at least two parties. This definition of contract only shows you the overt meaning. To find the covert or occult meaning of the word contract, you may have to look below its surface, dissect its layers, study its origins, and inspect it from many different angles. Therefore, you may need to use the art of anagram to rearrange its letters or separate it into two words. Before dissecting and inspecting the word contract, it is important to investigate its legal meaning. *Black's Law Dictionary* (5th edition) defines the word **contract** using these exact words:

> An agreement between two or more persons which creates an obligation to do or not to do a particular thing. **Its essentials are competent parties, subject matter, a legal consideration, mutuality of agreement, and mutuality of obligation**. Lamoureux v. Burrillville Racing Ass'n, 91 R.I. 94, 161 A.2d 213, 215. Under U.C.C., term refers to total legal obligation which results from parties' agreement as affected by the Code. Section 1-201(11). As to sales, "contract" and "agreement" are limited to those relating to present or future sales of goods, and "contract for sale" includes both a present sale of goods and a contract to sell goods at a future time. U.C.C. § 2-106(1). [Bold emphasis added]

One of the first steps to finding the covert meaning of the word contract is to separate it into two words. When you separate the word "contract" into two words, you get the term "con tract". As a verb, **con** is defined as "to swindle; trick".[3] As a noun, **tract** is defined as "a brief treatise or pamphlet for general distribution, usually on a religious or political topic."[4] When you put the two definitions together and translate them in a certain way, they transform into the definition "a deceptive treatise" or "a treatise of trickery". Keep in mind that the definition thereof does not define a valid contract; instead, it reveals that a contract can be used to deceive you. Every time you sign a "contract" with a corporation (e.g., bank and government agency), you often agree to a deceptive treatise which is not really a contract. The good news is that most contracts created by corporations and government agencies are not really valid because they do not come with full disclosure; furthermore, they often do not meet the requirements of a contract. For a contract to be truly valid, it needs to have an agreement with mutual understanding, competent parties, valuable consideration, and full disclosure of material facts.

Another word that judges and attorneys like to use to trick you in court is the word understand. "Do you **understand** the charges against you?" In court, when you hear the judge asks the question thereof, you should think twice before answering it. If you were to answer "yes", you would agree to allow the judge and the court to have jurisdiction over you. When you separate the word "understand" into two words, you get the term "under stand". To find the occult meaning of the term "under stand" you need to switch the words **under** and **stand** around. When you do this, the term "under stand" becomes "stand under". By saying to the judge that you **understand** the charges, you are also telling the judge that you **stand under** the charges.

One of the most common words that they like to use to trick you in court is the word **person**. The word person is a general word for the reason that it can mean a legal person, a natural person, a corporation, a partnership, or any fictitious entity. Most of the time when the judge asks you for your name he is asking for your legal name which is the designation of a legal person, also known as a legal fiction. A legal person can also be a corporation. A corporation is a "corp-o-ration" or "corpse-o-ration". The plural form of the word corporation can be written as corps. Phonetically, the word **corps** sounds similar to the word **corpse** which is defined as "a dead body, usually of a human being."[5] The legal system sees you as a **corpse** to be used as a **ration** to feed the artificial matrix of the Dark Forces. Hence, the word corporation/corp-o-ration/**corpse**-o-**ration**. Do you remember what I said in Chapter 2 about why the government sees you as a **legally dead** person because you are considered lost at sea or dead at sea?

A very important information that is beneficial for you to know about the legal system is that most, if not almost all, of its courts are operating under admiralty law and maritime law. The courts of the legal system deal with fictional characters (e.g., legal fictions and corporations), which is why their "laws" are called "acts" and "statutes". As a verb, the word **act** is defined as "to perform as an actor".[6] The agents of the legal court system are **actors** acting in a play known as the legal system. Whether they realize it or not, they are still just actors playing a game to con you. Even though it is a game, it is a very serious game because you could end up in jail. The court system and the legal system have to operate together as a **game** because they are dealing with **fictional things**. Because of this, if you are served with a Writ of Summons commanding you to appear in court, the court is NOT summoning you, the living man or woman made of flesh and blood. Instead, it is summoning the legal fiction associated with your legal name, which is the fictional entity used by the government to do business with you. However, the court's goal is to trick you to play the role of the legal fiction. This legal fiction is a fictional entity because it only exists on paper and in your mind, just like the government. Because of this, if you were to agree to accept a Writ of Summons, you would agree to **act** in the **capacity** of a **legal fiction**, allowing the court to summon you to appear in the magic play/game called the legal system. Once the court tricks you to act as a legal fiction, it has jurisdiction over you and can use the art of presumption to charge you with fines.

When you are in court, you are not only in a game arena to play "legal games" but also in a room to play "magic games". This is why the judge is also known as the **magistrate** and the letter that the court uses to notify you to "appear" in court is called a Writ of **Summons**. What do witches do when they want to call spirits of the dead to "appear" in front of them? They **summon** them! They did not call the letter commanding you to **appear** in court a Writ of **Summons** for no reason. Do you need more evidence showing that courtrooms are places for casting magic spells? Read further and I will show you more evidence than you may need.

Have you ever wondered why nearly all court documents have seals on them? The reason that they have seals is because seals are sigils which can be used to seal magic. Have you also ever wondered why a judge is sometimes called a magistrate? Judges are magistrates because they are religious priests dressed in black robes. In legal terms, the word **magistrate** is defined as "any individual who has the power of a public civil officer or inferior judicial officer, such as a Justice of the Peace."[7] **Magistrate** can also be defined as "a civil officer charged with the administration of the law."[8]

Phonetically, the word "magistrate" sounds very similar to "magistrait" or "magi-strait". One of the origins of the word **magi** is the Latin word *magi* (plural of *magus*), meaning "magician, learned

87

magician".[9] As for the word **strait**, it means "a narrow passage of water connecting two large bodies of water."[10] The word **strait** has a strong connection to the word **canal**. Do you remember what I said in Chapter 2 about the relationship between the **berth** canal and the **birth** canal? Sometimes you need to investigate the phonics of a word to find the hidden meanings of that word.

Because judges are magistrates/"magistraits", their hidden role in court is to administer your body/ship/vessel to "port" and cast magic spells on you. An important information that you need to know about the word **magistrate** is that it is also used to define presidents and governors. "The president of the United States is the chief magistrate of this nation; the governors are the chief magistrates of their respective states."[11] On a deeper level, a **courtroom** of the legal system is like a **shiproom** (storage space on a ship). It is like a shiproom because nearly every court of the legal system is operating under admiralty law, the law of the **sea**. This law deals with seamen and ships (vessels). The body, the vessel, or the product in the courtroom/shiproom is you! The legal system sees you as a vessel or a product and not as a man or a woman. This is why there is often little or no justice in nearly every court throughout Western and Eastern countries.

It is important to know that "courts" are also "banks" which is why they have "benches" and "bars". One of the origins of the word **bench** is the Old High German word *bank*, meaning "bench".[12] In English, the word **bank** can mean a few different things. One of its meanings is "an institution for receiving, lending, exchanging, and safeguarding money and, in some cases, issuing notes and transacting other financial business."[13] The word **bank** can also mean "a **bench** for rowers in a **galley**" or "a row or tier of **oars**" or "the sloping side of any hollow in the ground, esp when bordering a **river**" (bold emphasis added).[14] Hence, the word **riverbank**. The word **galley** is defined as "a seagoing **vessel** propelled mainly by **oars**, used in ancient and medieval times, sometimes with the aid of sails" (bold emphasis added).[15] Back in the old days, galleys were often rowed by slaves and **convicts**. Do you remember what I said in Chapter 2 about the relationship between the words **ore** and **oar**? In Chapter 2, I said that the word **ore** means "a metal-bearing mineral or rock". I also said that it sounds similar to the word **oar** which is "a long shaft with a broad blade at one end, used as a lever for rowing or otherwise propelling or steering a **boat**" (bold emphasis added).[16] Please be aware that most of the words in bold **font** in the previous few pages are directly or indirectly related to **water**. Why water? Because it has to do with admiralty law (law of the **sea**) and commerce. Even the word **font** is related to **water**. The word **font** means "a receptacle for baptismal water".[17] In printing, the word **font** means "a complete assortment of type of one style and size."[18] I can go on for pages about how all these words are related to water, but I think you should get the point by now.

In one of the previous paragraphs, there is a sentence that says, "Back in the old days, galleys were often rowed by slaves or convicts". The word "convict" is often used in the legal system to identify people who have been found "guilty" of a crime and is serving a sentence in prison. What most people do not know about the word convict is that there is a deeper meaning to this word. Most people are aware of the overt definition of the word **convict** which is "a person proved or declared guilty of an offense."[19] This definition only defines the word convict at the surface. To find the deeper meaning of the word convict, you need to separate it into two words (con vict) and then switch them around. When you do this, the term "con vict" transforms into "vict con". The word **vict** is derived from the Latin root *vict*, which means "conquer", and is related to the root *vinc*.[20] This is where we get the word victim from. One of the definitions of the word **victim** is "a person who is deceived or cheated, as by his or her own emotions or ignorance, by the dishonesty of others, or by some impersonal agency" or "a person or animal sacrificed or regarded as sacrificed".[21]

To connect the dots, a convict/con-vict/vict-con is "a **victim** of a **con** who has been conquered, deceived, and sacrificed because of his or her ignorance." This is the covert or occult definition of the word convict. So, what is the con? The **con** is the **legal system**, not the whole legal system but a large percentage of it. Convicts are victims of the con known as the legal system. This system is used by the flesh and blood minions of the Dark Forces to con living men, women, and children to temporarily give their natural rights and spiritual powers away to the DEAD. A convict gets to serve a sentence in prison because he has agreed to act out a play or story known as the Legal Name Game. Whether the convict realizes or not, he is just an **actor** or a **character** in a **story**. This is why the word **sentence** is used to communicate information that tells him how long he may have to stay in prison. Please keep in mind that the words actor, character, story, and sentence are all related to a **story**book. To take this concept to another level, men and women are **acting** out a **story** and the stage that they practice their acting lessons is Earth. This is why their

89

activities are categorized into the word history. When you separate the word "history" into two words, it transforms into the term "his tory" which is phonetically "his **story**". What are some of the most important elements in a story? Characters or "char**actors**"! Did you notice that the words **act**or, **act**ivities, and char**act**ers have the word **act** in them?

Let us focus our attention back to the word sentence. A **sentence** is "a grammatical unit of one or more words that expresses an independent statement, question, request, command, exclamation, etc."[22] In a **book**, sentences are used to communicate information and ideas to a reader. The word **sentence** comes from the Latin word **sententia**, meaning "thought, way of thinking, opinion; **judgment**, decision" (bold emphasis added).[23] The previous definition gives us some clues as to why judges give sentences to convicts or people who have violated the "law". Judges give **sentences** because one of their acting roles is to give **judgments**. When a judge gives a sentence (judgment) to a convict, he acts in the capacity of a religious magician whose job is to **write** a **sentence** and record or register it in a book of records as history/his-story. Phonetically, the word **write** sounds very similar to the word **rite** which means "a formal or ceremonial act or procedure prescribed or customary in religious or other solemn use".[24] Please keep in mind that a sentence is made of words and words can be used as magic spells. The book that is used by a judge to record/register/write sentences/judgments is a book of the DEAD. This book has no life because it contains records of artificial persons (corporations/corpses) and characters.

A **book** is defined as "a handwritten or printed work of fiction or nonfiction, usually on sheets of paper fastened or bound together within covers."[25] It can also mean "a record of bets, as on a **horse race**" (bold emphasis added).[26] This definition shows another connection to the horse theme. As a verb, the word **book** means "to enter in a book or list; record; register."[27] An important information that is beneficial for you to know about a book is that it has **chapters** and **pages**. The word **chapter** means "a main division of a book, treatise, or the like, usually bearing a number or title" or "a branch, usually restricted to a given locality, of a society, organization, **fraternity**, etc." (bold emphasis added).[28] As for the word **page**, it means "one side of a leaf of something printed or written, as a book, manuscript, or letter."[29] It also means "to **summon** formally by calling out the name of repeatedly" (bold emphasis added).[30] To summon someone or something by repeatedly calling out his, her, or its name is a form of magic spell!

One of the words in the previous paragraph that you need to pay attention to is **fraternity**. Today, nearly all secretive societies are fraternal orders controlled by mostly men which is why the term "fraternal orders" is used to define them. The word **fraternal** has a strong connection to the word **fraternity**, a word that comes from the Latin word *fraternitatem* (nominative *fraternitas*), meaning "brotherhood".³¹ The word fraternal also has a strong connection to the legal system because this system is controlled by the Jesuits, one of the **fraternal** secretive societies controlled by the Pope of the Holy Roman Empire.

It is important to be aware that the legal system is full of magic spells and tricks because it relies heavily on the art of word magic and presumption. Furthermore, it employs attorneys and judges who are trained in the magic art of legalese. These attorneys and judges are skillful at conning people and convicts to pay money to the legal system. Most convicts are not really criminals for the reason that they have been conned by the agents of the legal system. Many of these agents mock the victims of their legal system by calling them convicts (victims of a con). The fact is that many agents of the legal system are committing more "crimes" than convicts. Unlike convicts, their crimes can enslave and destroy a nation. Let us turn our attention back to the courtroom. In a courtroom operating under commercial laws, there is a section called a bar. Here is an excerpt from Wikipedia.org explaining what a **bar** is:

> The origin of the term **bar** is from the barring furniture dividing a medieval European courtroom, similar to the origin of the term **bank** for the **bench**-like location of financial transactions in medieval Europe. In the USA, Europe and many other countries referring to the law traditions of Europe, the area in front of the **barrage** is restricted to participants in the trial: the judge or judges, other court officials, the jury (if any), the lawyers for each party, the parties to the case, and witnesses giving testimony. The area behind the bar is open to the public. This restriction is enforced in nearly all courts. In most courts, the bar is represented by a physical partition: a railing or barrier that serves as a bar. [Bold emphasis added][32]

During a trial, as a defendant or plaintiff, you are required to stay within the **bar** (**bar**rier) of the courtroom. Only attorneys, judges, and certain court officials are allowed to go pass the bar. Why is that you may ask? Because the court, referring to a court operating under commercial laws, sees you as a **prisoner**. Where do they lock up prisoners? In a jail or prison cell. What is a jail or prison cell made of? Iron **bars** or steel **bars** and **bar**red doors! *Black's Law Dictionary* (5th edition) even defines the word **bar** as, "A particular part of the court-room; for example, the place where prisoners stand at their trial, hence the expression 'prisoner at the bar.' " Today, most courts that are operating under the legal system are admiralty courts enforcing military laws; therefore, when you go to court, you are treated as a **war criminal**. This is why they require you to stay within the **bar** in a courtroom. It is right in your face and hidden in plain sight! Keep in mind that on a deeper level the word **bar** represents the **veil** between the living and the dead.

Another definition of the word **bar** is "an ingot, lump, or wedge of gold or silver."[33] This definition shows another relationship between the words court and bank. The word **bar** can also mean "a counter or place where beverages, especially **liquors**, or light meals are served to customers" (bold emphasis added).[34] Have you ever heard someone say, "let's go drink at the bar"? One of the words that you need to pay attention to in this paragraph is liquor. The word **liquor** is derived from the Old French word *licor*, meaning "fluid, liquid; sap; oil".[35] It is also derived from the Latin word *liquorem* (nominative *liquor*), meaning "liquidity, fluidity", or "a liquid, liquor; wine; the **sea**" (bold emphasis added).[36] One of the English dictionaries defines the word **liquor** as "a distilled or spirituous beverage, as brandy or whiskey, as distinguished from a fermented beverage, as wine or beer."[37] Did you notice that all the words in bold font in this paragraph are also related to water or the sea? Even their definitions are related to water. By the end of this chapter, you will know why water plays such an important role in commerce. In addition, you will know why the word **sea** has a strong connection to the word **energy**.

Another word that is related to water is alcohol, a substance found in liquor. "Alcohol" is an interesting word because it is connected to the word "spirit". Once you know why they are connected, you will realize that alcohol is a substance that can be used to extract your essence, the spirit (breath of life) made of spiritual energy. The word **spirit** means "the principle of conscious life; the vital principle in humans, animating the body or mediating between body and soul."[38] To find some of the hidden meanings of the word alcohol, you need to investigate its origins and its relations to other words. Two origins of the word **alcohol** come from the Medieval Latin word *alcohol*, meaning "powdered ore of antimony" and the Arabic word *al-kuhul*, meaning "the fine metallic powder used to darken the eyelids".[39] Today, the Arabic word *al-kuhul* is termed "kohl". Some etymological researchers believe that the word "kohl" is connected to the word "ghoul", a word that is derived from the Arabic word *ghul*, meaning "an evil spirit that robs graves and feeds on corpses".[40] In English, the word **kohl** means "a powder, as finely powdered antimony sulfide, used as a cosmetic to darken the eyelids, eyebrows, etc."[41] This word comes from the Arabic word *kuhl*.[42] Another term that has a strong connection to alcohol is **aqua vitae** which is "an alchemical term for unrefined alcohol."[43] In Latin, it literally means "water of life".[44] This can be translated as "water with spirit".

Alcohol is an important substance for alchemists and herbalists because it has the ability to extract the essence of an entity. This is why it is heavily used to extract the essence of plants to make essential oils. Because of the extracting effect of alcohol, when you drink enough of it to make you drunk, it can temporary extract the essences of your body, which are your spirit and life force energy. This weakens your spirit and makes your body more susceptible to being possessed by foreign spirits. Why do you think certain "alcoholic beverages" are called "spirits" and people who drink too much alcohol often experience blackouts, causing them to have memory loss during those blackouts? Have you ever looked into a friend's eyes when he or she is drunk and sensed a different being inside his or her body? Many bad things happen to people who drink too much because their drinking habits attract many self-serving spirits that cannot wait to possess them when they are drunk.

Let us focus our attention back to the hidden roles of judges. Have you ever wondered why judges wear black robes? The black robe uniform is a symbol for representing a priest who works for the Jesuits or has a connection to the Jesuit order, the Vatican's private army. The **black** robe uniform can also represent a worshiper of the ancient god Saturn. During ancient times, **Saturn** was associated with the **god** of **law** and **justice**. Today, many secretive societies still worship Saturn as the god of law and justice. According to Jordan Maxwell, the symbol that was used in a religious context for Saturn was the **square** and its symbolic color was **black**.[45] This is one of the reasons that judges wear **black robes**. It is their way of showing respect to Saturn, the god of law and justice. Another reason is because they work for Satan, the god of the dead. In legalese, the dead is made up of corporations, persons, and citizens. The color of the dead is **black** because it represents death. Whether judges realize it or not, they are religious priests who are trained in the magic art of legalese to cast magic spells on people in a courtroom. Do you innerstand now why judges wear black robes?

Besides judges, priests also wear a uniform similar to a black robe. Their uniform is known as a cassock. The word **cassock** is defined as "a long, close-fitting garment worn by members of the clergy or others participating in church services" or "an ankle-length garment, usually **black**, worn by priests and choristers" (bold emphasis added).[46] Whether priests realize it or not, a significant percentage of the time they are acting in the capacity of magicians. Many of them have been tricked to work for the Dark Forces to control and manage people at the spiritual level. Because of this, when these priests are preaching religious words to people in church, they are often casting magic spells on them, similar to how judges/magistrates/"magistraits", which are religious priests, cast magic spells on people in court. This does not mean that all priests and judges are wicked. Most of them do not know that they have been trained and conditioned to cast certain magic spells. Keep in mind that there are many priests and judges who work for the Light Forces. Because judges are religious priests, there is no separation of church and state. Furthermore, most churches have been incorporated; therefore, the churches thereof belong to the State.

So, where do attorneys fit into this magic and black robe cult? In many ways, attorneys are also acting in the capacity of magicians because they know how to use the magic art of legalese to cast magic spells on people. However, they do not have as much power as judges. An important information that is beneficial for you to know about attorneys is that most of them work for the Crown Temple and therefore are Templar agents. A way to tell Templar attorneys from non-Templar attorneys is to ask them if they are members of the Bar Association. This association is controlled by the Crown Temple, a secretive society that operates under Roman law.

Whether Bar attorneys realize it or not, they are often committing atrocities in The United States of America, Canada, Australia, and other countries under the color of law (appearance of law). Bar attorneys work for the same secretive organizations (the Crown of

94

England and the Crown Temple) that tried to enslave the American people in the 1700s. These two secretive organizations were heavily involved in killing Americans during the American War of Independence. Today, the Crown of England and the Crown Temple still have the same desire to control Americans. Sadly, they have already conquered the court and the political systems of The United States of America over 100 years ago. These two secretive organizations are controlled by the Vatican, a city-state of the Holy Roman Empire. The good news is that a small percentage of the American people is still standing, and therefore the American government is also still standing. Because of this, Americans can still repopulate their constitutional court and political systems, restoring the power of their government.

Many people who are working for the legal system are unknowingly or knowingly abetting fraud. A significant percentage of this system is run by corrupt attorneys and judges working for the commercial courts of the Crown of England, the Crown Temple, and the Vatican. Therefore, the Crown of England, the Crown Temple, and the Vatican are responsible for the acts of their employees. Because of this, they are obligated to take serious actions to stop corrupt attorneys and judges from practicing law. Many of these corrupt judges working for commercial courts do not deserve to be called "your honor". In fact, they are not really judges but are **executive administrators**. By now you should know that the legal system is full of magic spells. You should also know why judges of the legal system and priests of churches are often acting in the capacity of magicians, especially judges. This is why judges wear black robes and "summon" people to "appear" in their courts, so they can trick them using the art of word magic. Please be aware that magic can be used for good or evil.

Why Commerce Is a Game of Battery for Draining Your Energy

On certain levels, the commerce game used by the Dark Forces to enslave mankind is a sick and evil game. However, when you learn how this game really works and know a significant percentage of its hidden in plain sight rules, you can find ways to prevent the Dark Forces from enslaving your family. You can even transform it into a game that works in your favor. The Dark Forces like to use the commerce game to con and trick you to temporarily give up your natural rights, spiritual power, and **energy**. This is why before they can summon you to go to court, they need to **charge** you first. When it comes to the legal system and commerce, the words charge, battery, and currency play a very big role for powering the commerce game and keeping it "alive".

In legal terms, when someone gets **beaten** up, that person is often referred to as a victim of **battery**. If the victim knows who the perpetrator is and presses **charges**, the perpetrator who did the **battery** will be summoned to appear in court to face the **charges**. In business, when a company outsells or outperforms its competitors, one of the common words that is used to describe this process is the word beat.[47] When the suffix "ing" is added to the word "beat", it changes to the word "beating". For example, company A is **beating** company B in sales. The commerce game is a game of **battery**, and therefore one business team or many business teams will eventually get **beaten** by the winner. Sports are also games of **battery**. In baseball, the combination of the pitcher and the catcher is called the **battery**. The evidence of this can be found in one of the definitions of the word **battery**: "the pitcher and catcher considered as a unit."[48] Have you ever heard someone say "batter up" in baseball? Add the letter "y" to the word "batter" in the term "batter up" and you get the term "**battery** up"![49]

The concept of **battery** is an important idea in commerce and law because it plays an important role in the process of harnessing the **energy** of mankind. This concept is one of the many concepts that the Dark Forces like to use to **drain** living people's **energy**. After collecting their energy using magic spells, the Dark Magicians and their masters (the Dark Forces) use it to **charge** their corporations (corpses or dead entities), banks, and other commercial entities that they control, so they can keep their game of conning mankind alive. Without living people's energy to **charge** their corporations and commercial systems, their commerce game will not have enough **power** to stay on or in business.

As living people, we are being used as "batteries". This is why before they can summon us to appear in court they have to "charge" us first. After the court **hearing** and trial, the judge reads the **charges** and **charges** them off or **discharges** them after a verdict or judgment is made. A court meeting between the defendant and the plaintiff before a trial is called a **hearing** because when a person is charged with something and summoned to appear in court he or she is called the defendant. Phonetically, the word "defendant" is "**deaf-end**-ant" which is a "deaf" person who is "a ward of the court" and is about to meet his "end" by the judge.[50] Hence, the word defendant/deaf-end-ant.

The phrase "a ward of the court" refers to an incompetent person or a person who is unable to care for himself, so the court must assume responsibility for his or her well-being. This is how most courts see you: a **deaf** and ignorant child who does not know the definition ("**deaf**-inition") of words. This is why they often summon you to appear at a **hearing** before a trial. The court hearing is done to test your **hearing** and understanding of words. If your hearing and understanding of words are not good, they know that it is most likely safe to treat you as a ward of the court, making it easier for them to charge you with fines and drain your energy. If you (the defendant/deaf-end-**ant**) agree to the charges, in a sense, you agree to make an **oath** to give up some of your energy to the judge and his masters because the word **ant** means "oath" or "a promise to oneself, resolution" in Turkish.[51] The judge has also sworn an oath, but his oath is to the god Saturn. Remember what I said earlier about why judges wear black robes? It is their symbolic way of paying respect to Saturn, the god of law and justice.

Remember, the symbol that is used in a religious context for Saturn is the **black square**. This black square can be found in the teachings of Islam. Have you ever heard of the **sacred black cube** in Mecca called the Kaaba or Kabah? This sacred black cube that Muslims pilgrimage to represents the god Saturn. The black mortarboard (graduation cap) that high school and college students wear when they graduate also symbolizes the god Saturn. Saturn was and is still such an important god that a day of the week has been dedicated to Saturn, which is known as "**Saturn**-day" or Saturday. It is right in your face! Saturn is also known as the **Lord** of the **Rings**. When a man and a woman get married today, they often use two rings as symbols of their marriage. What they do not realize is that rings also symbolize the god Saturn. This ancient god plays an important role in the ring ritual of a wedding. What you need to know about rituals is that they have energetic binding forces attached to them. These binding forces are often not dependent upon personal knowledge or beliefs. By simply taking the action to perform the religious ring ritual, you consent to whatever the ring ritual is designed to do.

During ancient times, Saturn was also known as **El**, the Hebrew word for **God**. "In the Hebrew Bible there are four words translated "God": El, Elah, Elo'ah, Elohim. The oldest Semitic word meaning "God" is El. Linguists believe its base meaning is strength or power. "El" is the Strong One, or the Deity (God)."[52] "When translating names that contain the segment אל (*'el*), it usually refers to אלהים (*'elohim*), that is Elohim, or God, also known as אלה (*'eloah*)."[53] An important information that you need to know about the four Hebrew words for God (i.e., El, Elah, **Elo'ah**, and Elohim) is that they have a strong connection to the name of the Islamic God called Allah. In fact, the name **Allah** comes from "Arabic **Allah**, contraction of **al-Ilah**, literally "the God," from **al** "the" + **Ilah** "God," which is cognate with Aramaic **elah**, Hebrew **eloah**" (bold emphasis added).[54]

> Saturn being El, was under the domination of Egypt. That whole area had its philosophies, ideas, and its people being dominated by Egypt. So Isis was the first main divinity. Now, with the coming of Ahknaton, the worship was then changed to the worship of Amen-Ra, the sun. This is where we get sun-ray from – from Amen-Ra. Amen-Ra was worshiped in the temples as God's Sun/Son. At the end of the service, they would say Amen, because they were sending a prayer to God through Amen-Ra, God's Sun/Son. So they would say Amen when they sent the prayer through God's Sun/Son. The ancient Egyptians said nobody had seen God, and perhaps, there is nobody who is ever going to see God. But when you have seen the sun, you have seen the Father. And when you pray to the Father, you pray directly to the Father, but you send your prayer through God's sun, Amen-Ra. So at the end of the prayer you say, Amen.[55]

Today, after Christians pray to God, they say "amen". Unfortunately, their pronunciation of the word amen may not be accurate. Some spiritual teachers and etymological researchers have said that "amen" is pronounced "aah-mon" or "aah-men". What Christians do not realize is that they have been conditioned to say amen to an **external** god which weakens their connection to the true Amen-Ra (Jesus) within them. Another important information that most Christians do not realize is that their religion is full of pagan beliefs. Furthermore, they do not know that their religion has many similarities to Islam.

The information in the previous few paragraphs is evidence of this. On the surface, Islam and Christianity seem to be different religions; however, below the surface they have similar messages and many of their words have the same origins.

Let us focus our attention back to the court hearing process. During a court trial, when the defendant loses the case, the judge often "orders" the defendant to pay the court and the plaintiff with "currency". The word **order** is defined as "a command of a court or judge."[56] It can also mean "a command or notice issued by a **military** organization or a **military** commander to troops, **sailors**, etc." (bold emphasis added).[57] Do you remember what I said earlier about why most courts operating under the legal system are **military** courts? They are military courts because they fall under the jurisdiction of the law of the **sea** (admiralty law). A word in this paragraph that is important to investigate is currency. One of the hidden definitions of the word **currency** is "flow of energy". In a battery, this "flow of energy" is called "electric current". On a deeper level, "electric current" can be translated as "currency of electricity". The word **currency** comes from the Latin word **currens**, the present participle of **currere**, which means "to run".[58] Now, why would they based the word currency on a Latin word that does not have a direct connection with paper money or coin? Because it is not really about the paper money or coin. Instead, it is about harnessing the **energy** of mankind!

To innerstand why currency has a strong connection to energy, you need to find the occult meaning of the word currency. To do this, you need to rely on the art of homophone and separate the word currency into two words. When spoken aloud, the word "currency" sounds similar to the term "current sea". What does a **current** do in a river? It **flows** or **runs** to the **sea**! Keep in mind that the Latin word **currens** means "to run". The word **current** means "a flowing; **flow**, as of a river" or "something that flows, as a stream" (bold emphasis added).[59] The flowing movement of currents is what causes the fresh water in the river to **flow** to the **sea**. Once the fresh water is in the sea, its "currents" are now part of the "current sea" or the "**current** of the **sea**". Hence, the term currency/current-sea. It is important to know that sea water has a lot of salt and therefore conducts electricity better than fresh water. In other words, as a medium, sea water (salt water) is better at transferring energy. Hence, the word electrolyte ("electro-**light**"). Light is energy! The word **electrolyte** is defined as "any substance that dissociates into ions when dissolved in a suitable medium or melted and thus forms a conductor of electricity."[60] Sea water is saturated with electrolyte/electro-light, just like blood. Therefore, sea water is the "blood" of Earth.

The word "currency" also sounds similar to the term "current chi". In Chinese, the word **chi** (*qi*) refers to natural energy and means "life force", or "energy flow".[61] Keep in mind that the Chinese word **chi** is pronounced somewhat similar to the English word **sea**. Based on the occult definitions of currency, the word **currency** means "flow of life force energy". When you really think about it, currency is a medium for exchanging or transferring life force energy which is why the Dark Forces are obsessed with using currency to drain your life force energy. An important information that is beneficial for you to know about the word **sea** is that it is strongly connected to admiralty law (the law of the **sea**) and Vatican City (home of the Holy **See**). The Vatican is heavily involved in the creation of many laws on Earth, such as admiralty, maritime, canon, statutory, and civil laws. When judges and attorneys talk about the word sea in admiralty law, whether they realize it or not, they are not always talking about water. On a deeper level, they are talking about **life force energy**. This becomes clear when you know that water carries the current/currency/current-sea/current-chi which is the life force energy needed to charge the dead matrix of the Dark Forces and their corporations/corpses. The life force energy in water is why water is essential for life to exist in the universe.

It is important to remember that currency is a medium of exchange. One of the definitions of the word **currency** is "something that is used as a **medium** of exchange; money" (bold emphasis added).[62] The word **medium** means "an intervening substance, as air, through which a force acts or an effect is produced."[63] It is important to know that the word **medium** can also mean "a person thought to have the power to communicate with the spirits of the **dead** or with agents of another world or dimension. Also called *psychic*" (bold emphasis added).[64] To connect the dots, currency/current-sea/current-chi is a medium that is used by agents of corporations/corpses to communicate with and transfer life force energy to the Dead.

The information in the previous paragraph becomes even more clear when you study the occult definitions of the word cryptocurrency. To find its occult definitions, you need to separate it into two words (crypto currency) and study their definitions. The prefix **crypto-** comes from the Greek word **kryptos**, meaning "hidden, concealed, secret".[65] As for the origin of the word **currency**, one of its origins is the Latin word *currens*, meaning "to run".[66] The definitions in this paragraph do not tell you the deeper occult meanings of the word cryptocurrency; therefore, you need to dissect it even further so it becomes the word **crypt**. One of the origins of the word **crypt** is the Latin word *crypta*, meaning "vault, cavern".[67] Another definition of the word **crypt** is "a subterranean chamber or vault, especially one beneath the main floor of a church, used as a burial place, a location for secret meetings, etc".[68] In simple terms, it is a place to bury the **dead**!

When you put all the occult definitions of the words cryptocurrency and currency together, you should realize that **cryptocurrency** is the **hidden digital currency** that the Dark Forces and their corporations/corpses want to use to control the global economy and drain mankind's life force energy. In other words, the word **cryptocurrency** (crypto-currency), which is made up of the words **crypt/crypto** (hidden vault for the dead) and **currency** (flow of energy), can be translated as "the hidden vault or chamber for storing energy for the Dead or flowing energy to the Dead". The good news is that if we can prevent the Dark Forces from abusing cryptocurrency and learn how to use it in harmony with nature, cryptocurrency can be an effective and convenient medium for exchanging goods and services. A very important information that you need to know about currency is that it is the Dark Magicians' favorite economic tool to use for draining your energy and using it to charge the Dead. The free manual *Silent Weapons for Quiet Wars* does a great job of explaining the relationship between energy and economics. Here are some paragraphs extracted from this manual that have some important information about energy and economics:

Energy is recognized as the key to all activity on earth. Natural science is the study of the sources and control of natural energy, and social science, theoretically expressed as economics, is the study of the sources and control of social energy. Both are bookkeeping systems: mathematics. Therefore, mathematics is the primary energy science. And the bookkeeper can be king if the public can be kept ignorant of the methodology of the bookkeeping.

All of the mathematical theory developed in the study of

one energy system (e.g., mechanics, electronics, etc.) can be immediately applied in the study of any other energy system (e.g., economics). ...

Mr. Rothschild had discovered that currency or deposit loan accounts had the required appearance of power that could be used to induce people (inductance, with people corresponding to a magnetic field) into surrendering their real wealth in exchange for a promise of greater wealth (instead of real compensation). They would put up real collateral in exchange for a loan of promissory notes. Mr. Rothschild found that he could issue more notes than he had backing for, so long as he had someone's stock of gold as a persuader to show his customers.

Mr. Rothschild loaned his promissory notes to individuals and to governments. These would create overconfidence. Then he would make money scarce, tighten control of the system, and collect the collateral through the obligation of contracts. The cycle was then repeated. These pressures could be used to ignite a war. Then he would control the availability of currency to determine who would win the war. ...

In this structure, credit, presented as a pure element called "currency," has the appearance of capital, but is in effect negative capital. Hence, it has the appearance of service, but is in fact, indebtedness or debt. It is therefore an economic inductance instead of an economic capacitance, and **if balanced in no other way, will be balanced by the negation of population (war, genocide)**. The total goods and services represent real capital called the gross national product, and currency may be printed up to this level and still represent economic capacitance; but currency printed beyond this level is subtractive, represents the introduction of economic inductance, and constitutes notes of indebtedness. [Bold emphasis added]

War is therefore the balancing of the system by killing the true creditors (the public which we have taught to exchange true value for inflated currency) and falling back on whatever is left of the resources of nature and regeneration of those resources. ... [Bold emphasis added]

Economics is only a social extension of a natural energy system. It, also, has its three passive components. Because of the distribution of wealth and the lack of communication and lack of data, this field has been the last energy field for which a knowledge of these three passive components has been developed.

In simple terms, the previous paragraphs in block quotation are basically telling you that currency can be used to steal people's energy and control them. To prevent this, people need to stop living beyond their means; they also need to use money wisely. It is important to know that paper or digital currency can be used for good or evil purposes. The problem is that the Dark Forces and their minions are in control of a large percentage of the global financial system; therefore, if they were to succeed at using digital currency to totally control the global economy, mankind would greatly suffer for many years.

Because cryptocurrency is a digital currency, it can be used to totally enslave people in the artificial matrix. This matrix is a hologram that is now being managed by a very advanced quantum computing system. It was created by the Dark Forces and their flesh and blood minions to control people. The artificial matrix of the Dark Forces is not really natural because it uses words and spells to manipulate people's minds to accept lies, creating beliefs that are based on lies. For example, they like to use movies and religious stories to brainwash people to think that they are weak and powerless. Movies and religious stories, which can be used for good or evil, are some of the most powerful mediums for casting words and magic spells. These words and magic spells are very powerful and effective for controlling the mind because they have the power to access and reprogram the subconscious mind. Because of this, they can easily be used to hypnotize and control people's minds, especially people who lack awareness and knowledge.

It is unfortunate that most people are ignorant of the power of words and spells. Because of their ignorance, the Dark Forces can effectively use words and spells to program and condition them to believe in lies and live as slaves in an artificial matrix, allowing the Dark Forces to use them as biological batteries. In other words, the **artificial matrix** is the **Hell on Earth**! Many people are worried that if they do not do good deeds and join a religion they may go to Hell after they die. What they do not know is that they are already living in Hell. It is called the artificial (dead) matrix which is the "land" or "sea" of the DEAD!

For you to innerstand how the artificial matrix is created, you need to know what the universe is made of. At the deepest level of the external reality, everything is energy and consciousness. When I say "external reality", I am talking about the reality in front of the fabric of space that is outside of you. The realm behind the fabric of space is known by scientists as "dark energy". Ancient civilizations referred to it as the ether. In certain occult teachings, the ether is known as the fifth element. In Sanskrit it is called akasha which is the essence of all things in the material world. One of the first levels of the external reality is made of crystallizations of "frozen light". Some spiritual teachings refer to them as "keylons". When these keylons are grouped together in grid-like patterns, they form the morphogenetic field crystal body. Morphogenetic field is an invisible and thought-form field that functions as the blueprint or template upon which matter is manifested. It is also a field that allows consciousness to create structure so it can experience itself.

To make it easier for you to innerstand, imagine that keylons are like light bulbs stacked side-by-side in grid-like patterns. When these keylons (light bulbs) are charged with energy, they light up in certain ways, creating light patterns. These are the energy or light codes of the universe. These light codes work similar to quantum computer codes or qubits. Your perception of reality is created when your body and mind process these light codes and project them as encoded light into the external world. This process occurs at the subconscious level. At the conscious level, you see these encoded light as matter. The Dark Forces are well aware of how keylons work. Because of this, they are able to use words and magic spells to create artificial light codes and manipulate people's bodies and minds to process these artificial codes. This process allows the Dark Forces to hijack their natural reality to a significant degree. It also allows them to "plug" their DNA into the artificial matrix, enslaving their minds inside an artificial reality that is now being managed by quantum computers.

The purpose of plugging people's DNA into the artificial matrix is to enslave their minds, so the Dark Forces can use them as biological batteries. The dead entities of the Dark Forces need to feed on people's life force energy to thrive and survive because they are not connected to the Eternal Life Force of God. This is why they like to order their flesh and blood minions to engineer wars. Wars create death and destruction, giving them the opportunity to feed on new dead bodies that still contain some life force energy. Because the dead entities of the Dark Forces need to feed on mankind's life force energy, they are "astral parasites" or "energy vampires". They are energy vampires for the reason that they need to feed on the energy of mankind to survive; furthermore, they need people's permission (consent) before they can do anything to them. In movies, vampires cannot enter a house unless they get permission from the owner. Now you know the origin of vampires.

It is important to know that there is a program behind all biological life, even reality has a program behind it. I will refer to this program as the Source Code. This code, which is made of symbols (e.g., letters and words), is written into the fabric of space by God and therefore is everywhere and is hidden inside everything. Some "lines" or "sentences" of the Source Code have been discovered by scientists. They like to refer to them as scientific laws. Geneticists have also found some sentences of the Source Code. They define them as genetic codes. In the mind, certain sentences of the Source Code are used to **command** thoughts, allowing them to be manifested into reality. When a certain percentage of the Source Code is "infected" with artificial programs, it can manifest a false reality (artificial matrix). Today, people's minds have been infected with so many artificial programs that most of them can barely tell the difference between the real world and the artificial world. The fact that most people believe that the government is real is evidence that they are living in a false reality known as the artificial matrix. There is NO government that is real because there is no living man or woman who is the government itself. There are only men and women acting as **agents** of the government. The sooner you realize this, the sooner you can free your mind from the artificial matrix.

It is also important to know that the DNA of man works similar to an antenna and the planets and the stars are like radio stations that emit signals (electromagnetic waves). These signals contain the codes of reality because they carry energy codes (information). When these signals reach people, they are processed by their minds and bodies in a way that allows their DNA to use the information to project the right frequencies of light (energy) into the external world. This process literally creates their perception of reality and material world. This is possible because matter is a projection of energy. In other words, the material world is a giant hologram. Keep in mind that the signals containing the codes of reality also come from within. Here is an excerpt from the book *Staradigm* (third edition) that explains this process further:

> To help simplify how our external reality is constructed through holographic projections of mind or energy, let us turn our attention to how a movie projector works. A movie projector basically works by continuously moving films along a path between a light source and a lens, causing a light effect that projects the image inside the films onto a screen. The movie projector can be metaphorically referred to as the observer's consciousness and the light can be associated with energy. Each film can be metaphorically referred to as a point in time, the lens acts like DNA, and the screen upon which the illusion is projected on is like the unified field from which all matter is manifested.

> When the film is not moving, everything is still and therefore there is no time or linear action. Once the projector is turned on and the film starts moving, there are movements on the screen, causing an illusion of linear actions and time. The illusion that is projected onto the screen (unified field) is caused by the light (energy) as it travels through the lens (DNA), causing it to project outward into the external world. The illusions that are projected can be likened to an observer's experiences. Some important things you need to know about time are that it does not move and it is not truly linear. Linear time is only achieved when an observer's consciousness moves through the unified field of time. When an observer's consciousness does not move through this unified field, time is simultaneous.

To trap man (male and female) in the artificial matrix, the Dark Forces and their flesh and blood minions created very advanced technology to obstruct certain natural signals of the planets and the Sun, allowing them to interfere with the natural communication process between nature and man. This also allows the Dark Forces to replace some natural signals of the planets and the Sun with their artificial light codes. These artificial light codes are the codes of their artificial matrix which is an artificial reality that is ruled by the DEAD. When the Dark Forces use certain words, spells, and technologies to broadcast the artificial light codes of the artificial matrix on Earth, people's DNA receives the codes and then the codes are processed into information by their minds. Once that process is finished, the information is projected as encoded light into the external world. This process alters their natural reality to a certain degree, allowing the Dark Forces to create a reality that they want. The artificial matrix that is used by the Dark Forces to overlay Earth's natural matrix or reality is one of their greatest technologies for controlling people's minds. The artificial matrix is very effective for controlling people because it looks very similar to the natural reality of Earth, and therefore most people have no idea that they live in an artificial reality or artificial hologram.

Is there evidence that the universe is made of light (energy) codes? To find some of the evidence, study the work of theoretical physicist Dr. James Gates Jr. Recently, he found evidence of "computer codes" in the fabric of space. "Working on a branch of physics called supersymmetry, Dr. James Gates Jr., discovered what he describes as the presence of what appear to resemble a form of computer code, called error correcting codes, embedded within, or resulting from, the equations of supersymmetry that describe fundamental particles."[69] He called these codes "adinkras".

A powerful system that is used by the Dark Forces to make it hard for people to delete the artificial codes of the artificial matrix and replace them with the natural codes of the universe is the distorted version of the alphanumeric system. Other tools that they like to use to prevent people from rising above the artificial matrix are false religion and the media. By using these tools to condition people how to think, they can control their thought patterns to a large degree. This allows them to create a reality that they want. When you know that mankind's collective consciousness is what creates man's reality on Earth, you will know why the Dark Forces want to control how people think. Reality is thought construction; therefore, when people collectively think in certain ways, their thoughts, beliefs, and actions shape and define what their reality will look like. This is possible because matter is a projection of energy and is focused into existence through the power of thought. As a collective, the people of Earth are, to a great extent, literally creating the reality of Earth. They are not aware of this creation process because it occurs in their subconscious minds.

The Dark Forces are well aware of how the universe works. This is because they know the language of the universe and how sacred geometry works. The language of the universe is based on frequency, light, sound, vibration, and sacred geometry. It is a very powerful communication and information system. In the wrong hands, a certain percentage of this universal language can be used to control people and hijack their reality. However, it can also be used to free them from the artificial matrix of the Dark Forces. The movie *The Matrix* (1999) was created to tell people that they have been enslaved by the Dark Forces. Sadly, most people are too brainwashed, ignorant, and spiritually "brain dead" to realize this.

Let us focus our attention back to the relationship between corporation and currency. When you go to work at a corporation, you are often paid hourly. Every hour is recorded to make sure that you are paid for investing your **time** and **energy** into the corporation. After you have worked for a certain amount of time, you are given a weekly or biweekly paycheck, usually on Friday. Once you take your paycheck to the bank to exchange it for currency, the **currency** now represents your **time** and **energy**. An important information that you need to know about the words **bank** and **currency** is that they are related to the word **river**. What does a river have on its two sides to prevent water from flowing out of it? River**banks**! Corporate banks are like riverbanks because they regulate currency/current-sea/current-chi. In other words, they regulate the flow of energy, just like how riverbanks regulate the flow of the energy of water. They did not combine the words "river" and "banks" to make the word "riverbanks" by accident.

To innerstand how currency is used to drain your energy on a deeper level, you need to know certain occult definitions of the word commerce. The word **commerce** is defined as "an interchange of goods or commodities, especially on a large scale between different countries (foreign commerce) or between different parts of the same country (domestic commerce) trade; business."[70] It can also mean "**sexual intercourse**" or "intellectual or spiritual interchange; communion" (bold emphasis added).[71] *Black's Law Dictionary* (4th edition) defines the word **commerce** using these words:

Commerce, in its simplest signification, means an

exchange of goods; but in the advancement of society, labor, transportation, intelligence, care and various mediums of exchange, become commodities and enter into commerce; the subject; the vehicle, the agent, and their various operations become the objects of commercial regulation. Lorenzetti v. American Trust Co., D.C.Cal., 45 F.Supp. 128, 132.

"Commerce" is not traffic alone, but is **intercourse between nations** and parts of nations in all its branches. Blumenstock Bros. Advertising Agency v. Curtis Pub. Co., 252 U.S. 436, 40 S.Ct. 385, 387, 64 L.Ed. 649. [Bold emphasis added]

The words "commerce" and "trade" are often used interchangeably; but, strictly speaking, **commerce** relates to intercourse or dealings with **foreign** nations, states, or political communities, while **trade** denotes business intercourse or mutual traffic **within the limits of a state or nation**, or the buying, selling, and exchanging of articles between members of the same community. Hooker v. Vandewater, 4 Denio, N.Y., 353, 47 Am. Dec. 258; Jacob; Wharton. [Bold emphasis added]

The word "commerce" is made up of two words which are "com" and "merce". The prefix or word-forming element **com-** etymologically means "with, together".[72] As for **merce**, it comes from the Latin word **merx** (genitive *mercis*), meaning "merchandise".[73] To find one of the deeper meanings of the word commerce, you need to investigate its origins. One of the origins of the word **commerce** is the Latin word ***commercium***, meaning "trade, **trafficking**" (bold emphasis added).[74] The word **trafficking** is defined as "the movement of vehicles, **ships**, persons, etc., in an area, along a street, through an air lane, over a **water route**, etc." (bold emphasis added).[75] It is derived from the Old Italian word ***traffico***, meaning "to engage in trade".[76] Therefore, trafficking has a strong connection to water, ships, and trade. Do you remember what I said in the beginning of this book about how your body is related to ship and water?

In legal terms, the word **trafficking** means "the carrying on of an **illegal** commercial activity such as selling drugs or substances that are banned" (bold emphasis added).[77] Because one of the definitions of the word commerce is "sexual intercourse" and the word commerce is related to trafficking, when people participate in commerce in an immoral way, they are, in a sense, selling their bodies for sex. The commerce system is one of the Dark Forces' favorite tools for "trafficking" people and tricking them to commit "adultery", giving the Dark Forces the excuse to use them as biological batteries. When people use the commerce system in a negative way, it allows the Dark Forces to trick them to commit sin and crime against mankind, Nature, and God, causing death to life. Hence, the biblical saying, "For the wages of sin is death".[78] Sin is debt/dead/death. Keep in mind that commerce can be use for good or evil.

One of the many systems that is a part of the commerce system is the stock market. This financial system is rigged and commits illegal and unlawful commercial activities on a daily basis. Every day, people are losing money in the stock market and therefore are being "screwed" by this system. Two slang definitions of the word **screw** (Chiefly British) are "an old broken-down **horse**" and "salary; wages" (bold emphasis added).[79] In American English, the slang definition of the verb **screw** means "to practice extortion", "to have **sexual** intercourse (with)", or "to have **coitus**" (bold emphasis added).[80] The word **coitus** means "sexual intercourse, especially between a man and a woman."[81] Remember, the word **commerce** can also mean "sexual intercourse". The definitions of the words in bold font in this paragraph and the previous few paragraphs show that the commerce system and the stock market are related to sex, money, and horse. The commerce system is full of sexual symbolism because the Dark Forces and their minions are not only after people's life force energy but also their sexual energy. This is why sexual symbolism is everywhere, especially in television commercials. Many agents of the Dark Forces are using the commerce system to steal people's sexual and life force energies, turning them into the whores/horses of Babylon.

In the stock market, the process of selling stocks is also known as stock trading. The people who trade stocks on the stock market are known as traders and therefore can be called traitors. Why is that you may ask? Because the word "trader" is phonetically "traitor". A **trader** of stocks is a **traitor** to man (male and female) because he or she is participating in the financial game to steal man's spiritual energy and enslave his mind and soul.[82] Until the stock market is transformed into an honest system, most "stock traders" are "stock traitors". The word **trader** means "dealer, **trafficker**, one engaged in commerce" (bold emphasis added).[83] The word **trader** can also mean "a **ship** used in trade, especially foreign trade" (bold emphasis added).[84] As for the word **traitor**, it means "a person who betrays another, a cause, or any trust" or "a person who commits treason by betraying his or her country."[85]

The definitions in the previous few pages show the connection between the words ship, water, and commerce. Remember, it is all about tricking people to agree to allow the Dark Forces to take their **energy** using commerce, maritime law (law of merchant), and admiralty law (law of the **sea**). Why the sea? Because the **sea** is made of mostly **water** and water carries the current/currency/current-sea/current-chi. Furthermore, people's bodies are also made of mostly water, which is the water that transports life force energy. This is the energy that is needed to charge currency, giving it value so it can be used as a medium of exchange in commerce.

When people use the commerce system in an immoral and greedy manner, they are, in a way, committing a crime against mankind. If you want strong evidence of this, study how some people immorally use the debt-based monetary system and the stock market to screw people over and over again with fraudulent debt. These two financial systems are based on greed and competition which are great for manifesting negative emotions, violence, and wars. For a man to make millions of dollars in the stock market, hundreds and possibly thousands of people have to lose a lot of money in that market. In other words, he has to screw people over and over again so he can take their soul energy, giving him enough stocks to become a millionaire. Until people learn to use the stock market in a harmonious way, it may be wise to stay away from the stock market.

Many people who make a profit from the stock market and other similar systems are helping certain corporations to enslave mankind and prevent poor countries from thriving. The people living in undeveloped countries are not poor because they are dumb or lazy. In fact, many of them are very intelligent and work a lot harder than many people living in rich countries. To a large extent, people living in poor countries lack wealth because it has been engineered that way by the Dark Magicians and their international bankers. The international bankers control many central banks throughout the world; therefore, they can prevent poor countries from thriving by charging them high interest rates and not giving them enough funds to invest in economic development projects. The good news is that the banking system of the world is starting to change into a more honest system. However, it is still men and women's responsibility to make sure that this change is for the better of mankind.

On a deeper level, the stock market is a financial system that sells or trades people's soul energy, which is why it is called a stock market. Many **stocks** in the stock market do not really represent the shares of corporations. Instead, they are linked to artificial persons which are legal fictions that are used by the legal system to represent **living men**, **women**, and **children**. The main reason that corporate stocks have value is because they are linked to living people. In other words, living men, women, children are the "livestock" or "living stock" that are sold ("souled") on the stock market by the traders/traitors of mankind. The word **stock** is defined as "a quantity of something accumulated, as for future use".[86] As for the word **livestock**, it is defined as "the **horses**, cattle, **sheep**, and other useful animals kept or raised on a **farm** or ranch" (bold emphasis added).[87] When you look at this situation from a higher view, it is not hard to see that people are the sheeple living on a "farm" called Earth which is a planet for domesticating people to be good little horses, cattle, and sheep. To be more specific, men, women, and children are the babies (bay-bees) raised on a farm to produce honey or golden fluid for the Dark Forces, so they can use it to extend their lifespans.

In a way, most people are not that much different from horses, cattle, and sheep because they have been domesticated by the Dark Forces to obey their Secret Government and blindly follow the masses. This is why when you talk to people about a conspiracy of the government, most of them look at you like you are crazy. Some of them may even physically attack you for telling them the truth. What a bunch of sheeple and domesticated animals! The sheeple are so brainwashed that they cannot see that they are being domesticated to behave like sheep and sold ("souled") on the stock market. To make matters worse, their soul energy is being stocked in the stock market, so it can be sucked out later by corporations/corpses and other dead entities. This is why one of the definitions of the word **stock** is "a quantity of something accumulated, as for future use".[88] One of the origins of the word **stock** is the Old French word **stocc**, meaning "stump, post, stake, tree **trunk**, log" (bold emphasis added).[89] The word **stock** has a connection to the word **trunk** which is derived from the Old French word **tronc**, meaning "trunk of a tree, trunk of the **human body**, wooden block" (bold emphasis added).[90] In English, one of the definitions of the word **trunk** is "the **body** of a **person** or an animal excluding the head and limbs; torso" (bold emphasis added).[91] It can also mean "the main channel, artery, or line in a **river**, railroad, highway, **canal**, or other tributary system" (bold emphasis added).[92]

The definitions in the previous paragraph reveal the relationship between the stock market, the physical body, and water. To connect the dots, your "body" is being sold on the stock market for currency/current-sea/current-chi. The currency that represents your time and energy. Do you remember what I said in Chapter 3 about why "the birth certificate bond is a financial contract that can be used to enslave your body, mind, and soul by turning you into collateral to backup the debt of the government"? I also told you that "your birth certificate is the bond with your legal name written on it in all capital letters; therefore, it is the financial document (security/capital) or insurance certificate that has the value of the bounty on your head. This is why your birth certificate can be used to issue bonds to trade on the stock market". In simple terms, your "birth certificate" is a registered security or a "**stock** certificate". Do you now innerstand why living people are the "livestock" or "living stock" of the stock market? When you sell or trade stocks, what you are really doing is selling or trading people's soul energy, thereby treating people like commercial products. Please be aware that I am not saying that the stock market is evil. With proper management and laws, the stock market can be transformed into a wonderful financial system that can greatly benefit mankind.

It is important to know that commerce is not the same as the process of living people trading goods and services with one another. **Commerce** deals with the charging of the DEAD and is business conducted between two or more incorporated entities. To be more specific, it is business conducted between incorporated corporations that are chartered by and insured as franchises of an incorporated corporation (e.g. United States, Inc.). On the other hand, in general, **trade** deals with unincorporated corporation. Keep in mind that a corporation can be incorporated or unincorporated. When living people trade goods and services with one another, they are mutually exchanging their energy. Because of this, they do not necessarily need to rely on corporations to do business. However, when living people participate in commerce, corporations act like middlemen to facilitate commercial transactions. If these corporations are run by greedy and immoral agents, they can be used to steal living people's energy. Today, many corporations are run by greedy and immoral agents which is why the commerce system is becoming more vampiric than ever.

A popular vampiric system that is part of the commerce system is the mortgage system. A mortgage is one of the most parasitic debts that you can get from a bank. To innerstand how parasitic and vampiric a mortgage is, you need to dig deep into the hidden layers of the word mortgage so you can find its occult (secret) meanings. The overt definition of the word **mortgage** is, "a conveyance of an interest in property as security for the repayment of money borrowed."[93] Another definition of the word **mortgage** is, "A legal agreement by which a bank, building society, etc. lends money at interest in exchange for taking title of the debtor's property, with the condition that the conveyance of title becomes void upon the payment of the debt."[94]

The two definitions of the word mortgage in the previous paragraph only define mortgage on the surface. To find its deeper meaning, you need to use an etymological dictionary to find the origins of the word mortgage. You also need to separate it into two words, so it transforms into the term "mort gage". The word mortgage/mort-gage is derived from two Old French words which are *mort* and *gage*. In Old French, *mort* means "dead"[95] and *gage* means "pledge".[96] As a verb, **pledge** etymologically means "to promise".[97] As a noun, it etymologically means "surety, bail".[98] According to *A New Dictionary of the English Language* (Richardson, 1839), the word **pledge** means, "To be, or become, surety or security; to undertake to answer for; to stake as a gage; to put in pawn; to warrant, to offer in warranty, or proof of good faith, of good fellowship." One of the modern definitions of the word **pledge** is "a solemn promise or agreement to do or refrain from doing something".[99]

To connect the dots, when you take out a mortgage, you unknowingly make a pledge (promise) to the Dead and become a surety of the Dead. This is one of the occult (secret) definitions of the word mortgage. So, what is the Dead? The Dead is made of the Dark Forces and their corporations (corpses). The word corporation has a strong connection to the Dead because its deeper meaning is "a dead body". Do you remember what I said earlier in this chapter that the plural form of the word **corporation** can be abbreviated as **corps** and is related to the word **corpse** which is defined as "a dead body, usually of a human being"?[100] According to *Black's Law Dictionary* (6th edition), a **corporation** is, "An artificial person or legal entity created by or under the authority of the laws of a state." An **artificial**

person is considered a **dead entity** because it does not exist in the real world. All corporations (e.g., banks and governments) are dead because they are not living and breathing beings made of flesh and blood.

Based on the information in the previous paragraph, the word **corporation** has a strong connection to the word **mortgage**. Both of these words also have a strong connection to the words **morgue** and **mortuary**. This is why the place where dead bodies (corpses) are stored is called a morgue. Mortgages are created in a way that makes them hard to pay off, so the people who have signed mortgages (dead pledges) have to work most of their lives to pay them off. This allows the debt-based monetary system to drain their life force energy and use it as currency to charge the Dead, allowing the Dead to feel "alive". This is the currency that people make from many hours of working at a corporation (dead body). Do you remember what I said earlier about why currency is a medium for exchanging or transferring life force energy? On a spiritual level, when people sign a mortgage, they sign a large percentage of their lives away to the Dead. They also make a promise to the Dead to charge it with their energy, so the Dead can stay alive. In other words, they agree to make a solemn pledge to the Dead to ensure that the Dead will be paid with life force energy.

Phonetically, the word **dead** sounds similar to the word **debt**. Furthermore, the word **debt** has a strong connection to the word **mortgage**. Every time you get a mortgage (debt/dead pledge), you commit **sin**. If you want evidence of this, go to Merriam-Webster.com and search for the definition of debt and you should see the word sin as one of its definitions. The word **sin** is derived from the Old English word *synn*, meaning "moral wrongdoing, injury, mischief, enmity, feud, guilt, crime, offense against God, misdeed".[101] Sin is also the name of an ancient moon-god or moon-goddess. The reason that you commit a sin (death) when you get a debt (e.g., mortgage) is because you bring more debt (death) into the economy, decreasing the purchasing power of the country's currency and causing death to the economy. As debt/death spreads throughout the economy, it strengthens the power of the Dark Forces, allowing them to enslave mankind. The debt system is controlled by the Dark Forces and they are using it to drain the energy of mankind and destroy their home called Earth, causing death to life. Maybe this is why the Bible verse Romans 6:23 starts with the clause, "For the wages of sin is death".[102] Sin is debt/dead/death.

If you want to innerstand the sin of debt a little deeper, you need to know how the words mortgage, debt, dead, and battery are all related to the "dollar" which is also known as "legal tender". The term **legal tender** etymologically means "currency which by law must be accepted **from** a **debtor**" (bold emphasis added).[103] An important word in the previous sentence that you need to investigate is legal. In Chapter 3, I said that "the word legal has nothing to do with true law". This is because the word "legal" deals with the "color of law". *Black's Law Dictionary* (5th edition) defines the word **color** using these exact words: "An appearance, semblance, or *simulacrum*, as distinguished from that which is real. A *prima facie* or apparent right. Hence, a **deceptive appearance**; a plausible, assumed exterior, concealing a lack of reality; a disguise or pretext" (bold emphasis added). In other words, **legal** tender is not really money; it is debt that has the **appearance** of money. This is why on the front of every Federal Reserve Note there is this statement: "THIS NOTE IS LEGAL TENDER FOR ALL DEBTS, PUBLIC AND PRIVATE". A **note** is basically an I.O.U. which is **evidence of debt**.

The words sin, mortgage, note, debt, and dead are all related to the dollar because the dollar is **legal tender** or **dead money**. What do people do with some of their legal tender? They "bury" it in the banks! What you need to know about the word **bank** is that it is related to the word **currency**. Furthermore, both of these words are related to the word **river**. Do you remember what I said earlier about the relationship between the words "river" and "bank"? What does a river have on both of its sides to prevent water from flowing out of it? Riverbanks! Corporate banks are like riverbanks because they regulate currency (current-sea). Corporate banks regulate the flow of the energy of people; riverbanks regulate the flow of the energy of water. Banks need to regulate the flow of energy in order to control the currency/current-**sea**/current-chi (flow of energy) to charge the dead/debt. This is why when the dead/debt is not paid the banks may send a loan **shark** after people who have refused to pay the dead/debt. A **shark** is a large fish that lives in the **sea**. They did not use the term "loan shark" for no reason. It is all about water and energy because water carries the current/currency/current-sea/current-chi which is needed to charge the dead/debt with life force energy.

By now you should know why the words sin, legal, stock, mortgage, note, debt, dead, currency, corporation, bank, riverbank, commerce, battery, and charge are all related to the process of harnessing the energy of mankind. The Earth Matrix Drama is all about tricking mankind to consent to be a biological battery, so the Dark Forces and their flesh and blood minions can drain the life force energy of men and women to charge their dead matrix system. The good news is that we have the power to change this destructive and unpleasant drama into a harmonious and pleasant drama. One of the keys to doing this is to control and balance the dark and light forces inside each of us. The main reason that the Dark Forces are out of control is because the dark force inside each of us is also out of control.

What Banks Do Not Tell You About Mortgages and Loans

Today, nearly all banks do not lend out lawful money; instead, they lend out notes or checks that are backed by a promise to pay. Before lending out these notes or checks, the borrower has to sign documents that have terms and conditions written on them, along with a price tag (the amount of money the borrower agrees to pay back). These documents are called "negotiable contracts", "loan agreements", or "promissory notes". After you sign a "loan" agreement with a bank, it **legally** binds you to the terms and conditions of that agreement. What banks do not tell you is that when you sign a loan agreement or promissory note you give value to that loan or note. You give it value because it is backed by your promise to pay. An important fact that you need to know about a valid agreement (contract) is that it is a mutual agreement. A mutual agreement cannot be truly valid without **full disclosure**.

Nearly all bank loan agreements of today are not truly mutual agreements because they do not come with full disclosure. As a result, they are often invalid agreements and therefore have no legal or lawful standing. Almost all bank loan agreements may not be valid because the credits created from those loan agreements are created out of thin air. In a way, this way of creating credit can help the economy thrive because it allows people to access their future earnings; however, when people are irresponsible and greedy, it can destroy the economy.

After you are approved for a bank loan (e.g., mortgage), the bank requires you to sign a promissory note. After signing it, the bank deposits your promissory note into its account as money. To be more specific, it accepts your promissory note in exchange for credit to your transaction account, thereby creating new money. In other words, YOU are the CREDITOR, not the debtor, and therefore the bank is only loaning you your future earnings. The bank is the debtor and therefore cannot loan you any money. However, because of the way the banking system is set up today, the bank's role is to trick you to think that the bank is the creditor. After using your promissory note to create money, the bank turns around and lends you that same money as a bank loan. Did the bank tell you in advance that it was going to lend you your own money? Did you agree to allow the bank to lend you your own money? If your honest answer is "no", then it was not a mutual agreement.

By lending you your own money, the bank makes 100 percent profit every time you pay your monthly payment. If you add the interest (rent) into the equation, the bank makes more than 100 percent profit. This is how banks steal your money and energy without your knowledge. If you and I were to do this, they would throw us in jail for a very long time. Once you innerstand how banks create money out of thin air, you will know that most banks have been committing fraud for decades. For evidence that banks use promissory notes to create credit, read page 6-7 of *Modern Money Mechanics* by the Federal Reserve Bank of Chicago. On page 6-7, you should find a sentence that says, "What they do when they make loans is to accept promissory notes in exchange for credits to the borrowers' transaction accounts". When the sentence thereof refers to "they", it refers to "banks"!

If you have a mortgage or are planning to take out a mortgage, you need to know that you are NOT legally the owner of your house. This is because the mortgage contract appoints you as the **tenant** and not the owner of the house. As a result, you do not hold legal title to the land and the house. A **tenant** is defined as, "An individual who occupies or possesses land or premises by way of a grant of an estate of some type, such as in fee, for life, for years, or at will. A person who has the right to temporary use and possession of particular real property, which has been conveyed to that person by a landlord."[104] Another definition of the word **tenant** is "a person who occupies real property owned by another based upon an agreement between the person and the landlord/owner, almost always for rental payments."[105] As a tenant, you do not legally own your house and land. Furthermore, you are required to pay **rent** which is the **interest** of the mortgage (debt/dead pledge). In simple terms, the interest payment of the mortgage is the monthly rent! Banks do not tell you this because they want you to think that you are the owner of your house. Once you innerstand how the mortgage system really works, you will know that there is not that much difference between renting a house and buying a house via a mortgage. In a way, buying a house via a mortgage is worse than renting a house.

After you buy a house, you are required to pay property tax which is the rent owed by your landlord to another landlord. As a "homeowner", your landlord is the bank and the bank's landlord is the State. The State owns the land by claiming that the land is controlled and owned by them through their land registry. The State can make this claim because people do not rebut it, and therefore it becomes a fact. This is one of the ways that the State controls the land in most countries, especially in the United States. According to certain laws and documents of the United States, citizens (individuals) do not have the "right" to own property. If you want strong evidence that you (United States citizen) do not **legally** own anything, read Senate Document 43, 73rd Congress 1st Session. According to this document, citizens (individuals) do not own any property. Here is an excerpt of a paragraph from Senate Document 43 that basically said that individuals have no right to own property:

> The ultimate ownership of all property is in the State; individual so-called "ownership" is only by virtue of Government, i.e., law, amounting to mere user; and use must be in accordance with law and subordinate to the necessities of the State.

The secret that the State does not want you to know about the previous statement is that the State and its government cannot own any **real** property, just like United States citizens. They cannot own any real property because they are not living; instead, they are **corporations** which are **dead bodies**. A corporation is legally defined as "an artificial person", which is a **dead** and **fictional** entity that does not exist in the real world. Can a fictional entity own real property? NO! Because of this, the statement that the "ultimate ownership of all property is in the State" is fictitious with respect to the **real** world. In the imaginary world of legal fictions and corporations, the State can own property. However, in reality, only living men and women can own real property. Keep in mind that a citizen is also a corporation (artificial person) and therefore cannot own real property.

By now you should know why taking out a mortgage is a sin. Taking out a mortgage is like asking for a death sentence. If you have a

119

mortgage and want to know how to free yourself from it, you need to first know how to defend and exercise your natural rights. You also need to learn how the legal system works. You do not need to know everything about the legal system. However, the more knowledge you have about the legal system, the easier it is for you to overcome your fear of the legal system and find effective ways to remove yourself from its jurisdiction. Two websites that have interesting information about the legal system are AnnaVonReitz.com and YouAreLaw.org. Another interesting source of information is Bill Turner. He has some very informative seminars and videos on YouTube that you can watch. Besides these sources, KurtisRichardKallenbach.xyz and my website EsotericKnowledge.me are two other interesting sources of information.

Most people are not aware of the information in this book because they have relied too much on TV for information. The acronym TV stands for television or "tell a vision" which can be written as "tell **lie** vision". Many TV shows are **telling** you **lies** through the power of **vision** to brainwash you. This is why **TV shows** are called **TV programs**. They are using TV **programs** to condition and **program** your mind, so they can control how you think. It is right in your face and hidden in plain sight! Some of the solutions: Stop watching so much television/tell-a-vision/tell-lie-vision; study how words and spells are used to reprogram your mind; and learn to defend and exercise your natural rights.

Chapter 6
Word Magic and the Forbidden
Secrets of Religion

Religion is one of the most powerful systems for empowering and disempowering us. Because it is powerful, in the wrong hands, it can be used to control us and make us believe that religion is the only source for divine truth. To make matters worse, society has conditioned us to blindly follow religion like a flock of sheep, so we do not question the teachings of religion. By not questioning the teachings of religion, we made ourselves vulnerable to being controlled by the Dark Forces. This negative side of religion has manifested misery and sorrow to mankind. However, it has taught mankind many important lessons in life, giving mankind the knowledge and courage to travel into a new age.

For millennia, most religious teachings have taught people to rely on certain **external** saviors to save them. This has created a world full of people with slave mentality, making it easier for the Dark Forces to control and enslave mankind. The external savior program is one of the most successful mind control programs ever created by the Dark Forces. This is why the external savior program is found in almost all religious stories, myths, and movies. Today, nearly every movie that comes out of Hollywood has a savior or a group of saviors. This also applies to most Eastern and non-Hollywood movies.

Many religious teachings like to use the power of fear to scare people to obey their versions of God. They do this by conditioning and programming people to believe that if they do not submit themselves to their religious teachings, they will be banished from the kingdom of God and suffer for eternity. This fear tactic is designed to keep people living in a constant state of fear and compliance, allowing the people working in high positions of the religious system to rule the world. To be fair, religion does have a lot of empowering and enlightening knowledge. However, most of it is occulted (hidden) behind stories that are full of myths, parables, allegories, and riddles; therefore, to access the empowering and enlightening knowledge in religion, you need to decipher its myths, parables, allegories, and riddles. By the end of this chapter, you will know why it is often not wise to read and interpret the stories of religion in a literal way.

A very important information you need to know about the religious system is that it is heavily involved in the art of magic. For example, the Christian religion is heavily based on the teachings of the holy and magic book called the Bible. This holy book is not only a sacred book full of religious stories; it is also a holy book full of magic spells. This is why the first four books of the New Testament are called Gospels. In Chapter 4, we found out that the word **gospel** originated from the Old English word **godspel**, literally meaning "good spell".[1] Therefore, the word "Gospels" can be translated as "God spells" or "spells of God". The fact that the Bible has allegories, parables, fables, and sacred words is evidence that it is a magic book full of word magic. Every religion on Earth has word magic embedded into its teachings, especially the major religions of the world.

In this chapter, I will concentrate mostly on Christianity for the reason that I am more knowledgeable in Christianity than other religions. When I was a child, I went to a Baptist church for a few years. During those years, I read many verses of the King James Bible and was introduced to many Christian beliefs, so I am aware of the teachings of Christianity. Before I expose some dirty secrets of the church, I want to make it clear to you that my intention is not to offend anyone. The main reason that I am doing this is to show you the facts; it is up to you to accept them as truths. Another reason is to increase your awareness, so you are less vulnerable to being manipulated by certain religious leaders. My intention is not to spread fear but to inform you of the facts, so you can become more awake and aware. Becoming more awake and aware is one of the first steps to achieving spiritual freedom.

For you to innerstand how the church system works, you need to study its history. According to some religious scholars, the early churches were pagan churches; therefore, their teachings were heavily focused on the worshiping of pagan gods. In general, Paganism is a religion that worships many gods and goddesses and tends to be nature oriented. During the time of the Roman Empire, Christianity was a minority religion, but it soon became popular and spread throughout Rome. This religious movement became so strong that it threatened the Roman religion, which was heavily based on Polytheism and Paganism. As Christianity became more and more popular, it caused a lot of conflicts between the Christian and Roman religions, so Emperor Constantine ordered that the basic principles of the Roman religion and the Christian religion be merged into one religion. This is one of the reasons that many pagan beliefs can be found in Christianity and holidays celebrated by Christians. For example, Christmas and Easter have a strong connection to Paganism. Most Christians do not know this because the pagan beliefs and stories are encoded into Christianity to prevent Christians from knowing that their religion is full of pagan ideology. Do you need evidence of this? Read further and I will show you more evidence than you may need.

Why Christmas Is a Pagan Holiday For Worshiping the Sun

Christmas is a time when most people, especially people living in Western countries, like to get together to celebrate a day full of evergreen trees, colorful lights, and delicious food. Today, Christmas is often viewed as a holiday for giving and receiving gifts. Sadly, most people have no clue as to what Christmas is really about because they have not investigated the origins of Christmas and the symbols associated with it. When you investigate the origins of Christmas and learn to decipher the symbols of Christmas, you will realize that Christmas is not what most people think it is. Furthermore, you will notice that Christmas is full of pagan ideology.

Besides giving and receiving gifts, many people, especially Christians, like to celebrate Christmas to commemorate the birth of Jesus Christ. What most Christians do not know is that Christmas, on a deeper level, is a holiday for worshiping a **solar** deity. Hence the Bible verse John 8:12 (ESV), "Again Jesus spoke to them, saying, 'I am the light of the world. Whoever follows me will not walk in darkness, but will have the light of life.' "[2] The person named Jesus in the Bible is not really a man with a body made of flesh and blood; instead, Jesus is the name of a biblical character who represents the light principle. When an author writes a book about a man, his pen or pencil transcribes the man thereof into a character, allowing the character to exist inside a book. Therefore, the character is not the man. In other words, they are not one and the same.

When the Bible refers to Jesus, a significant percentage of the time it refers to the Sun that rises in the East and sets in the West. Most of time, it refers to the Light-Principle. Jesus is also known as the **Son** of God. Phonetically, the word **son** sounds almost, if not exactly, like the word **sun**. Without the Sun, we cannot survive because we need the energy (sunlight) of the Sun to keep us warm and grow food. Therefore, Jesus or the Sun/Son of God is our savior and the light of the world. Sometimes you have to pay attention to the phonics of words to find their occult meanings. When you innerstand that Jesus represents the Sun, the light of the world, then many of the stories of the Bible will make more sense. When you go through the process of accepting the idea that Jesus is a metaphor for the Sun and represents the Light-Principle, you may feel angry at the church and the Bible. However, the more you decode the Bible, the more you will realize that it has many empowering knowledge. To access the empowering knowledge of the Bible, you need to learn how to decipher its content. Here are some verses of the Bible (ESV) that I will decode to help you see the hidden knowledge within them:

As long as I am in the world, I am the light of the world." (John 9:5)[3]

Again Jesus spoke to them, saying, "I am the light of the world. Whoever follows me will not walk in darkness, but will have the light of life." (John 8:12)[4]

And then they will see the Son of Man coming in clouds with great power and glory. (Mark 13:26)[5]

So Jesus came out, wearing the crown of thorns and the purple robe. ... (John 19:5)[6]

When the Bible says that **Jesus** is "the light of the world", it refers to the **Sun** that lights up the world when it rises in the morning. This is why the Bible talks about Jesus "coming in clouds" and "wearing the crown of thorns and the purple robe". The **thorns** symbolize the **rays** of the **Sun** and the **purple robe** represents **royalty**. Hence, the clause "the light of the world" and the title "King of kings". Do you need more evidence that Jesus is a metaphor for the Sun? To find more evidence, look at the images of Jesus in books or on the Internet and you will see that many of them have a halo or a sun symbol behind Jesus's head. When you see an image of Jesus with a halo or a sun symbol behind his head, it symbolically shows that Jesus is a metaphor for the Sun. The word "Sun" is capitalized because it is the name of a star, just like Earth is the name of the planet we live on. Keep in mind that Jesus also represents the light within us. To find another evidence that Jesus is a metaphor for the Sun, you need to investigate the biblical phrase "crown of thorns" and study the occult meaning of the word crown. The Latin word for **crown** is *corona*.[7] In English, the word **corona** is defined as "a white or colored circle or set of concentric circles of light seen around a luminous body, especially around the sun or moon."[8]

Based on the definitions and information in the previous few paragraphs, the phrase "crown of thorns" means "a set of concentric circles of light rays". Once you innerstand that Jesus represents the Sun, the story of Jesus being born on December 25 in Bethlehem and the story of the Three Kings following the brightest star in the sky to find Jesus will make more sense. To keep it simple, the **Three Kings** represent the **three stars** of Orion's Belt, and the **brightest star** in the sky represents the star called **Sirius**. "Orion's Belt or the Belt of Orion, also known as the Three Kings or Three Sisters, is an asterism in the constellation Orion. It consists of the three bright stars Alnitak, Alnilam and Mintaka."[9]

Certain branches of Christianity like to teach their followers that Jesus was born on the 25th of December. This religious story of Jesus being born on the 25th of December is more evidence that Jesus represents the Light-Principle or the Sun, the light of the world and the savior of mankind. As the winter solstice approaches from the Northern hemisphere, the days become shorter and shorter until it reaches the shortest day of the year, which occurs on December 21. On the day after December 21, which is December 22, the Sun stops moving south for three days. Hence, the belief that Jesus died for three days. On December 25, the Sun moves about one degree north; therefore, it was said that the Sun/Son of God died for three days and was resurrected on December 25. This one degree movement of the Sun is very subtle but can be measured using very sensitive equipment. This movement of the Sun is one of the deeper meanings of Christmas, a holiday for celebrating the resurrection of the Sun or the Light-Principle. Christmas is also a holiday for celebrating the

Dark-Principle. I will elaborate on this in more detail later in this chapter.

An important information that is beneficial for you to know about December 25 is that on this date the Three Kings (three stars of Orion's Belt) line up in a way that points toward Sirius, the brightest star in the sky. When you draw an imaginary line through the three stars of Orion's Belt and Sirius, it points to the area where the Sun rises over the horizon. This is why the Three Kings followed the brightest star (Sirius) in the sky to find Jesus. Sirius showed the Three Kings where the Sun would rise over the horizon on December 25, the "birthday" of the Sun/Son/Jesus.

> Sirius is always easy to find. It's the sky's brightest star! Plus, anyone familiar with the constellation Orion can simply draw a line through Orion's Belt to find this star. Sirius is roughly eight times as far from the Belt as the Belt is wide.[10]

By now you should know that the biblical character Jesus represents the Light-Principle and is a personification of the **Sun**. This fact is even more obvious when you innerstand why Christians go to church on Sunday. When you separate the word "Sunday" into two words, it transforms into the term "Sun day" which means "**day** of the **Sun**". This is why Christians go to church on Sunday (day of the Sun), so they can worship the Sun/Son/Jesus, the light of the world. It is right in your face and hidden in plain sight. If you still need more evidence that the biblical character Jesus is a personification of the Sun, study the sun-gods of ancient mythology and you will notice that Jesus has similar characteristics to those ancient sun-gods. Here are some popular characteristics of sun-gods:

> In some areas, the calendar originally began in the constellation of Virgo, and the Sun would therefore be "born of a Virgin."

> The Sun is the "Light of the World."

> The Sun "cometh on clouds, and every eye shall see him."

> The Sun rising in the morning is the "Savior of mankind."

126

The Sun wears a corona, "crown of thorns" or halo.

The Sun "walks on water." [When watching the Sun rise in the morning or set at night, the moment when the Sun touches the water of the sea is known as the Sun/Son/Jesus "walking" on water. This is one of the occult meanings of the biblical story of Jesus walking on the water.]

The Sun's "followers," "helpers" or "disciples" are the 12 months and the 12 signs of the zodiac or constellations, through which the Sun must pass.

The Sun at 12:00 noon is in the house or temple of the "Most High"; thus, "he" begins "his Father's work" at "age" 12.

The Sun enters into each sign of the zodiac at 30°; hence, the "Sun of God" begins his ministry at "age" 30.

The Sun is hung on a cross or "crucified," which represents its passing through the equinoxes, the vernal equinox being Easter, at which time it is then resurrected.[11]

Many characteristics of Jesus were copied from ancient religious stories and myths about solar deities. Because of this, Jesus is the modern version of ancient solar deities, going all the way back to ancient Egypt, Babylonia, and beyond. Some of those ancient solar deities are Horus, Ra, Osiris, Attis, Helios, and Baal. Because Jesus is a solar deity, he has similar characteristics to Lucifer. The word **lucifer** comes from the Latin word *lucifer*, meaning "morning star".[12] It literally means "light-bringing".[13] According to a very informative book titled *Fire & Ice* (written by Stephen E. Flowers), Lucifer is the higher octave of Saturn and the Light Bearer for mankind.[14] Jesus is the Son/Sun (the light of the world) and bears light to mankind; therefore, in a way, Jesus and Lucifer are similar.

One of the main reasons that ancient civilizations worshiped the Sun is because it is an intelligent creator. Some researchers of occultism have said that the Sun plays an important role in the creation of the planets and the elements in our solar system, and also plays a crucial role in creating our holographic reality. In a way, the Sun is the physical manifestation of the "fire" of God. This fire is the creative spiritual force that manifests light of which everything in the visible and material universe is made. Once you know that the Sun is a loving and intelligent creator, then the idea of using a character named Jesus to represent the Sun is a creative and brilliant concept. Furthermore, the idea of worshiping the Sun makes sense. However, be aware that when you worship a being or an object outside of you, you give your power away to that being or object. Instead of worshiping the Sun, acknowledge it as an intelligent creator and thank it for sending its light to heal the world. In addition, respect the Sun because without it life cannot exist on Earth.

At this point it should be obvious that Jesus is a name that is used as a symbol to represent certain essential things in nature and important principles of life. This does not mean that there was not a man from the past who taught people about the Christ principles. In fact, there were many great spiritual teachers from the past who taught people about their spiritual powers and the Christ inside each of them.

Let us investigate the name Jesus Christ more closely to find more of its occult meanings. To do this, we need to separate the name "Jesus" into two words "je sus". In French, **je** means "I".[15] Phonetically, the letter **I** sounds exactly like the word **eye**. This is referring to the all-seeing eye/optic thalamus/eye of Jesus/eye of Horus/Sun/Star. As for **sus**, it is a Latin word for "a fish".[16] In astrology, the **fish** symbolizes the **Age of Pisces**. Based on these occult definitions, Jesus is the Sun/Star of the Age of Pisces. This is why the name Jesus is sometimes enclosed inside a fish symbol. Another French term that has a strong connection to Jesus is *je suis* which means "I am".[17] Some researchers of occult knowledge have said that "I Am" means "Son of Man". The title "Son of Man" is used over a dozen times in the Bible and is often used to represent Jesus. YourDictionary.com defines the term **i am** using these exact words: "God, seen as self-sufficient and self-existent."[18]

As for the word **Christ**, it is derived from the Greek word χριστος (*christos*), meaning "anointed or sovereign".[19] This can be translated as "messiah". The word **messiah** comes from the Hebrew word *mashiah*, meaning "the anointed".[20] Phonetically, the Greek word χριστος (*christos*) sounds like the word **crystal**. This has a connection to the crystal brain and the pineal gland. It is important to remember that the Greek word χριστος is used to describe "someone who is a sovereign: someone who answers only to the Creator and not to any human."[21] Another important information to remember about the Greek word thereof is that it has a strong connection to the holy oil. This holy oil, also known as the holy chrism, is esoterically the oil secreted by the brain. To be more specific, it comes from the claustrum, flows down into the olivary fasciculus, and eventually goes into the spinal cord where it is stored. When the holy oil is refined by the body, it transforms into the "Christed Seed" or "Christed Jesus". Keep in mind that **Jesus** is esoterically known as the Word or **Seed**.

If the Christed Seed is able to travel back to the brain without being totally consumed by sexual activities and toxins, it can be used by the brain to heal the whole body. This is only possible when you learn how to use certain exercise and meditation techniques to raise the kundalini energy up to your brain, allowing it to interact with the Christed Seed. Once the Christed Seed **cross**es the nerves at the **skull**-shaped hill called Golgotha, which etymologically means "skull" and esoterically refers to the brain, it is crucified in that area of the brain (skull). Hence the saying, "Jesus Christ died on the **cross**". In other words, Golgotha (skull-shaped hill) is a metaphor for the area within the skull where the Christed Seed (Jesus Christ) is crucified.

To crucify, means to add to or increase a thousand fold. When electric wires are crossed, they set on fire all inflammable substances near them. When the Christed seed crossed the nerve at Galgotha, the vail of the temple was rent and there was an earthquake, and the dead came forth, *i. e.*, the generative cells of the body were quickened or regenerated.[22]

The process of crucifying the Christed Seed in the brain causes it to ignite, producing high vibrational energy that energizes the pineal gland which in turn significantly increases its vibration. This causes the electrons of the pineal gland to produce more electrical energy and transmit it along the optic nerve to the optic thalamus (eye of the chamber), illuminating the optic thalamus and giving it the power to become all-seeing. This process also fills the whole body with light. In other words, the **optic** within the thalamus is the **single eye** of which the Bible speaks. Etymologically, the word **optic** means "of sight or seeing". Hence, the Bible verse Matthew 6:22 (KJV): "The light of the body is the eye: if therefore thine eye be single, thy whole body shall be full of light."

It is important to know that the word Christ has more than one meaning. From the perspective of the physical body, the word Christ is used to represent the holy oil produced in the brain. In certain spiritual teachings, the Christ is the mind of pure intelligence and the embodiment of enlightenment and reason. It is through these principles of the Christ that mankind will gain the knowledge to achieve spiritual freedom and enlightenment.

Why Christmas Is a Holiday Full of Occult and Satanic Symbolism

People celebrate Christmas for many reasons but what most of them do not know about Christmas is that it is a holiday full of satanic and occult ideologies. Please be aware that just because Christmas contains occult ideology does not mean that Christmas is evil. The word **occult** etymologically means "hidden, concealed, secret".[23] Before we explore the satanic and occult ideologies of Christmas, I need to tell you some of the origins of the word Christmas. Knowing where the word Christmas is derived from will make it easier for you to see its occult (hidden) meaning. One of the origins of the word **Christmas** is the late Old English term **Cristes mæsse**. Christmas has a strong connection to a medieval custom of the Roman Church called **Mass**, a religious event that was celebrated at midnight on the eve of December 25.[24] Put the words "Christ" and "Mass" together and you get the word "ChristMass" or "Christmas". The word **Mass** is defined as "public celebration of the Eucharist in the Roman Catholic Church and some Protestant churches."[25] This word comes from the Middle English words **messe** and **masse**, and from the Old English word **mæsse**, meaning "eucharistic service"; it also comes from the Vulgar Latin **messa** ("eucharistic service") and Late Latin **missa** ("dismissal").[26] As for the word **Christ**, it is derived from the Greek word **khristos** (*christos*), meaning "the anointed".[27] Based on these definitions, the word **Christmas** means "eucharistic service of the anointed". What most Christians do not know about a mass is that it is also a magic ritual for acknowledging and worshiping the dead.

Christmas is sometimes referred to as Xmas. The letter X is the Greek symbol for the 22nd letter of the Greek alphabet which is "chi", the initial letter in the word **Χριστός**, meaning "Christ".[28] An important information that is beneficial for you to know about Christmas/Xmas is that it has a lot of sexual symbolism. For example, the letter X is sometimes used to represent sexual activity, which is why the letter X sounds like sex. This is also why adult movies are rated X. In Latin, the adjective word *mas* means "manly, virile, brave, noble" or "masculine, of the **male sex**" (bold emphasis added).[29] In the Greek alphabet, the letter X (chi) is sometimes used as a Christogram. Hence, the word Xmas.

Based on the definitions and information so far in this subchapter, Christmas/Xmas is not only a holiday for celebrating the birth of the Son/Sun/Jesus, but also for celebrating male sexuality and dominance. This is obvious when you know that light (Jesus/Sun) represents order, power, and the conscious mind, which are attributes of the Divine Masculine Energy. More evidence of the relationship between sex and Christmas can be found in the Roman holiday called Saturnalia. According to certain historians, Saturnalia was a week-long ancient Roman festival in honor of the ancient god Saturn. During the festival, which was celebrated around the time of the winter solstice, Roman courts were closed and Roman Citizens were allowed to do almost anything because it was a period of lawlessness.

> The ancient Greek writer poet and historian Lucian (in his dialogue entitled Saturnalia) describes the festival's observance in his time. In addition to human sacrifice, he mentions these customs: widespread intoxication; going from house to house while singing naked; rape and other sexual license; and consuming human-shaped biscuits (still produced in some English and most German bakeries during the Christmas season).[30]

In the English alphabet, the letter **X** is the **24th** letter. This may be related to December **24** which is Christmas Eve or **X**-mas Eve. Another letter that may be related to Christmas is Y, the 25th letter of the English alphabet. What you need to know about the letters X and Y is that they can be used to represent the X and Y chromosomes in cells. According to geneticists, males and females have 23 pairs of chromosomes. The numbered pairs (1-22) are called autosomes and they are the same in males and females.[31] The pair that is different is the 23rd pair, also known as the sex chromosomes. In the cells of males, the 23rd pair chromosome has an X chromosome and a Y chromosome. As for females, the 23rd pair chromosome has two X chromosomes. The word **chromosome** comes from the Greek words χρῶμα *(chroma)* and σῶμα *(soma)*. In general, the word **chroma**

131

means "color"[32] and the word **soma** means "body".[33] The DNA and body of man are made of different colors or frequency bands, just like the different colors of the chakras. This is why a man or a woman is sometimes called a human. Phonetically, the word "human" sounds almost exactly like the phrase "hue man". The word **hue** is defined as "a gradation or variety of a color; tint".[34] When the words "hue" and "man" are joined together, they transform into the word "hueman" which is phonetically "human".

To connect the dots, the act of decorating evergreen trees with Christmas lights and putting gifts under them symbolizes the sacred changes that happen in the physical body during Christmas. Symbolically, the colorful Christmas lights represent the different colors of the DNA and the chakras. As for the evergreen tree and the gift, they represent the spine and the holy oil respectively. To connect the dots even further, we need to study the word Christmas more closely. In the beginning of this subchapter, there is a sentence that said, "the word Christmas means 'eucharistic service of the anointed' ". The word **eucharistic** is derived from the word **eucharist** which etymologically means "thanksgiving, gratitude".[35] Therefore, Christmas is a religious service for giving thanks to Christ, the anointed. According to Lexico.com, the word **eucharist** means, "The Christian service, ceremony, or sacrament commemorating the Last Supper, in which **bread** and **wine** are consecrated and consumed" (bold emphasis added).[36] Esoterically, the bread, also known as manna, is the seed of life. According to the Bible, manna was the bread that God provided to the children of Israel when they traveled in the desert during the forty-year period following the Exodus. The word **manna** is etymologically defined by EtymOnline.com using these exact words:

> Old English borrowing from Late Latin *manna*, from Greek *manna*, from Hebrew *man*, probably literally "substance exuded by the tamarisk tree," but used in Greek and Latin specifically with reference to the substance miraculously supplied to the Children of Israel during their wandering in the Wilderness (Exodus xvi.15). Meaning "spiritual nourishment" is attested from late 14c. Generalized sense of "something provided unexpectedly" is from 1590s.[37]

The bread/manna is the seed of life because it represents Jesus.

Hence, the Bible verse John 6:51 (KJV): "I am the living bread which came down from heaven: if any man eat of this bread, he shall live for ever: and the bread that I will give is my flesh, which I will give for the life of the world." Jesus is the seed of life because he is the word of God. Hence, the Bible verse Luke 8:11 (KJV): "Now the parable is this: The seed is the word of God." An important ingredient for the bread/manna is the holy oil, also known as the holy chrism. The Greeks sometimes called it the Christ. Certain esoteric teachings used the term "**Santa** Claus" to define this holy oil. In Spanish, the word *santa* means "saint" in English.[38] The word **saint** is derived from the Latin word *sanctus*, meaning "holy, consecrated".[39] Therefore "Santa Claus" or "Saint Claus" means "holy claus". The word **claus** can be found in the word **claus**trum, the area of the brain where the holy oil is secreted, according to certain esoteric and occult teachings. When the holy oil travels down the spinal cord and is refined and is able to travel back to the brain without being destroyed, it becomes highly vitalized, allowing it to be crucified in the brain, giving the brain the power to regenerate the body. It is said that this holy oil, when the body reaches a certain state of vibration, has the power to heal the body of all diseases. In other words, the bread/manna (Jesus) and the holy oil (Christ), which is the precious and sacred "gift" secreted by the claustrum, have the potential to prevent death and therefore save mankind from sin (death). This is one of the reasons that Jesus Christ is the savior of mankind.

One of the most popular symbols of Christmas is the evergreen tree. Symbolically, the **evergreen tree** represents the **spine**, also known as the "tree of life" in certain esoteric teachings. The tree of life can represent a few different things, but when it comes to Christmas it symbolizes the spine. The spine connects to the **skull**, the house with a **dome** that houses the pineal/"**pine**-al" gland. This is your kingdom or "kingdome" which is located between the **temples** of your head. Maybe this is why kings and queens wear a crown on top of their heads to symbolize their kingdoms between their temples. The information in this paragraph is telling you that the kingdom of God is located within the head. Because of this, you will never find it in a religious temple or church outside of you. This is why the Bible verses Luke 17:20-21 (KJV) say:

And when he was demanded of the Pharisees, when the kingdom of God should come, he answered them and said, The kingdom of God cometh not with observation:

Neither shall they say, Lo here! or, lo there! for, behold, the kingdom of God is within you.

The Bible verses Luke 17:20-21 are talking about the "house" inside your skull and between your temples, which is your kingdom or temple of God. The word **house** is derived from the Gothic word *gudhus*, meaning "temple" or "god-house".[40] The Bible and many religious stories throughout the world are telling you that the kingdom of God is located between your temples, inside your pineal gland, and within your body, not out in the external world. Sadly, most people read the Bible and other religious books in a literal manner, thereby preventing themselves from seeing the deeper knowledge hidden in these religious books.

The pineal gland is shaped like a **pine** cone. Hence, the name pineal/**pine**-al gland. An important information that is beneficial for you to know about the word **pine** is that it has a connection to the word **spine**. When you move the letter "s" in the word "spine" a space away from the rest of the letters, the word "spine" becomes "s **pine**". The letter "s" looks like the spine. Symbolically, the letter "s" is the spine that connects to the skull that houses the pineal gland. Hence, the word spine/s-pine and its connection to the word pineal/pine-al and the term pine cone. Have you ever wondered why **pine** trees are used as Christmas decorations in homes? The hidden reason that they are used to decorate homes during Christmas is because they symbolize the **spine**, which is the bone structure that connects to the skull. The structure inside the skull is the holy temple that houses the pineal/pine-al gland. This is your kingdom or temple of God. Symbolically, the **pine cones** of pine trees represent the **pineal gland**. According to some occult teachings, the spine is the structure of the physical body that stores golden fluid, also known as ichor. In Greek mythology, ichor was a gold-colored fluid used to increase longevity by alien gods, allowing them to live for thousands of years. This is one of the reasons that the spine is sometimes referred to as the tree of life.

Some researchers of ancient knowledge believe that alien gods drink ichor to prevent death; furthermore, they believe that ichor plays an important role in ascension. Some of them even believe that alien gods are false gods existing in the minds of people. If this is true, then these alien gods are thought-forms that exist in people's minds; therefore, they can consume their ichor or spiritual energy during their journey of ascension. Maybe this is why ascension is sometimes referred to as "the harvest". One of the definitions of the word **harvest** is "to gather (a crop or the like); **reap**" (bold emphasis added).⁴¹ The word **harvest** etymologically means "to gather, pluck".⁴² This definition comes from the Latin word *carpere*. The best time to harvest something is when it is **ripe**, and therefore ascension would be the best time to harvest people. The word **ripe** comes from the Old English word *ripe*, meaning "ready for **reap**ing, fit for eating, mature" (bold emphasis added).⁴³ Remember, one of the definitions of the word harvest is "reap". Please be aware that I am not saying that ascension is all about the harvesting of people. What I am saying is that ascension is the time when the Dark Forces like to trick people, allowing their corporations and agents to harvest people's energy, turning them into biological batteries to power the artificial matrix. They like to harvest people during ascension because it is the time when their bodies and souls are ripe.

One of the origins of the word **ascension** is the Latin word *ascensionem* which means "a rising".⁴⁴ Another of its origin is the noun of action from the past participle stem of *ascendere*, meaning "to mount, ascend, go up". Based on these definitions, the word ascension means "to go up or rise". An important information about ascension is that it involves a spiritual process, a scientific process, and the Laws of Nature to assist spiritual beings to ascend to higher states of consciousness. This process allows all spiritual beings to eventually ascend out of time and space to unite with their higher identities of pure consciousness. The process of ascension involves increasing the particle pulsation rhythm of the body, allowing the body to absorb high frequency energy into its morphogenetic field, thereby increasing its frequency. A term that is sometimes used to define the process of increasing the body's frequency is "frequency accretion". This process causes people's bodies to become lighter and less dense. It also causes their consciousness to expand, allowing them to ascend to higher levels of consciousness.

Every religion of mankind has its own version of ascension. For example, some religions teach their followers that only the chosen people can ascend or only God can make someone ascend. Other religions (e.g., the New Age) have said that extraterrestrials (ETs) will come from outer space to help us to ascend. In Christianity, it is taught that Jesus will one day come from heaven to save his people and bring them back to the kingdom of God. With so many different versions of ascension, how do you know which one is correct? To know if the ascension technique you are using may help you achieve spiritual freedom and ascend to heaven, ask yourself this question: does this version of ascension teach me knowledge of empowerment and truth, and how to be responsible for my spiritual growth? If your answer is no, you should stay far away from it. Any teaching that teaches you to rely on an **external** savior to save you will not empower you to achieve spiritual freedom. This type of teaching is often used by the Dark Forces to condition you to think and act like a slave. The idea that an external messiah or an ET race will soon come to save certain groups of people is a psychological operation that is used by the Dark Forces to keep people living in a state of mental slavery.

To find more evidence that the Dark Forces may be planning to harvest people during ascension, we need to investigate and study some of the hidden messages in the movie *Jupiter Ascending*. Before we do this, it is important to be aware that the Dark Forces and their flesh and blood minions like to use many movies and TV shows to disclose what they are doing or planning to do to mankind. *The Matrix* is one of the best examples of a movie that reveals to people the agendas of the Dark Forces in plain sight. One of the main reasons that the Dark Forces and the Dark Magicians disclose their agendas in movies and TV shows is because they do not want to violate people's free will. Furthermore, most people do not take the messages in movies and TV shows seriously. This allows the Dark Forces to show their agendas in plain sight without worrying about people becoming aware of their evil deeds. Be aware that they also like to use other media to reveal their agendas, such as video game, music video, newspaper, and magazine. By telling people what they are doing to mankind through movies, TV shows, music videos, video games, etc., the Dark Forces and their flesh and blood minions are giving people many chances to say no. When people ignore the Dark Forces' messages and choose not to say anything, it means that they do not care enough to exercise their power of consent; therefore, the Dark Forces can use that as an excuse to proceed with their diabolical plans. Remember, silence is a form of consent.

For you to not blindly give the Dark Forces your implied consent, you need to be aware of what they are doing. Your awareness is one of your most important spiritual powers for stopping the Dark Forces. When you become aware of what they are doing, you can say no. If enough of us say no, the Dark Forces will have to back off. If they refuse to back off and take actions to harm us, they will have to face the cosmic forces and the justice system of God. All thoughts, intentions, and actions are known by God and there is no escaping His Laws.

Let us focus our attention back to the movie *Jupiter Ascending*. Shortly after the halfway point of this movie, there is a scene where Titus shows Jupiter a room full of thousands of vials that are filled with youth serums. By drinking the serums, it allows Titus and his people to live for thousands of years. The shocking thing about the serums is that they are made from harvesting dead people. Based on my research on ancient knowledge, the secret ingredient that gives the serums the healing effect of longevity is ichor, the golden fluid that is believed to be stored in the spine. The following content is an excerpt of the movie script *Jupiter Ascending*. This part of the script talks about the youth serums that allow Titus and his people to live for thousands of years.

[Titus:] Come with me.

[Jupiter:] What is that?

[Titus:] It has many names. Regenx, recell, nectar. There are various levels of usefulness and quality, but this is the most pure and most valuable solution made by the house of Abrasax.

[Jupiter:] Kalique came out of a bath.

[Titus:] Naturally, my sister didn't explain what it is or where it comes from. It comes from people. Each unit is refined from approximately a hundred human beings.

[Jupiter:] What?

[Titus:] Your planet is a farm, Jupiter. There are thousands of planets like yours set up by families like mine to supply an ever increasing demand for more time.

[Jupiter:] Are you saying you killed a hundred people to make this?

[Titus:] Not me, but...yes, someone did. Not unlike

butchering a herd of cattle.

[Jupiter:] Oh, my God.[45]

When Titus says to Jupiter that planet Earth is a **farm** for supplying an ever increasing demand for more time, he is telling her that people are being raised as **livestock**, so when they are ripe or ready for reaping they are killed to make youth serums. Do you remember what I said in Chapter 5 that living people are the "livestock" or "living stock" of the stock market? This does not literally mean that the Dark Forces are killing people to make youth serums; however, it is not hard to see that the Dark Forces are using the power of words to trick people to give some of their life force energy to them, turning people into biological batteries. When you take a step back and look at the big picture, Earth is being used as a farm for raising people to be used as biological batteries. This farm is the artificial matrix! This matrix is used to imprison people's minds and drain their life force energy. Maybe this is why the Dark Forces created many programs to brainwash people to raise and sacrifice animals for food. When people raise and sacrifice animals for food, it gives the Dark Forces the excuse to sacrifice people for food too. Like they say, "karma is a bitch!" Knowing about these programs should make you seriously think about becoming a vegan or a vegetarian.

By now you should know why the Dark Forces created the external savior program. If you still do not know why, I will explain it in more detail because it is very important that you innerstand what the external savior program is secretly about. The teaching that ETs will come save the world or a messiah will descend from the clouds to rapture the chosen people to heaven is a **psychological operation** and **magic spell** for tricking people to consent to live in the artificial matrix, allowing the Dark Forces to harvest their bodies for energy without directly violating their free will. The good news is that the Dark Forces can only harvest you and feed on your life force energy with your CONSENT so stop giving them your consent as much as possible. To do this effectively, you need to learn how to defend and exercise your natural rights. An informative website that can teach you how to defend and exercise your natural rights is YouAreLaw.org. My website EsotericKnowledge.me is also another informative website that can teach you how to defend and exercise your God-given rights.

Let us focus our attention back to Christmas. Another popular symbol of Christmas is the star. Symbolically, the **star** on top of the

138

Christmas tree/pine tree/spine is the **optic thalamus** which is the **all-seeing eye** or **mind's eye**. When it is opened, it acts like a conduit, allowing you to connect to your Christ/God-consciousness. When activated and used wisely, the optic thalamus, also known as the Eye of Horus, can lead you to true enlightenment. Here is an excerpt from Freemasons-Freemasonry.com that explains what the star represents in more detail:

> Within the Craft degrees, the figure of the Pentagram may also be seen in the image of the 5 rayed Blazing Star. According to Albert Pike, the pentagram is synonymous with the Blazing Star of Masonic Lodges:

> *The Blazing Star in our Lodges, we have already said, represents Sirius, Anubis, or Mercury, Guardian and Guide of Souls. Our Ancient English brethren also considered it an emblem of the Sun. In the old Lectures they said: 'The Blazing Star or Glory in the centre refers us to that Grand Luminary the Sun, which enlightens the Earth, and by its genial influence dispenses blessings to mankind. It is also said in those lectures to be an emblem of Prudence. The word Prudentia means, in its original and fullest signification, Foresight: and accordingly the Blazing Star has been regarded as an emblem of Omniscience, or the All-Seeing Eye, which to the Ancients was the Sun.*[vi]

> He further associates this star with the *"Divine Energy, manifested as Light, creating the Universe."*[vii]

> The Masonic scholar Rex Hutchins asserts that the Pentagram

> *is the symbol of the Divine in man... The five-pointed star with a single point upward represents the Divine. It also symbolizes man for its five points allude to the five senses, the five members (head, arms and legs) and his five fingers on each hand, which signify the tokens that distinguish Masons.*

Furthermore he writes that this figure

is the symbol of the Microcosm, the universe where humans dwell. Since the pentagon which encloses the pentagram may be formed by connecting the five points of the human body, for many centuries the symbol was also used to represent humanity in general.

Within this symbol then is a representation of humanity, and our Divine role in the Universe as co-creators of eternity.[46]

By now you should know that there is more to Christmas than meets the eye. To find other hidden meanings of Christmas, we need to turn our attention to the name **Santa Claus** and dissect it to find its occult meanings. After doing this, you will know why Christmas is not only a holiday for celebrating the Sun/Son/Jesus, but also for celebrating Satan, the personification of darkness. In other words, Christmas is a holiday for celebrating polarity, such as light and darkness, masculine and feminine, and "good" and "evil". Two origins of the character Santa Claus can be found in the mythology of ancient Egypt and Greece. In Egyptian mythology, the sun-god Osiris was born on the 25th of December. During the anniversary of his birth, he would ride through the heavens in his chariot.[47] The Greek sun-god Helios was also said to be born on the 25th of December. Helios would also ride through the heavens in his sun chariot pulled by horses during the anniversary of his birth. Today, we have a similar character named Santa Claus who flies across the sky in his reindeer-drawn chariot on Christmas Eve.

To find one of the hidden meanings of Santa Claus, you need to use the art of anagram to shuffle the letters of the word "Santa" around. When you do this, you will eventually transform the word **Santa** into the word **Satan**. Santa is an anagram for Satan! Have you ever wondered why Santa wears a red suit? The color red is sometimes used to represent the **Devil**, meaning "the supreme spirit of evil; **Satan**" (bold emphasis added),[48] which is why the Devil is often red in color. The name "Satan", which can be anagrammatically written as "Santa", is a symbol that represents the principle of darkness. On the other hand, the name "Santa" represents the principle of light. In other words, Santa can be "good" or "evil", depending on if you have been good or bad. An important fact that you need to know about the color red is that it has a connection to Saturn. The **dark characteristics** of Saturn are associated with the entity **Satan**, which is why Saturn is sometimes known as Satan. On the other hand, the **light characteristics** of Saturn are associated with the entity **Lucifer**. In ancient Egypt, the color red was sometimes viewed as bad or evil for the reason that it was occasionally associated with the Egyptian god Set. Today, this Egyptian god is known as Satan in many Western countries. This is why Satan is often depicted as red in color.

Is it hard for you to accept that a big belly old man in a red suit can represent Satan or the Devil? Santa is also known as Saint **Nick**. The word **nick** is etymologically defined as "the devil".[49] As for the word **saint**, it is derived from the Latin word *sanctus*, meaning "holy".[50] Phonetically, the word **holy** sounds somewhat similar to the word **holly**. One of the definitions of the word **holly** is "any of numerous trees or shrubs of the genus *Ilex,* as *I. opaca* (American holly), the state tree of Delaware, or *I. aquifolium* (English holly), having glossy, spiny-toothed leaves, small, whitish flowers, and red berries."[51] The wood of holly trees was used by the Druids to make magic wands. The Druids believed that holly trees had magical powers, which was why they used them to make magic wands. Today, certain magicians who practice real magic still create magic wands out of the wood of holly trees.

An organization that has a strong connection to magic, holly trees, Christmas, Santa, Satan, Lucifer, Jesus, and the word holy is the Holy See, the central governing body of the Roman Catholic Church. The Holy See is located in Vatican City (the Vatican), a city-state controlled by the Holy Roman Empire. This empire is alive and well today. Any phrase, name, or title that has the word **holy** in it is often connected to the Vatican and the **Holy** Roman Empire. The Vatican is a city-state that is governed by the **Holy See**, also known as the **See of Rome**. In Italian, the Holy See is called *Santa Sede* and in Latin it is known as *Sancta Sedes*, meaning "holy chair" or "holy seat".[52] It is interesting to know that the Latin word *sanctus* means "**holy**" and is the source of the Spanish words *santo* and *santa*.[53] Maybe this is why the pope (**holy** father) sometimes wears a red suit similar to the red suit of **Santa** Claus. Could the pope be the representative of Santa/Satan?

Another word that has a strong connection to the words **holy** and **holly** is **holiday**, which is "holy day" or "holly day", meaning "a sacred day of magic". Most, if not all, holidays are magic rituals that can be used for good or evil purposes. Because of this, the Dark Forces like to use holidays to cast magic spells on people. Christmas is one of the best examples of a holiday that is full of magic rituals. This is why the stems, leaves, and berries of **holly** trees are often used as Christmas decorations. When the word "holly" is translated into Norwegian, it transforms into the word "kristtorn".⁵⁴ When you separate the word "kristtorn" into two words, it becomes "krist torn". Phonetically, the word "krist" sounds similar to the word "Christ". Remember, the word **Christ** is derived from the Greek word χριστος *(khristos)*, meaning "the anointed".⁵⁵ The occult definitions in the previous few paragraphs show the connection between the words holy, holly, holiday, magic, saint, pope, Satan, Santa, Christ, and Christmas.

Because you now know some of the occult meanings of the word Santa, let us explore the hidden meanings of the word Claus. By exploring and investigating this word, it will make it easier for you to innerstand the deeper meanings of the name and character Santa Claus. The word **Claus**, from the name **Santa Claus**, is related to the word **claustrum** which is defined as "the one of the four basal ganglia in each cerebral hemisphere that consists of a thin lamina of gray matter separated from the lenticular nucleus by a layer of white matter".⁵⁶ Take out the letters "t", "r", "u", and "m" from the word "**claus**trum" and you are left with the word **claus**.

Keep in mind that the word **claus** sounds like the words **claw** and **clause**. The word **claw** means "a sharp, usually curved, nail on the foot of an animal, as on a cat, dog, or bird."⁵⁷ As for the word **clause**, it means "a distinct article or provision in a **contract**, treaty, will, or other formal or **legal written document**" or "a group of **words**, consisting of a subject and a predicate including a finite verb, that does not necessarily constitute a sentence" (bold emphasis added).⁵⁸ Satan, the evil side of Santa, is often portrayed with **claws** and likes to use **contracts** and **words** to trick people to agree to certain obligations. Here is an excerpt from the book *God-Man: The Word Made Flesh* that does a great job of explaining the connection between the words Claus and claustrum and the religious character Santa Claus/Saint Nick:

The claustrum is a thin sheet of isolated gray matter, found just medial to the Island of Reil. Santee says it "is a sheet of peculiar gray substance, and is made up of fusiform (spindle shaped) cell-bodies." It is from this claustrum that contains yellow substance within its outer grayish exterior, that the wonderful, priceless OIL is formed that flows down into the olivary fasciculus, "descending with the rubro-spinal tract through the reticular formation in the pons and medulla to the lateral column of the spinal cord. It terminates in the gray matter of the spinal cord, probably giving off collaterals to corresponding nuclei in the brain stem."—*Santee*. This is the OIL, the precious gift of which the Bible speaks, "Thou anointest my head with oil."

And not only is there oil manufactured within this special laboratory of the brain, but there is actually an *olive tree*, which bears actual olives—so named in any anatomy. The two olives are two infinitesimal eminences on either side of the medulla, with the Pyramid between. They are one-half inch in length. It is found well developed only in the higher mammals. They are RELAY (Santee) stations between the cerebrum and the cerebellum and between the spinal cord and the cerebellum.

This oil is the most sacred substance in the body—it is the quintessence of gold—the "Gold of Ophir"—most truly a rare gift. Globules of oil are found in the vital fluid, the semen, and when the prodigal son has wasted his substance, he finds that it takes a long time to replace the deficiency and make good the looted bank account.

... The olives, which contain the oil, are the reservoirs—the relay stations, of course, which furnish the oil for the lamp, the pineal gland, at the top of which is the flame or eye. When the Kundalini, the serpent fire that lies concealed within the sacral plexus is awakened, burns up the dross within the spinal cord, and reaches the conarium, it sets fire to this oil and thus lights the "perpetual lamp," which "Gives the light to the whole house."[59]

Based on the information in this subchapter, the word **Claus** represents the sacred and precious **oil** that is secreted in the **claus**trum of the brain. This part of the brain has a very strong connection to Santa Claus. Remember, the Spanish word *santa* means "saint" and the word **saint** is derived from the Latin word *sanctus*, meaning "**holy**, consecrated". Therefore, "Santa Claus" or "Saint Claus" esoterically means "holy oil". When this holy oil flows down the spinal cord, some of it spreads to certain areas of the body. The spinal cord is protected by the **spine** which is symbolically the **chimney** that is used by the holy oil (Santa Claus) to travel up and down the body. When this holy oil reaches the pineal gland and interacts with the kundalini energy, it lights and activates the **optic thalamus/single eye/lamp**, causing it to become all-seeing or illuminated. Symbolically, this is the all-seeing eye on the back of the one dollar bill. The symbol of the all-seeing eye is often used by the Illuminati to represent their secretive society. The all-seeing eye can be found in the Bible verses Matthew 6:22-23 (KJV):

The light of the body is the eye: if therefore thine eye be single, thy whole body shall be full of light.

But if thine eye be evil, thy whole body shall be full of darkness. If therefore the light that is in thee be darkness, how great is that darkness!

The Bible, Matthew 6:22 (ESV), even says, " 'The **eye** is the **lamp** of the body. So, if your eye is healthy, your whole body will be full of light" (bold emphasis added).[60] This verse of the Bible is talking about the **optic thalamus** which is the **single eye**. When the holy oil within the pineal gland is ignited by the kundalini energy, it produces high vibrational energy which then travels to the optic thalamus and lights it like a **lamp**, giving light to the whole body. Sometimes the verses of the Bible are written in riddles, so if you want to find the really important knowledge hidden in the Bible, you need to learn how to decipher its riddles.

To connect the dots, the main reason that Santa Claus comes during Christmas/Xmas Eve is to give children his precious and sacred gift, which is the holy oil. This **holy oil** is the **ichor** (golden fluid) that has the potential to give eternal life to men and women. In other words, Santa Claus can give you life by supplying your body with the sacred gift/holy oil; however, when you have been bad, Santa Claus becomes "evil" and diminishes your life by not supplying your body with the sacred gift/holy oil. When you have been bad, Santa becomes Satan (Saint Nick) and gives you coal, diminishing your life force energy. You become "bad" by masturbating too much, having excessive sex, and not living a healthy lifestyle. An unhealthy lifestyle is great for destroying the holy oil, turning it into "coal". On a deeper level, the Christmas story about Santa Claus coming down the chimney (spine) to give gifts to children is a magical story about the Seed/Bread/Jesus's journey to become "christed" (baptized with the holy oil) and return to the **temple**, which esoterically represents the brain located between the **temples** of the head, so he can be crucified as nourishment for the brain. This is the secret meaning of Christmas/ChristMass (Mass of Christ).

When you contemplate the information in this subchapter, you should realize that the esoteric (internal) version of Christmas is the true version. Therefore, the false version of Christmas is the exoteric (external) version. The external version of Christmas teaches people to cut down pine trees and decorate them with Christmas lights and ornaments. Furthermore, it teaches people to buy toys and wrap them as gifts and put them under Christmas trees. By participating in the external version of Christmas without investigating what it means on an esoteric and spiritual level, people prevent themselves from acknowledging and accepting the most precious and sacred gift of Christmas, which is the holy oil within them that has the potential to heal all diseases, giving them the power to rise above death (sin).

What most people do not know about the false or external version of Christmas is that it is a religious ritual. The supporters of this ritual, which are the Dark Forces, like to use it to trick people to give their holy oil (ichor) to them. An important information that you need to know about rituals is that they have energetic binding forces. These binding forces are not very dependent upon personal knowledge or beliefs. By blindly performing the holiday (magic day) ritual known as Christmas (external version), it can bind you to whatever the ritual is designed to do. When you ignore the internal version of Christmas and only participate in the external version of Christmas, you are telling the Dark Forces that you care more about external gifts than the sacred gift (holy oil) within you. This makes it easier for the Dark Forces to consume your holy oil, preventing it from returning to your brain, the temple of God. Keep in mind that the Dark Forces are entities that exist within the minds and the energy fields of all men, women, and children. One of the best ways to prevent them from consuming your ichor is to stop being afraid of the darkness, so you can learn to control your deepest fears.

To attract people to participate in the external version of

Christmas and distract them from seeking the internal version of Christmas, the Dark Forces made Christmas very appealing to the senses. This is why there are so many cute creatures, colorful decorations, delicious foods, sweet candies, and cheerful music during Christmas and other holidays. The purpose for doing this is to attract people to mostly focus their awareness and attention on external things that are appealing to the senses. This makes it easier for the Dark Forces to seduce and hypnotize their minds, allowing them to drain their energy. The Dark Forces are masters of manipulation and are very cunning.

If you plan to participate in the external version of Christmas, it would be wise to meditate before doing so. During meditation, focus your awareness inside your head and pray to God that your act of participating in the external version of Christmas does not mean that it is more important than the internal version of Christmas. Furthermore, sincerely tell God that you are celebrating Christmas because you cherish spending time with your families and friends. Energize your prayer with love and joy and let God know that the love that you share with your families and friends is more important than any external gift. When you say this prayer, it produces healing energy within you that can protect you from the Dark Forces during Christmas. As for external gifts, there is nothing immoral about giving external gifts to friends, family members, or strangers; however, it is wise to not spend too much time on external gifts, so you have more time to appreciate the sacred gift within you, which is the holy oil of Christ-Mass/Christmas. An important act that you should do during Christmas is to meditate for at least 30 minutes; while meditating, focus your awareness on the holy oil (Christ) within you and thank God for sending this sacred gift to heal your body.

It is important to remember that Christmas is a magic holiday (holy day) that teaches you why it is important to be "born again", not of the flesh but of the spirit, so you can rise above death and be free from sin. It is about the Son/Sun of Man within you and your journey to achieve spiritual freedom and eternal life. Please be aware that the stories and religious rituals of Christmas can be used to empower or disempower you. When you accept the stories literally and believe that they only teach you important things about the external world, they can weaken your spirit. However, when you innerstand that the stories of Christmas are full of parables that teach you important facts about your body and the internal world, they can raise your consciousness and empower your spirit.

Remember, the external version of Christmas is the false version. It is false in the sense that it lacks empowering truths. The false version of Christmas often teaches you to mostly concentrate on material things and value things outside of you. It also teaches you to rely on an external savior to save you. Unlike the false version of Christmas, the true version of Christmas (the internal version of Christmas), teaches you about the sacred process within your body that allows you to rise above sin and achieve spiritual freedom. This version of Christmas teaches you that the Christ and the kingdom of God are within you. So, if you plan to celebrate Christmas this year, remember that the most precious gifts of Christmas are not outside of you but are inside of you. Your mind, spirit, and Christ (holy oil) are some of your most precious and sacred gifts so cherish and love them. Thank God for giving you these sacred gifts and value them more than material things. When you value your internal sacred gifts more than external material gifts, you will sooner or later know that there is no mystery or no marvel in the external world that is greater than the internal world of your body. Furthermore, you will sooner or later know that you are a son of God. The word **son** etymologically means "descendant", and therefore all of us are sons/descendants of God.

The Occult Meanings of Easter

Another popular holiday that people like to celebrate is Easter. This holiday (holy day/magic day) has a strong connection to Christmas. Like Christmas, Easter is also full of occult symbolism and important parables. Two of the origins of the word **Easter** are the Old English word *easterdæg* and the Proto-Germanic word *austron*, meaning "dawn".[61] *Austron* is also the name of a goddess of fertility, spring, and sunrise whose feast was celebrated at the **spring equinox**. One of the common definitions of **Easter** is "an annual Christian festival in commemoration of the resurrection of Jesus Christ, observed on the first Sunday after the first full moon after the vernal equinox, as calculated according to tables based in Western churches on the Gregorian calendar and in Orthodox churches on the Julian calendar."[62]

To find the occult meanings of Easter, you need to know what Jesus represents in the religious story of the resurrection of Jesus Christ. In this religious story, the character Jesus does not really represent a physical man; instead, he represents the Light-Principle and the Sun that rises in the East and sets in the West. Because of this, one of the occult (secret) meanings of Easter is a holiday for celebrating the Sun and the spring equinox. To be more specific, Easter is a holiday for celebrating the light overpowering the darkness, which occurs during the spring equinox. After the spring equinox, the days get longer and the nights get shorter. This holiday can be celebrated anywhere from March 22 to April 25. Easter does not have a fixed date for the reason that it is celebrated on the first Sunday following the full moon that occurs on or following the spring equinox (March 21).

Two of the most popular symbols of Easter are the rabbit and the egg. These two symbols are used to represent fertility. Easter is not literally about the resurrection of a man named Jesus Christ because Jesus Christ is a name or a symbol, like a logo of a corporation, that is used to represent many important principles in life. However, this does not mean that there was not a man from the past who taught about the Christ principles. What most people do not know about Easter is that certain ancient civilizations celebrated this holiday long before the existence of Christianity.

It was during the 6th-7th centuries AD when this original pagan holiday was incorporated into Christianity and the Catholic Church. It would officially become a Christian Holiday and would be assigned in the bible of the New Testament to the day of Christ's resurrection and thereafter was called Easter.

The English word Easter is derived from an Old English or Anglo-Saxon word *Ēastre* or *Ēostre* (or *Estarte/Astarte*), who was an ancient fertility Goddess that various Anglo-Saxon Tribes worshiped during the start of this Sixth Age when they had celebrated this time of year as the suns Passover time, and to whom sacrifices were annually offered.

Before the Anglo-Saxons had worshiped Estarte, she was called by the Sumerian Inanna and later the Akkadian Ishtar, whose temple priestesses were the "women of Ishtar"; ishtaritum and sacred "prostitution" was part of this religion or cult and their temples served as houses of prostitution, in which the priestesses were prostitutes. In the East, to the Phoenicians, Canaanites and Babylonians she was the Goddess that was known as Astoreth or Ishtar. She was also the Babylonian Venus or Goddess of love and the consort of the pagan Fire God, Baal.[63]

Here is an excerpt from an interesting article published on LastTrumpetMinistries.org that explains the deeper meaning of Easter in more detail:

In those ancient times, there was a man named Nimrod, who was the grandson of one of Noah's son named Ham. Ham had a son named Cush who married a woman named Semiramis. Cush and Semiramis then had a son named "Nimrod."

... Nimrod became a god-man to the people and Semiramis, his wife and mother, became the powerful Queen of ancient Babylon. Nimrod was eventually killed by an enemy, and his body was cut in pieces and sent to various parts of his kingdom.

Semiramis had all of the parts gathered, except for one part that could not be found. That missing part was his reproductive organ. Semiramis claimed that Nimrod could not come back to life without it and told the people of Babylon that Nimrod had ascended to the sun and was now to be called "Baal", the sun god.[64]

The article then talked about how Satan helped Semiramis to deceive the people to accept her as a goddess. To influence the people with her ideas, Semiramis created a mystery religion and claimed that she was immaculately conceived. She taught the people that the "moon was a goddess that went through a 28 day cycle and ovulated when full". Semiramis also taught the people that "she came down from the moon in a giant moon egg that fell into the Euphrates River". This event happened during the first full moon after the spring equinox. Semiramis, one of the main characters of the ancient "Easter" story, became known as "Ishtar" and her "egg" became known as "Ishtar's egg". As Ishtar, which is pronounced similar to "easter", she told the people that the rays of the sun-god Baal impregnated her, causing her to conceive and birth a son named Tammuz. An important characteristic of Tammuz was his affection for rabbits. This ancient Easter story said that Tammuz, the son of the sun-god Baal, became a hunter and was eventually killed by a wild pig. After he died, his mother (Queen Ishtar) told the people that her son ascended to be with his father (Baal) and "the two of them would be with the worshippers in the sacred candle or lamp flame as Father, Son and Spirit".

The queen told the worshippers that when Tammuz was killed by the wild pig, some of his blood fell on the stump of an evergreen tree, and the stump grew into a full new tree overnight. This made the evergreen tree sacred by the blood of Tammuz.

She also proclaimed a forty day period of time of sorrow each year prior to the anniversary of the death of Tammuz. During this time, no meat was to be eaten.

Worshippers were to meditate upon the sacred mysteries of Baal and Tammuz, and to make the sign of the "T" in front of their hearts as they worshipped. They also ate sacred cakes with the marking of a "T" or cross on the top.

Every year, on the first Sunday after the first full moon after the spring equinox, a celebration was made. It was Ishtar's Sunday and was celebrated with rabbits and eggs. [65]

By now you should know that Easter is a holiday full of occult and sexual symbolism. In addition, you should know that it is a holiday for celebrating the Sun, the light of the world and the savior of mankind. Why is the Sun the savior of mankind? Because it produces sunlight and ejects it towards mother Earth to nourish and "fertilize" her, so she can produce food and life during the spring season. An important information that you need to know about ancient myths that have a lot of occult symbolism is that many of them were created to teach people important moral lessons. However, many of them were also created to poison people's minds with disempowering ideas. Another information that is important for you to know about ancient myths is that many of them have empowering truths. These truths are often hidden behind allegories and riddles. Because of this, it would be wise for you to study ancient myths and take them seriously. You can learn a lot about life and reality from deciphering ancient myths and studying their occult (hidden) knowledge.

Ancient myths are still relevant today because many of them are found in modern holidays and religious stories. Because of this, they are still shaping the culture of mankind. The problem is that many holidays are used by the Dark Forces to take advantage of people's free will, preventing them from discovering who they really are and their divine connection with God. The Law of Free Will plays a very important role in the Earth Matrix Drama. Within this law holds one of the keys for freeing mankind from the artificial matrix. When most of us innerstand that the Dark Forces cannot enslave us without our consent and participation, we can end this drama in no time by removing our consent and support. Once enough of us do this, it is game over for the Dark Forces and their version of the New World Order.

Twenty Solutions to Free Mankind

There are many solutions to free mankind from the artificial matrix of the Dark Forces. Based on my research, knowledge, and experience, some of the best solutions involve self-responsibility and God's Law. If the following solutions work for you, I highly encourage you to share them with other people. The more people who know how to free their bodies, minds, and souls from the artificial matrix, the faster we can restore our freedom and sovereignty. Here are 20 effective solutions to empower you to achieve spiritual freedom. It would be wise for you to study the solutions that resonate with you and then learn to apply and adapt them to your situations.

1. True Freedom Requires Great Responsibility

With freedom comes great responsibility. Freedom and responsibility are like two sides of one coin. You cannot have true freedom without responsibility, especially self-responsibility. If you were to be given too much freedom without self-responsibility, you would eventually harm yourself or worse harm another living being (i.e., man, woman, or child). Harming a living being thereof is a direct violation of God's Law. The consequence of harming a living being is very serious. Here is a great example of a situation that shows why freedom requires self-responsibility. Pretend that you have a 5-year-old child. Would you be willing to leave your 5-year-old child at a mall or a state fair by himself? Let me guess, your answer is no, right? A 5-year-old child is too **irresponsible** to be given that kind of freedom. When you lack self-responsibility, you are like an incompetent child who always relies on authorities and government institutions to govern you. Because of this, you will never be able to achieve true spiritual freedom.

2. Learn How to Use Words Wisely

On a deeper level, words are spiritual symbols that are used by the collective mind to create the program of the world. This program or software exists within the subconscious mind of every man, woman, and child. Words and symbols can be used to create 3D software, such as Maya and 3ds Max. These 3D animation and modeling software can be used by 3D artists to create a 3D world that looks real. However, on a deeper level, the 3D world thereof is basically made of words and symbols. The reality known as the natural world works similar this. Unlike a 3D world, the natural world or the earth was first programmed into existence by God. After God created man (male and female), He gave man dominion over all the earth, giving man the natural right to remodel it. Remodeling the earth without proper communication was unproductive so a language was developed, allowing man to use words to reprogram his subconscious mind. This gave man great power, allowing man to control and manipulate matter and reality to a large degree. Today, the knowledge to use the right ancient words to control and manipulate reality is only known by a very small percentage of men and women. Unfortunately, some of them have used this knowledge to reprogram people's minds, allowing them to create an artificial matrix to control people and harness their energy.

Besides programming the subconscious mind, words have the power to define things and give **mean**ing to life. This is why when a man does not innerstand a word or an idea, he sometimes says, "what does it **mean**?" Because reality and life are programmed into existence through the power of words, when you say something to an agent of the government, pay close attention to the words that come out of your mouth. For example, when you say these words, "I am a **citizen** of the United States", you just agreed to define yourself as a citizen of a corporation, conveying yourself into a world of fiction. This is possible because **your words create your reality**. When you say that you are a citizen, in law, you are no longer a man and therefore have no natural rights (God-given rights). As a **citizen**, which is a **subject** of the government, the rights that you have are artificial rights. They are **artificial** because they are created and given to you by the government which is an **artificial** person, also known as a corporation (a dead body). Keep in mind that accepting citizenship status does not mean that you cannot restore your natural status as a **man**. Furthermore, you do not have to act as a citizen all the time, as long as you know the right words to use.

A very important and powerful word in the previous paragraph that you need to know its deeper and spiritual meaning is man. The word man is so powerful that when you know how to use it wisely most judges will be afraid to speak to you in court. Besides being powerful, the word man is very sacred; the knowledge hidden inside it is worth more than all the gold on earth. This is because the word **man** secretly means "holy trinity" or "god". To find evidence of this, you need to decipher the capital letters that make up the word man, which are M, A, and N. To effectively decipher these three letters, you need to investigate and study their origins.

The first letter that you need to investigate and study is **M** (m), the thirteenth letter of the English alphabet; it is derived from *mem* which is the thirteenth letter of the proto-Sinaitic alphabet. In its original form, it represents a "stream of water" or "waves in the sea", and looks like waves that are drawn like shark teeth.[1] The letter M is the initial letter of the Hebrew word *mayim*, meaning "water". The modern Hebrew word for water is מים which is pronounced "mayim". It is important to remember that in Hebrew "water" is always in the plural ("waters"). Keep in mind that the suffix *ayim* means "dual".[2] Therefore, *mayim* can be translated as "duality of waters", "dual water", or "two waters".[3] It is important to know that Hebrew words that end in *im* (e.g., *mayim* and *elohim*) indicate a **masculine** plural. Because the letter M represents "water" and "waves", it is used to symbolize "life", "purification", "movement", and "action". In other words, the letter **M** represents the **masculine** principle of **water**. Keep in mind that the letter M (m) is the initial letter of the word man.

The next letter that you need to decipher is A. This letter is the **first** letter of the English alphabet and is derived from the *aleph*, the first letter of the proto-Sinaitic alphabet. *Aleph* means "ox" or "bull" in Hebrew and Semitic languages.[4] One of its original forms is the head of an ox. Throughout millennia, the *aleph* eventually changed into the letter **A**. Its original meaning is "**primal** energy", but its derivative meanings are "strength", "man" and "beginning". The word **primal** etymologically means "belonging to the earliest age"; it is derived from the Latin word *primus*, meaning "**first**".[5] In Greek, the *aleph* was changed to the *alpha*.

c. 1300, from Latin *alpha*, from Greek *alpha*, from Hebrew or Phoenician *aleph* (see aleph). The Greeks added -*a* because Greek words cannot end in most consonants. Sense of "**beginning** of anything" is from late 14c., often paired with *omega* (the last letter in the Greek alphabet, representing "the end"); sense of "first in a sequence" is from 1620s. In astronomy, the designation of the brightest star of each constellation (the use of Greek letters in star names began with Bayer's atlas in 1603). *Alpha male* was in use by c. 1960 among scientists studying animals; applied to humans in society from c. 1992. [Bold emphasis added][6]

Based on the information about the letter **A**, this letter has a strong connection to the concept of **beginning**, **first**, and **alpha** and **omega**. Jesus also has a strong connection to the concept of beginning, first, and alpha and omega. **Jesus** is sometimes known as the **Word**. Hence the Bible verse John 1:1 (NKJV), "In the **beginning** was the **Word**, and the Word was with God, and the Word was God" (bold emphasis added). Jesus is also known as "the Alpha and the Omega". Hence the Bible verse Revelation 22:13, "I am the **Alpha** and the **Omega**, the **Beginning** and the End, the **First** and the Last" (bold emphasis added). In addition, Jesus is known as the **first**born. Hence the Bible verses Colossians 1:15-18 (NKJV):

He is the image of the invisible God, the **first**born over all creation. [Bold emphasis added]

For by Him all things were created that are in heaven and that are on earth, visible and invisible, whether thrones or dominions or principalities or powers. All things were created through Him and for Him.

And He is before all things, and in Him all things consist.

And He is the head of the body, the church, who is the **beginning**, the **first**born from the dead, that in all things He may have the preeminence. [Bold emphasis added]

An important information that you need to know about Jesus, the firstborn, is that one of his title is "Son of God". In other words, he is God's firstborn. The evidence that Jesus is the Son of God can be found in the Bible verse Mark 1:1 (NKJV): "The beginning of the gospel of Jesus Christ, the Son of God." Remember, the word **son** etymologically means "descendant". The word "descendant" is made up of the word "descend" and the suffix "-ant". The word **descend** comes from the Latin word *descendere*, meaning "come down, descend, sink".[7] Jesus said, "I am the bread which came down from heaven."[8] Therefore, Jesus is the Son/Descendant of God. It is important to remember that a descendant can be a man or a woman. Keep in mind that the letter A (a) is the second letter of the word man.

The last letter of the word man that you need to decipher is the letter N (n). This letter is the fourteenth letter of the English alphabet; it is derived from the *nun* which is the fourteenth letter of the proto-Sinaitic alphabet. In its original form, the *nun* "represents a serpent, snake, water serpent, or eel".[9] The letter N (n) is the initial letter of the Hebrew word *nun*, representing "a fish, a sea snake, or a game fish".[10] Its original meaning is "that which is **hidden** in the ocean depths, a fish" and its derivative meanings are "**hidden**, intimate, **feminine**, place where one can crouch, place that contains, fish, fetus in the waters of the fetal sac, spark of life, life, forthcoming birth, infant, growth, production, product, advent, continuation, to grow, to stretch, to push, opening, twisted, to twist" (bold emphasis added).[11] The letter *nun* has a strong connection to the English word **nun** which is etymologically defined using these exact words:

> Old English *nunne* "**woman** devoted to religious life under vows of celibacy, poverty, and obedience to a superior," also "vestal, pagan priestess," from Late Latin *nonna* "nun, tutor," originally (along with masc. *nonnus*) a term of address to elderly persons, perhaps from children's speech, reminiscent of *nana* (compare Sanskrit *nona*, Persian *nana* "**mother**," Greek *nanna* "aunt," Serbo-Croatian *nena* "mother," Italian *nonna*, Welsh *nain* "grandmother;" see nanny). [Bold emphasis added][12]

An important information that you need to know about the word **nun** is that it has a strong connection to the biblical character **Jesus**. In fact, this connection can be seen when you decipher the "sus" in the name "Je**sus**". In Latin, the word *sus* means "a fish".[13] Remember, in Hebrew, *nun* means "a fish, a sea snake, or a game fish". It is interesting to realize that the letter *nun* and the word **fish** have a strong connection to the **fetus**. In the first two months of fetal development, the fetus looks like a fish. Another interesting information about the word **nun** is that it is the name of a goddess. "BEFORE THERE WAS anything, there was the Nun, the great primal waters of Nothing-ness. And in them, Eternity flowed. One day, from this nothing there arose something: Atum, the Perfect and Complete One, arising as the First Hill out of the waters of the Nun."[14] Here is some more interesting information that shows the connection between the letter *nun*, the word nun, and the biblical character Jesus:

> Every twenty-nine and one-half days, when the moon is in the sign of the zodiac that the sun was in at the birth of the native, there is a seed, or Psycho—Physical germ born *in* the, or *out of*, the Solar Plexus (the Manger) and this seed is taken up by the nerves or branches of the Pneumo gastric nerve, and becomes the "Fruit of the Tree of Life," or the "Tree of good and evil"—viz.: *good*, if *saved* and "cast upon the waters" (circulation) to reach the Pineal Gland; and *evil*, if *eaten* or consumed in sexual expression on the physical plane, or by alcoholic drinks, or gluttony that causes ferment—acid and even alcohol in intestinal tract—thus—"No drunkard can inherit the Kingdom of Heaven" *for acids and alcohol cut, or chemically split, the oil that unites with the mineral salts in the body and thus produces the monthly seed.*

> This seed, having the odor of fish, was called Jesus, from Ichtos (Greek for fish) and Nun (Hebrew for fish)—thus "Joshua the son of Nun,"—"I am the bread of life;" "I am the bread that came down from heaven;" "Give us this day our daily bread."[15]

Based on the information about the letter **N**, this letter represents the **feminine** principle of **water**. Remember, one of the original meanings of the letter N is "that which is **hidden** in the ocean depths, a fish" (bold emphasis added). When you look at the water of a river or a sea, you can see what is on or near the surface of the water, but beneath the surface of the water everything is **hidden**. This is especially true in deep water where there is no light. Deep water is dark and may look dead; however, hidden in it is nourishment that is essential for life. This dark water that conceals everything from sight represents the **feminine** principle, also known as darkness. Keep in mind that the letter N (n) is the last letter of the word man.

157

To connect the dots, the word man is made up of the letters M/m, A/a and N/n. **M** = **masculine** principle of water; **A** = beginning, first, or **alpha** (Jesus, Son of God); **N** = **feminine** principle of water. When the letters M, A, and N are combined into one word, they become MAN or man which secretly means "M = masculine water (**father**), A = alpha (**son**), N = feminine water (**mother**)". This is the **Holy Trinity**, meaning "the Father, the Son, and the Holy Spirit existing as one God".[16] Within every man (male and female), there exists the Holy Trinity/God. When you really think about it, man is a god in the flesh. In other words, you are a son of God in the flesh; however, you still have a lot of learning and growing up to do before you can ascend and be united with God. Hence, the saying, "Man know thyself; then thou shalt know the Universe and God."

Because every man (male and female) has the Holy Trinity within him, man has the ability to use the power of the Christ to command atoms, elements, matter, and the government to do what he wants them to do, as long as he is not in violation of God's Law. When a man says that he is a **citizen**, through the power of his words, he temporarily give up his godly status (man) and become a **subject** of the government, allowing the government to be his master. Because of this, as a citizen (subject) he has no right to tell the government what to do. Keep in mind that agreeing to **act** as a citizen does not mean that you are acting as a citizen all the time. There is nothing evil about acting in the capacity of a citizen whenever you need to; however, when you become too identified with it and forget your true and natural nationality, it can be used to imprison you in the artificial matrix. The word man is a very sacred word so cherish it and do not allow people to persuade you to think that it is a sexist word. People who think that the word man is sexist have no idea what they are talking about and are making it easier for the Dark Forces to enslave mankind. Please remember these words: **Man** secretly means "father, son (descendant), mother" or "Holy Trinity", and is your **natural nationality**. In other words, we (descendants of God) make up the nation of man.

> Then God said, "Let Us make man in Our image, according to Our likeness; let them have dominion over the fish of the sea, over the birds of the air, and over the cattle, over all the earth and over every creeping thing that creeps on the earth." So God created man in His own image; in the image of God He created him; male and female He created

them. (Genesis 1:26-27, NKJV)

The first man was of the earth, made of dust; the second Man is the Lord from heaven. As was the man of dust, so also are those who are made of dust; and as is the heavenly Man, so also are those who are heavenly. And as we have borne the image of the man of dust, we shall also bear the image of the heavenly Man. (1 Corinthians 15:47-49, NKJV)

Do you not know that you are the temple of God and that the Spirit of God dwells in you? If anyone defiles the temple of God, God will destroy him. For the temple of God is holy, which temple you are. (1 Corinthians 3:16-17, NKJV)

3. Be Wary of Disharmonious and Disempowering Music

The art of music is one of the most powerful arts for casting magic spells. Music has the power to affect your vibration; it also has the power to affect the fundamental architecture of your body, which is formed based on sacred geometry. Furthermore, music can energize words, making them more powerful and allowing those words to reprogram your mind easier than words without music. In other words, music can be used to hypnotize your mind. Certain music can cause the frequencies of your mind and body to not synchronize properly, causing you to feel depressed, sad, or angry. For example, many heavy metal, hip hop, techno, and rap music are great for disharmonizing the frequencies of your mind and body. Because of this, it is wise to greatly reduce the amount of time you listen to these types of music.

4. Avoid Fighting the Dark Forces

It is not wise to fight the Dark Forces because fighting them produces negative energy for them to feed on. In addition, fighting them generates the right kind of energy to power the artificial matrix. This is why they like to promote wars and conflicts between nations and ethnic groups. Even though it is not wise to fight the Dark Forces, be aware that you do have the right to defend yourself. An important information that you need to know about the Dark Forces is that they cannot be stopped using physical weapons. The Dark Forces are non-physical beings; therefore, physical weapons are not very effective against them. Instead of fighting them, use the power of knowledge, words, thought, intention, and God's Law to discipline them. In addition, reduce your support for the artificial matrix as much as possible. Just like how any corporation needs your support to stay in business, the artificial matrix also needs your support to function. When enough of us remove our support, the artificial matrix will become weak and powerless. You also need to support people who are creating systems that work in harmony with nature. These systems are important for empowering mankind to transcend the artificial matrix.

5. Stop Voting for Treasonous Politicians

As a United States citizen, your right to vote is not a right but is a privilege. To be a United States citizen means that you are an "employee" of the United States of America (incorporated) and therefore are considered a legal fiction, also known as a corporation (artificial person). A corporation is a fictitious entity that has no natural rights. In other words, every time you vote in a corporate election, you agree to be a legal fiction (dead/artificial person). Furthermore, you agree to allow the U.S. government, which is another corporation, to have jurisdiction over you. The right to vote in the United States of America is a big fat sham because the voting system is rigged so bad that your vote does not really matter. To make matters worse, the presidential candidate you vote for is actually running for office of a **foreign** corporation. It is foreign because it is not part of The United States of America (**un**incorporated). If you are not a resident of the United States of America, the voting system in your state is most likely rigged too.

6. Do Not Ignore the Dark Forces

You need to be aware of what the Dark Forces are doing, so you can protect yourself from them by rebutting their false presumptions and saying no to the magic spells that they broadcast via television and other media. Ignoring the Dark Forces only makes it much easier for them to enslave mankind. One of the main reasons that the world is on the brink of destruction is because most people have ignored the Dark Forces. Remember, silence is a form of consent and ignorance is not a good enough excuse, especially in the Information Age (Computer Age).

7. Study God's Law (Natural Law)

When it comes to spiritual freedom, educating your mind with the knowledge of God's Law and **applying** the knowledge to your life are two of the most important things you can do. Why is that you may ask? Because learning how to live in harmony with God's Law is a requirement for ascending to a higher level of consciousness that is beyond time and space. It is also a requirement to ascend into the kingdom of God. As you ascend to higher levels of consciousness, it allows your body to hold more high frequency energy, causing your spiritual powers (e.g., love, thought, awareness, and consciousness) to strengthen exponentially. Eventually, your spiritual powers will become so strong that you will be able to destroy planets and stars. Do you think God will allow you access to that kind of power without being responsible and knowing how to live in harmony with nature? With great power comes great responsibility.

8. Study Man's law and the Legal System

Besides studying God's Law, it is also wise to study man's law, such as contract law, trust law, common law, statutory law, corporate law, admiralty law, maritime law, and U.C.C. In addition, study how the legal system works from behind the scene. Doing these things will help you find effective ways to defend and exercise your artificial rights and natural rights. You do not have to learn everything about the laws created by man, but you should study them to the point where you are comfortable using them to defend and exercise your rights. It is important to remember that the legal system uses an ancient magic art that relies on words to trick you to reside in the realm of the dead. Today, this ancient magic art is known as legalese. Because the magic art of legalese is heavily used by the legal system, it is important that you study how magic works, so you can protect yourself from the magic spells of legalese.

When you learn to use God's Law and man's law to defend and exercise your rights, you can effectively put the Dark Forces and their minions in checkmate every time they harm you and your property. This is how you can tame and control them without violent revolutions. A very important information that the Dark Forces do not want you to know is the fact that God has His own law and justice system. God's intelligence and awareness are infinite, and therefore He can easily know every being's thoughts, intentions, and actions. As long as you properly exercise your God-given rights whenever the Dark Forces and their minions cause harm to you, they will have to face the Law and Justice System of God.

Whenever the Dark Forces harass or harm you, use the art of meditation to summon them by focusing your awareness inside your head and sending your thoughts and intentions to the Spirit of God that dwells between the temples of your head. Sincerely ask God to summon the beings who have harmed you to appear in front of the judge of His court for the violation of your natural rights. You can also summon Christ to command them to appear in front of God. For example, you can say, "In the name of Christ, I command the spirits who have harmed me to appear in front of the Supreme Judge of the universe ..." If you know their names, you can replace "the spirits" with their names. Remember to ask God to judge them for the violation of your natural rights. When you do this properly, they will run away from you like scared little kids.

9. Stay Away from All Public Protests

Many people have been conditioned to think that protesting is the way to restore freedom or create beneficial change. Unfortunately, they do not realize that protesting is not going to really change anything for the better, especially when it comes to freedom. When you join a protest and speak out against the government, what you are really doing is telling the government that you want change, but you want the government to do it for you. In other words, you are still an incompetent child who does not want to take full responsibility for your life and future. Without full responsibility, there is no real freedom!

If you want to change the world into a place full of freedom and prosperity, you need to first change yourself in a way that allows your energy to attract and support freedom and prosperity. When enough people do this, the government will have no choice but to support freedom and prosperity. It is important to remember that the government is a reflection of the people. Because of this, when people protest against the government, they are, to a significant degree, protesting against themselves. This is a foolish thing to do. Instead of protesting against the government, people should lead by example by showing other people that they are responsible and teaching those people to be responsible like them. Remember, with freedom comes great responsibility.

10. Arm Yourself with Knowledge of Empowerment

The right knowledge is power; however, you have to learn how to use it wisely or you will not be able to access its power. Knowledge is the key to empower you to overcome your fears and achieve spiritual freedom. One of the main reasons that you are fearful of something is because you lack the knowledge to innerstand it. Once you gain the right knowledge to innerstand it, your fear will eventually subside to the point where it cannot control you anymore. Because of this, it is essential for you to seek the right knowledge to empower you to innerstand the Dark Forces, so you can rise above the artificial matrix and achieve spiritual freedom. Remember, physical weapons are not very effective for stopping the Dark Forces; however, the right knowledge is. Once you learn to wisely use the right knowledge to exercise your God-given rights (natural rights) and strengthen your spiritual powers, the Dark Forces cannot stop you from leaving the artificial matrix.

11. Stop Relying on an External Savior to Save You

The external savior program was created by the minions of the Dark Forces to enslave your body, mind, and soul. When you rely on an external savior to save you, you subconsciously tell the universe that God did not give you the required spiritual powers to achieve spiritual freedom. This is an insult to God. If you think that you need to rely on an external savior to save you, you are not using your spiritual powers wisely. Furthermore, you are thinking like a cowardly slave. Remember these words: the true savior has always been inside you.

12. Stop Supporting Wars and Crimes Against Mankind

Most, if not all, the major wars on Earth have been engineered by the Dark Forces and their flesh and blood minions. The Dark Forces are obsessed with wars for the reason that wars create a lot of negative energy for them to feed on. To prevent wars, support peace and teach other people to live in harmony with God's Law and His Ten Commandments.

13. Spend Money Wisely

Money is a medium that represents your labor which is your time and energy. It is also an instrument for measuring choices. These choices have the power to direct energy to flow in a way that creates **change**, meaning "the act or fact of changing; fact of being changed".[17] In simple terms, when money is used by people, it has the power to create **change**, which is why the "money returned when a payment exceeds the amount due" is called **change**.[18] Because money has the power to create change, if you want to make the world a better place, stop spending your money (time and energy) on companies that do not care about truth, justice, freedom, peace, rights, and nature. This is one of the easiest ways to effectively change the world for the better. Every time you spend money on a product or a service, you are making a choice and telling the universe that you support that choice. The more money you use to support that choice, the more energy is directed by the universe to support products and services that are related to that choice. In other words, you create your own reality through your choices which can be expressed through money.

An important information about money that most people do not know is that their irresponsible use of money is one of the major causes of their suffering. The world has a lot of corruption and disease because of people's irresponsible financial choices. For example, using money to buy junk food instead of healthy food, and using money to buy conventional food instead of organic food. Food that is conventionally grown is often contaminated with environmental toxins (e.g., pesticides) and GMOs. By buying conventional food, you are, in a way, supporting environmental toxins. Remember, money is an instrument for measuring choices. Do you want to change the world for the better? If your answer is "yes", make responsible choices and use money wisely.

If the prices of organic food are preventing you from buying organic food, be aware that conventional food is cheaper because it has less regulation and receives government subsidies. In other words, some of the money collected from taxpayers is being used to make conventional food cheaper than organic food. The hidden purpose of this is to motivate people to eat more conventional food, resulting in more sick people. A sick and unhealthy society is easier for the Dark Forces and their minions to control. Another great way to use money wisely is to shop at locally-owned stores and farmers' markets more often. By doing this, you will reduce the power of big corporations, which can prevent them from destroying small and family-owned businesses.

14. Claim Your Sovereignty and Correct Your Status

Shortly after you were born your parents accepted a birth certificate with your legal name on it, thereby agreeing to allow you to participate in commerce. If your parents used your birth certificate, on your behalf, as evidence of your identity, they unknowingly created a presumption, allowing the government to presume that you are the person (legal fiction) designated with the legal name on your birth certificate. This process transformed you into the **debtor** of your birth certificate, which was a mistake because you were supposed to be the **beneficial owner**. By transforming you into the debtor designated with the legal name on your birth certificate, you became a legal property of the State, making you a corporate slave. To correct this mistake, you need to notify the right government agent and let him know that you are the beneficial owner and not the debtor of your birth certificate, which is a certificate of a trust.

Before taking any action, it would be wise for you to explore the following three websites because they have important information that teaches you how to claim your sovereignty, correct your status, and nullify certain legal contracts. The three websites are AnnaVonReitz.com, Freedom-School.com, and YouAreLaw.org. It is important to know that to be able to effectively free yourself from the Earth Matrix Drama, you need to learn how to use the power of God's Law to defend and exercise your natural rights. Furthermore, you need to know how to rebut and nullify fraudulent claims and false presumptions. My website EsotericKnowledge.me is a great place to learn empowering knowledge that teaches you how to defend and exercise your natural rights, and nullify fraudulent claims and false presumptions using the power of God's Law. To effectively claim your sovereignty, you (the living man) have to claim your dominion and know how to exercise the power of God's Law. Remember, God gave man dominion over all the earth. However, for man's dominion to become really effective, he has to claim it and prove that he is responsible enough to exercise it.

15. Learn How Contracts Work

A very important information that you need to know about a contract is that it can be used to bind you to its terms and conditions. Because of this, it is important to learn how contracts work. The Dark Forces and the Dark Magicians like to use contracts to trick you to participate in the world of legal fictions and corporations (artificial persons). By contracting with corporations, it makes it easier for them to imprison you in the artificial matrix; however, if you know how to use contracts wisely and innerstand how contract law works, you can negotiate or change the terms and conditions of contracts so they are more fair. If negotiating or changing the terms and conditions of the contract is not acceptable, you can use the power of contract law to take control of the contact. This is why it is important that you study contract law and learn how to use contracts wisely. Keep in mind that contracts are not evil but can be used for evil purposes.

16. Stop Relying on Politicians to Create Change

Many politicians in Western and Eastern countries are bought off by the Dark Magicians and their corrupt bankers. Because of this, serving the people is not in their best interest. Furthermore, many politicians are often addicted to money and power. The Dark Magicians are well aware of this, which is why they pay a lot of money to politicians and give them certain special privileges. In other words, politicians live like royalty and can get away with many illegal activities. Because of the benefits thereof, many politicians would rather protect the current system than change it. Most politicians are comfortable where they are at; therefore, the last thing they want is for the system to change in a way that empowers the people. When the people become empowered, the government loses power, causing politicians to also lose power.

17. Invest in Alternative Energy Technology

Many alternative energy devices have the potential to reduce the cost of living by 50 percent or more. Some of them can produce electrical energy without consuming any fossil fuel, especially free energy devices. Because of these features, alternative energy technology is a threat to the oil cartel. As soon as alternative energy devices are used by most of us to power our homes and vehicles, we can significantly reduce our support for the oil industry. Oil is one of the top sources of revenue for the Dark Magicians. If we can mostly or completely stop using oil as an energy source, the Dark Magicians will have less money to finance their corporate greed and wars.

18. Learn to Live Peaceably

The Dark Forces and their minions rely heavily on wars and violence to keep the artificial matrix operating efficiently. Because of this, it is wise to live peaceably with other people and support the unification of mankind. As long as we, the people of the world, are united in peace and love, the Dark Forces and their minions will not be able to achieve their dark agendas.

19. Write Your Own Waiver to Protect Your Natural Rights

A well-written waiver can protect your natural rights and remove your consent to be a subject of the government. Visit this link (https://esotericknowledge.me/waiver/) to see an example of a well-written waiver.

20. Live Like Small Communities

Have you ever been to small towns where people have their own doctors, teachers, mechanics, markets, farms, etc.? These small communities are self-sufficient and independent, and the people often know how to live in harmony with nature. Because they are independent, they do not need to rely heavily on the government to survive. If we want to free ourselves from the artificial matrix, one of the things that we need to do is learn how to live like small communities. This does not mean that we need to move out of the city. Imagine living in a city where almost everyone knows how to live in harmony with nature and is responsible. A city like this would thrive so well that there would be no poverty and the people would not need to worry about crimes. Without poverty and crimes, there is no desire for a big government. There is nothing dangerous about a government that is balanced in size; however, when a government becomes too big, it often becomes tyrannical.

Some Words of Encouragement

If you have read most of this book or all of its pages, I congratulate you for having the courage to explore beyond the conventional paradigm and seek the truth. I know that walking the path of truth and standing up for the truth are not easy, but it is the truth that will set you free. Do not ever forget that. By now you should know that mankind has been enslaved for a very long time and is being used as a biological battery to power the artificial matrix. Sadly, most people are still spiritually asleep; furthermore, they lack the courage to face the truth. As a living man or a living woman who is spiritually awakened, it is up to you to decide if you want to share the knowledge in this book with other truth seekers to wake them up from the artificial matrix. This book does not have all the answers, but it has enough empowering knowledge to make the Dark Forces very nervous.

The solutions in this chapter are effective for reducing the power of the Dark Forces; however, to free mankind from the artificial matrix requires a large number of people to use the solutions wisely. If we can get about 15 percent of the world's population to apply most of the 20 solutions to their lives, we can restore a significant percentage of our freedom and sovereignty in less than one generation. As soon as this happens, it is just a matter of time until we, the people of the world, free ourselves from the artificial matrix. Some of you may think that there is no way we can free enough people's minds to restore our freedom and sovereignty, because the Dark Forces control nearly everything that we do and have gatekeepers guarding every important entrance to the mainframe or control room of the artificial matrix. Do not let the Dark Forces intimidate you. In truth, **when it comes to law and order**, darkness will always surrender to light. Darkness is a state of randomness and chaos. When light comes in contact with darkness, it gives order to that chaos, causing it to structuralize. This process "melts" the darkness away, showing that when it comes to order light has more authority than darkness.

It is important to know that darkness is not evil. The darkness is the subconscious of God. It is chaotic because it is a field of infinite possibility. The **darkness** is the field where light is born and therefore is the attribute of the **Divine Feminine Energy**. The material world cannot exist without the darkness and the light because when one of them is missing forms and colors cannot manifest. It is also important to know that the Dark Forces do not represent all of the darkness. However, they like to hide in the darkness and use it to scare people because they know that most people are afraid of the unknown. The Dark Forces are only succeeding because most people believe they are powerless. The truth that they do not want you to know is that you are a spiritual being with

infinite potential. You literally have the spiritual power to create planets, stars, and even universes. One of the reasons that you do not have access to the full potential of your spiritual power is because you lack knowledge, wisdom, love, experience, self-responsibility, courage, and faith. This causes you to become less aware of who you truly are and how to use your spiritual power wisely.

The artificial matrix and the Dark Forces can only flourish on Earth with the support of living men and women. You are one of those men or women, so reduce your support for the Dark Forces as much as possible. If you can, stop supporting them to teach them a lesson. Furthermore, take action to educate men, women, and children who want to know the truth about the history of mankind. Also, learn to defend and exercise your natural rights, and support the men and women who are creating systems and organizations to transcend the artificial matrix. Once there are enough men and women working together to transcend the artificial matrix, we can stop supporting it and leave it to disappear. Without the support of men and women, the artificial matrix will eventually disappear or shrink to near nothingness, and therefore the Dark Forces will not be able to use it to control us anymore. This is how we can free mankind without violent revolutions. The fact that you are living on Earth during the end of this age is proof that you have an important role to play in the Earth Matrix Drama. It is time to wake up and remember your duty, so you can play your role in helping to free mankind. Once mankind is free, you will also be free because your family (mankind) is no longer imprison in the artificial matrix. Be strong and fearless, and may you be protected on your journey to spiritual freedom and enlightenment.

References

Chapter 1

1. Gnostic Teachings. *The Elements in Spiritual Growth.* http://gnosticteachings.org/courses/alchemy/3071-the-elements-in-spiritual-growth.html

2. Dictionary. *Whirl.* https://www.dictionary.com/browse/whirl

3. Lat Dict. *Neo.* http://latin-dictionary.net/search/latin/neo

4. You Tube. *The Golden Web Part 1.* https://www.youtube.com/watch?v=5PgX8l9AgzE

5. Online Etymology Dictionary. *Whir.* https://www.etymonline.com/word/whir

6. Dictionary. *Whir.* https://www.dictionary.com/browse/whir

7. Online Etymology Dictionary. *Language.* https://www.etymonline.com/word/language

8. You Tube. *The Golden Web Part 1.* https://www.youtube.com/watch?v=5PgX8l9AgzE

9. Online Etymology Dictionary. *English.* https://www.etymonline.com/word/English

10. Dictionary. *English.* https://www.dictionary.com/browse/english

11. Dictionary. *English.* https://www.dictionary.com/browse/english

12. Wikipedia. *Angles.* https://en.wikipedia.org/wiki/Angles

13. Dictionary. *Angle.* https://www.dictionary.com/browse/angle

14. Dictionary. *Angel.* https://www.dictionary.com/browse/angel

15. Dictionary. *Angle.* https://www.dictionary.com/browse/angle

16. Dictionary. *Radian.* https://www.dictionary.com/browse/radian

17. Dictionary. *Radiant.* https://www.dictionary.com/browse/radiant

18. Online Etymology Dictionary. *Radius.* https://www.etymonline.com/word/radius

19. Merriam Webster. *Radiant.* https://www.merriam-webster.com/dictionary/radiant

20. Lexico. *Refract.* https://www.lexico.com/en/definition/refract

21. Dictionary. *Angle.* https://www.dictionary.com/browse/angle

22. Online Etymology Dictionary. *Angle.* https://www.etymonline.com/word/angle

23. Dictionary. *Angle.* https://www.dictionary.com/browse/angle

24. Dictionary. *Geometry.* https://www.dictionary.com/browse/geometry

25. Dictionary. *Alpha.* https://www.dictionary.com/browse/alpha

26. Dictionary. *Beta.* https://www.dictionary.com/browse/beta

27. Dictionary. *Alpha.* https://www.dictionary.com/browse/alpha

28. Dictionary. *Beta.* https://www.dictionary.com/browse/beta

29. Ouaknin, Marc-Alain. *Mysteries of the Alphabet.* Abbeville Press Publishers. New York, NY. 1999.

30. Online Etymology Dictionary. *Electro-.* https://www.etymonline.com/word/electro-

31. Online Etymology Dictionary. *Magnetic.* https://www.etymonline.com/word/magnetic

32. Online Etymology Dictionary. *Archangel.* https://www.etymonline.com/word/archangel

33. Online Etymology Dictionary. *Archon.* https://www.etymonline.com/word/archon

34. Online Etymology Dictionary. *Ethnarch.* https://www.etymonline.com/word/ethnarch

35. Encyclopaedia Britannica. *Archon.* https://www.britannica.com/topic/Archon-Gnosticism

36. Dictionary. *Arc.* https://www.dictionary.com/browse/arc

37. Merriam Webster. *Arc.* https://www.merriam-webster.com/dictionary/arc

38. Online Etymology Dictionary. *Arc.* https://www.etymonline.com/word/arc

39. Online Etymology Dictionary. *Arch-.* https://www.etymonline.com/word/arch-

40. Definitions. *Arche.* https://www.definitions.net/definition/Arche

41. Arvindus. *Contemplationam, Etymological and Esoteric Roots of 'Arch', 'Arc' and 'Ark'.* http://www.arvindus.com/publications/201103261.html

42. Ouaknin, Marc-Alain. *Mysteries of the Alphabet.* Abbeville Press Publishers. New York, NY. 1999.

43. Learner's Dictionary. *Trinity.* http://learnersdictionary.com/definition/trinity

44. Ouaknin, Marc-Alain. *Mysteries of the Alphabet.* Abbeville Press Publishers. New York, NY. 1999.

45. Abarim Publications. *Beth Meaning.* http://www.abarim-publications.com/Meaning/Beth.html#.XOEePKR7lPY

46. Wikipedia. *Lehem.* https://en.wikipedia.org/wiki/Lehem

47. Online Etymology Dictionary. *Sol.* https://www.etymonline.com/word/Sol

48. Online Etymology Dictionary. *Son.* https://www.etymonline.com/word/son

49. Online Etymology Dictionary. *Descend.* https://www.etymonline.com/word/descend

50. Dictionary. *-Ant.* https://www.dictionary.com/browse/-ant

51. The Free Dictionary. *Word.* https://www.thefreedictionary.com/word

52. Lexico. *Word.* https://www.lexico.com/en/definition/word

53. Lexico. *Vibration.* https://www.lexico.com/en/definition/vibration

54. Lat Dict. *Verbum, Verbi.* http://latin-dictionary.net/search/latin/verbum

55. Dictionary. *Verb.* https://www.dictionary.com/browse/verb

56. Dictionary. *Photon.* https://www.dictionary.com/browse/photon

57. MasonicDictionary. *The Letter "G".* http://www.masonicdictionary.com/gee.html

58. Masonic World. *The Letter "G".* http://www.masonicworld.com/education/articles/THE-LETTER-G.htm

59. Dictionary. *Gamma Ray.* https://www.dictionary.com/browse/gamma-ray

60. Dictionary. *Grammar.* https://www.dictionary.com/browse/grammar

61. Online Etymology Dictionary. *Magic.* https://www.etymonline.com/word/magic

62. Dictionary. *Magic.* https://www.dictionary.com/browse/magic

63. The Free Dictionary. *Words.* https://www.thefreedictionary.com/words

64. Your Dictionary. *Logos.* https://www.yourdictionary.com/logos

65. Merriam Webster. *Logos.* https://www.merriam-webster.com/dictionary/Logos

66. New World Encyclopedia. *Logos.* http://www.newworldencyclopedia.org/entry/Logos

67. Encyclopaedia Britannica. *Logos.* https://www.britannica.com/topic/logos

68. Online Etymology Dictionary. *Uni-.* https://www.etymonline.com/word/uni-

69. Online Etymology Dictionary. *Verse.* https://www.etymonline.com/word/verse

70. Leeds, Marty. *Pi & The English Alphabet (Vol. 1).* CreateSpace. 2014.

71. Leeds, Marty. *Pi & The English Alphabet (Vol. 1).* CreateSpace. 2014.

72. Merriam Webster. *Grammar*. https://www.merriam-webster.com/dictionary/grammar

73. Wikipedia. *Trivium*. https://en.wikipedia.org/wiki/Trivium

74. Online Etymology Dictionary. *Grammar*. https://www.etymonline.com/word/grammar

75. Online Etymology Dictionary. *Grimoire*. https://www.etymonline.com/word/grimoire

76. Dictionary. *Grimoire*. https://www.dictionary.com/browse/grimoire

77. Bible Gateway. *Genesis 1:3*. https://www.biblegateway.com/passage/?search=Genesis+1:3&version=KJV

78. Your Dictionary. *Logos*. https://www.yourdictionary.com/logos

79. Dictionary. *Homophone*. https://www.dictionary.com/browse/homophone

80. Online Etymology Dictionary. *Covenant*. https://www.etymonline.com/word/covenant

81. Online Etymology Dictionary. *Covenant*. https://www.etymonline.com/word/covenant

82. Dictionary. *Covenant*. https://www.dictionary.com/browse/covenant

83. Dictionary. *Coven*. https://www.dictionary.com/browse/coven

84. Online Etymology Dictionary. *Coven*. https://www.etymonline.com/word/coven

85. Dictionary. *Ant*. https://www.dictionary.com/browse/ant

86. Dictionary. *Ant*. https://www.dictionary.com/browse/ant

87. Turkish Dictionary. *Ant*. http://www.turkishdictionary.net/?word=ant

88. Dictionary. *Lord*. https://www.dictionary.com/browse/lord

89. Dictionary. *Ant*. https://www.dictionary.com/browse/ant

90. Dictionary. *Baptism*. https://www.dictionary.com/browse/baptism

91. Dictionary. *Rite.* https://www.dictionary.com/browse/rite

92. Online Etymology Dictionary. *Ritual.* https://www.etymonline.com/word/ritual

93. Dictionary. *Write.* https://www.dictionary.com/browse/write

94. Lexico. *Sigil.* https://www.lexico.com/en/definition/sigil

95. Bible Gateway. *John 3:5.* https://www.biblegateway.com/passage/? search=john+3%3A5&version=NKJV

96. Bible Gateway. *1 Corinthians 3:16.* https://www.biblegateway.com/passage/? search=1%20Corinthians+3:16&version=NKJV

Chapter 2

1. The Free Dictionary. *Berth.* https://www.thefreedictionary.com/berth

2. Online Etymology Dictionary. *Umbilical.* https://www.etymonline.com/word/umbilical

3. Dictionary. *Naval.* https://www.dictionary.com/browse/naval

4. The Free Dictionary. *Dock.* https://www.thefreedictionary.com/dock

5. Dictionary. *Ore.* https://www.dictionary.com/browse/ore

6. Dictionary. *Oar.* https://www.dictionary.com/browse/oar

7. Online Etymology Dictionary. *Hospital.* https://www.etymonline.com/word/hospital

8. Dictionary. *Hostile.* https://www.dictionary.com/browse/hostile

9. Merriam Webster. *Ward.* https://www.merriam-webster.com/dictionary/ward

10. Dictionary. *Cell.* https://www.dictionary.com/browse/cell

11. You Tube. *The Golden Web Part 1.* https://www.youtube.com/watch?v=5PgX8l9AgzE

12. Online Etymology Dictionary. *Au.* https://www.etymonline.com/word/Au

13. You Tube. *The Golden Web Part 1.*
https://www.youtube.com/watch?v=5PgX8l9AgzE

14. You Tube. *The Golden Web Part 1.*
https://www.youtube.com/watch?v=5PgX8l9AgzE

15. Online Etymology Dictionary. *Christ.*
https://www.etymonline.com/word/Christ

16. You Tube. *The Golden Web Part 1.*
https://www.youtube.com/watch?v=5PgX8l9AgzE

17. AntiCorruption Society. *The Orchestrated Plan to Deceive and Enslave the American People.*
https://anticorruptionsociety.files.wordpress.com/2014/08/the-orchestrated-plan-to-deceive-and-enslave-the-american-people-pdf.pdf

18. Investopedia. *Beneficial Interest.*
https://www.investopedia.com/terms/b/beneficial-interest.asp

19. Maxwell, Jordan. *Matrix of Power: Secrets of World Control.* The Book Tree. San Diego, CA. 2000.

20. Black, Henry C. *Black's Law Dictionary* (fifth edition). West Publishing Co. St. Paul, MN. 1979.

21. Dictionary. *Government.*
https://www.dictionary.com/browse/government

22. The Law Dictionary. *What Is Government?*
https://thelawdictionary.org/government/

23. Online Etymology Dictionary. *Government.*
https://www.etymonline.com/word/government

24. Online Etymology Dictionary. *Govern.*
https://www.etymonline.com/word/govern

25. Online Etymology Dictionary. *-Ment.*
https://www.etymonline.com/word/-ment

26. The Latin Lexicon. *Mentum.*
https://latinlexicon.org/definition.php?p1=2035672

27. Online Etymology Dictionary. **Men-.*
https://www.etymonline.com/word/*men-

28. Online Etymology Dictionary. *Mentation.*

https://www.etymonline.com/word/mentation

29. Online Etymology Dictionary. *Men-*.
https://www.etymonline.com/word/*men-

30. Dictionary. *Mnemonic*.
https://www.dictionary.com/browse/mnemonic

31. Dictionary. *Mnemonic*.
https://www.dictionary.com/browse/mnemonic

32. Online Etymology Dictionary. *Mnemonic*.
https://www.etymonline.com/word/mnemonic

33. Online Etymology Dictionary. *Cop*.
https://www.etymonline.com/word/cop

34. Online Etymology Dictionary. *Cop*.
https://www.etymonline.com/word/cop

35. Dictionary. *Cop*. https://www.dictionary.com/browse/cop

36. Dictionary. *Cop*. https://www.dictionary.com/browse/cop

37. Dictionary. *Cop*. https://www.dictionary.com/browse/cop

38. Bible Gateway. *Matthew 6:24*.
https://www.biblegateway.com/passage/?
search=Matthew+6%3A24&version=KJV

Chapter 3

1. Fam Guardian. *Legal v. Lawful*.
http://famguardian.org/Subjects/LawAndGovt/LegalEthics/LegalVL
awful.htm

2. Dictionary. *Signature*.
https://www.dictionary.com/browse/signature

3. AntiCorruption Society. *The Orchestrated Plan to Deceive and Enslave the American People*.
https://anticorruptionsociety.files.wordpress.com/2014/08/the-orchestrated-plan-to-deceive-and-enslave-the-american-people-pdf.pdf

4. You Tube. *The Golden Web Part 1*.
https://www.youtube.com/watch?v=5PgX8l9AgzE

5. Dictionary. *Ewe.* https://www.dictionary.com/browse/ewe

6. English Oxford Living Dictionaries. *Sheeple.* https://www.lexico.com/en/definition/sheeple

7. Dictionary. *Nag.* https://www.dictionary.com/browse/nag

8. You Tube. *The Golden Web Part 1.* https://www.youtube.com/watch?v=5PgX8l9AgzE

9. You Tube. *The Golden Web Part 1.* https://www.youtube.com/watch?v=5PgX8l9AgzE

10. Dictionary. *Groom.* https://www.dictionary.com/browse/groom

11. Dictionary. *Stable.* https://www.dictionary.com/browse/stable

12. Dictionary. *Stable.* https://www.dictionary.com/browse/stable

13. Dictionary. *Babylon.* https://www.dictionary.com/browse/babylon

14. Online Etymology Dictionary. *Babylon.* https://www.etymonline.com/word/Babylon

15. Online Etymology Dictionary. *Manage.* https://www.etymonline.com/word/manage

16. You Tube. *The Golden Web Part 1.* https://www.youtube.com/watch?v=5PgX8l9AgzE

17. Dictionary. *Manager.* https://www.dictionary.com/browse/manager

18. Dictionary. *Manger.* https://www.dictionary.com/browse/manger

19. Dicios. *Pony.* http://en.dicios.com/deen/pony

20. Dictionary. *Pony.* https://www.dictionary.com/browse/pony

21. The Law Dictionary. *What Is BOND, N?* https://thelawdictionary.org/bond-n/

22. Online Etymology Dictionary. *Sigil.* https://www.etymonline.com/word/sigil

23. Merriam Webster. *Sigil.* https://www.merriam-webster.com/dictionary/sigil

24. You Tube. *The Golden Web Part 1.* https://www.youtube.com/watch?v=5PgX8l9AgzE

25. Online Etymology Dictionary. *Capital.* https://www.etymonline.com/word/capital

26. Online Etymology Dictionary. *Capital.* https://www.etymonline.com/word/capital

27. Online Etymology Dictionary. *Democracy.* https://www.etymonline.com/word/democracy

28. Online Etymology Dictionary. *-cracy.* https://www.etymonline.com/word/-cracy

29. Dictionary. *Franchise.* https://www.dictionary.com/browse/franchise

30. Merriam Webster. *Franchise.* https://www.merriam-webster.com/dictionary/franchise

31. Dictionary. *Idol.* https://www.dictionary.com/browse/idol

32. Online Etymology Dictionary. *Vote.* https://www.etymonline.com/word/vote

33. Online Etymology Dictionary. *Vote.* https://www.etymonline.com/word/vote

34. Online Etymology Dictionary. *Vote.* https://www.etymonline.com/word/vote

35. Dictionary. *Vote.* https://www.dictionary.com/browse/vote

36. Collins Dictionary. *Vote.* https://www.collinsdictionary.com/us/dictionary/english/vote

37. Merriam Webster. *Suffrage.* https://www.merriam-webster.com/dictionary/suffrage

38. Dictionary. *Franchise.* https://www.dictionary.com/browse/franchise

39. The Law Dictionary. *What is Parent Corporation?* https://thelawdictionary.org/parent-corporation/

40. Dictionary. *Enfranchise.* https://www.dictionary.com/browse/enfranchise

41. Dictionary. *God.* https://www.dictionary.com/browse/god

42. Dictionary. *Idol.* https://www.dictionary.com/browse/idol

43. Lexico. *Abstract.* https://www.lexico.com/en/definition/abstract

44. Dictionary. *Idolatry.* https://www.dictionary.com/browse/idolatry

45. Dictionary. *Vote.* https://www.dictionary.com/browse/vote

46. Dictionary. *Pole.* https://www.dictionary.com/browse/pole

47. You Tube. *The Golden Web Part 1.* https://www.youtube.com/watch?v=5PgX8l9AgzE

48. Online Etymology Dictionary. *Vote.* https://www.etymonline.com/word/vote

49. Online Etymology Dictionary. *Elect.* https://www.etymonline.com/word/elect

50. The Free Dictionary. *Free Will.* https://www.thefreedictionary.com/free+will

51. Online Etymology Dictionary. *Elite.* https://www.etymonline.com/word/elite

52. New World Encyclopedia. *El.* https://www.newworldencyclopedia.org/entry/El

53. Dictionary. *Sig.* https://www.dictionary.com/browse/sig

54. Dictionary. *Signa.* https://www.dictionary.com/browse/signa

55. Online Etymology Dictionary. *Nature.* https://www.etymonline.com/word/nature

56. Online Etymology Dictionary. *Nature.* https://www.etymonline.com/word/nature

Chapter 4

1. Online Etymology Dictionary. *Kindergarten.* https://www.etymonline.com/word/kindergarten

2. Dictionary. *Garden.* https://www.dictionary.com/browse/garden

3. Online Etymology Dictionary. *Elohim.* https://www.etymonline.com/word/Elohim

4. Hebrew for Christians. *Hebrew Names of God.* https://www.hebrew4christians.com/Names_of_G-

d/Elohim/elohim.html

5. Hebrew Streams. *"Elohim" in Biblical Context.* http://www.hebrew-streams.org/works/monotheism/context-elohim.html

6. Online Etymology Dictionary. *Extra-.* https://www.etymonline.com/word/extra-

7. Online Etymology Dictionary. *Terrestrial.* https://www.etymonline.com/word/terrestrial

8. Lat Dict. *Siri.* http://latin-dictionary.net/search/latin/siri

9. Lat Dict. *Canus.* http://latin-dictionary.net/search/latin/canus

10. Lat Dict. *Canis.* http://latin-dictionary.net/search/latin/canis

11. The Free Dictionary. *Verse.* https://www.thefreedictionary.com/verse

12. Bible Gateway. *Matthew 13:34-35.* https://www.biblegateway.com/passage/? search=Matthew+13%3A34-35&version=NIV

13. Online Etymology Dictionary. *Adam.* https://www.etymonline.com/word/adam

14. Dictionary. *Atman.* https://www.dictionary.com/browse/atman

15. Online Etymology Dictionary. *Genesis.* https://www.etymonline.com/word/genesis

16. Online Etymology Dictionary. *Genuis.* https://www.etymonline.com/word/genius

17. Online Etymology Dictionary. *Gene.* https://www.etymonline.com/word/gene

18. Scitable. *The Language of DNA.* https://www.nature.com/scitable/blog/accumulating-glitches/the_language_of_dna

19. Techopedia. *Transhumanism.* https://www.techopedia.com/definition/31624/transhumanism

20. Gnostic Warrior. *From Atom to Adam to Red Man.* https://gnosticwarrior.com/atom-adam.html

21. The Illuminatus Observor. *The Garden of Eden as an Occult Construct.*

http://illuminatusobservor.blogspot.com/2008/05/garden-of-eden-as-occult-construct.html

22. You Tube. *The Golden Web Part 1.* https://www.youtube.com/watch?v=5PgX8l9AgzE

23. Online Etymology Dictionary. *Rapture.* https://www.etymonline.com/word/rapture

24. The Free Dictionary. *Bay.* https://www.thefreedictionary.com/bay

25. The Free Dictionary. *Colony.* https://legal-dictionary.thefreedictionary.com/colony

26. Online Etymology Dictionary. *Spell.* https://www.etymonline.com/word/spell

27. Encyclopedia. *Spells.* https://www.encyclopedia.com/philosophy-and-religion/other-religious-beliefs-and-general-terms/religion-general/incantations

28. Online Etymology Dictionary. *Gospel.* https://www.etymonline.com/word/gospel

29. Dictionary. *Spell.* https://www.dictionary.com/browse/spell

30. Dictionary. *Magic.* https://www.dictionary.com/browse/magic

31. Online Etymology Dictionary. *Magic.* https://www.etymonline.com/word/magic

32. Merriam Webster. *Sigil.* https://www.merriam-webster.com/dictionary/sigil

33. Dictionary. *Alchemy.* https://www.dictionary.com/browse/alchemy

34. Cambridge Dictionary. *Curse.* https://dictionary.cambridge.org/us/dictionary/english/curse

Chapter 5

1. Dictionary. *Bench.* https://www.dictionary.com/browse/bench

2. Online Etymology Dictionary. *Contract.* https://www.etymonline.com/word/contract

3. Dictionary. *Con.* https://www.dictionary.com/browse/con

4. Dictionary. *Tract.* https://www.dictionary.com/browse/tract

5. Dictionary. *Corpse.* https://www.dictionary.com/browse/corpse

6. Dictionary. *Act.* https://www.dictionary.com/browse/act

7. The Free Dictionary. *Magistrate.* https://legal-dictionary.thefreedictionary.com/magistrate

8. Dictionary. *Magistrate.* https://www.dictionary.com/browse/magistrate

9. Online Etymology Dictionary. *Magi.* https://www.etymonline.com/word/magi

10. Dictionary. *Strait.* https://www.dictionary.com/browse/strait

11. The Free Dictionary. *Magistrate.* https://legal-dictionary.thefreedictionary.com/magistrate

12. Online Etymology Dictionary. *Bank.* https://www.etymonline.com/word/bank

13. Dictionary. *Bank.* https://www.dictionary.com/browse/bank

14. Dictionary. *Bank.* https://www.dictionary.com/browse/bank

15. Dictionary. *Galley.* https://www.dictionary.com/browse/galley

16. Dictionary. *Oar.* https://www.dictionary.com/browse/oar

17. Merriam Webster. *Font.* https://www.merriam-webster.com/dictionary/font

18. Dictionary. *Font.* https://www.dictionary.com/browse/font

19. Dictionary. *Convict.* https://www.dictionary.com/browse/convict

20. Word Reference. *Vict.* https://www.wordreference.com/definition/-vict-

21. Dictionary. *Victim.* https://www.dictionary.com/browse/victim

22. Dictionary. *Sentence.* https://www.dictionary.com/browse/sentence

23. Online Etymology Dictionary. *Sentence.* https://www.etymonline.com/word/sentence

24. Dictionary. *Rite.* https://www.dictionary.com/browse/rite

25. Dictionary. *Book.* https://www.dictionary.com/browse/book

26. Dictionary. *Book.* https://www.dictionary.com/browse/book

27. Dictionary. *Book.* https://www.dictionary.com/browse/book

28. Dictionary. *Chapter.* https://www.dictionary.com/browse/chapter

29. Dictionary. *Page.* https://www.dictionary.com/browse/page

30. Dictionary. *Page.* https://www.dictionary.com/browse/page

31. Online Etymology Dictionary. *Fraternity.* https://www.etymonline.com/word/fraternity

32. Wikipedia. *Bar (Law).* https://en.wikipedia.org/wiki/Bar_(law)

33. Dictionary. *Bar.* https://www.dictionary.com/browse/bar

34. Dictionary. *Bar.* https://www.dictionary.com/browse/bar

35. Online Etymology Dictionary. *Liquor.* https://www.etymonline.com/word/liquor

36. Online Etymology Dictionary. *Liquor.* https://www.etymonline.com/word/liquor

37. Dictionary. *Liquor.* https://www.dictionary.com/browse/liquor

38. Dictionary. *Spirit.* https://www.dictionary.com/browse/spirit

39. Online Etymology Dictionary. *Alcohol.* https://www.etymonline.com/word/alcohol

40. Online Etymology Dictionary. *Ghoul.* https://www.etymonline.com/word/ghoul

41. Dictionary. *Kohl.* https://www.dictionary.com/browse/kohl

42. Online Etymology Dictionary. *Kuhl.* https://www.etymonline.com/word/kohl

43. Online Etymology Dictionary. *Aqua Vitae.* https://www.etymonline.com/word/aqua%20vitae

44. Online Etymology Dictionary. *Aqua Vitae.* https://www.etymonline.com/word/aqua%20vitae

45. Maxwell, Jordan. *Matrix of Power: Secrets of World Control.* The Book Tree. San Diego, CA. 2000.

46. Dictionary. *Cassock.* https://www.dictionary.com/browse/cassock

47. You Tube. *The Golden Web Part 1.*

https://www.youtube.com/watch?v=5PgX8l9AgzE

48. Dictionary. *Battery.* https://www.dictionary.com/browse/battery

49. You Tube. *The Golden Web Part 1.*
https://www.youtube.com/watch?v=5PgX8l9AgzE

50. You Tube. *The Golden Web Part 1.*
https://www.youtube.com/watch?v=5PgX8l9AgzE

51. Turkish Dictionary. *Ant.* http://www.turkishdictionary.net/?
word=ant

52. Hebrew Streams. *"Elohim" in Biblical Context.*
http://www.hebrew-streams.org/works/monotheism/context-
elohim.html

53. Abarim Publications. *The name El in the Bible.*
http://www.abarim-publications.com/Meaning/El.html#.Vt-
EouaYu4Q

54. Online Etymology Dictionary. *Allah.*
https://www.etymonline.com/word/Allah

55. Maxwell, Jordan. *Matrix of Power: Secrets of World Control.* The
Book Tree. San Diego, CA. 2000.

56. Dictionary. *Order.* https://www.dictionary.com/browse/order

57. Dictionary. *Order.* https://www.dictionary.com/browse/order

58. Online Etymology Dictionary. *Currency.*
https://www.etymonline.com/word/currency

59. Dictionary. *Current.* https://www.dictionary.com/browse/current

60. Dictionary. *Electrolyte.*
https://www.dictionary.com/browse/electrolyte

61. Wikipedia. *Qi.* https://en.wikipedia.org/wiki/Qi

62. Dictionary. *Currency.*
https://www.dictionary.com/browse/currency

63. Dictionary. *Medium.*
https://www.dictionary.com/browse/medium

64. The Free Dictionary. *Mediums.*
https://www.thefreedictionary.com/mediums

65. Online Etymology Dictionary. *Crypto.*
https://www.etymonline.com/word/crypto-

66. Online Etymology Dictionary. *Currency.*
https://www.etymonline.com/word/currency

67. Online Etymology Dictionary. *Crypt.*
https://www.etymonline.com/word/crypt

68. Dictionary. *Crypt.* https://www.dictionary.com/browse/crypt

69. You Tube. *Theoretical Physicist Finds Computer Code in String Theory.* https://www.youtube.com/watch?v=cvMlUepVgbA

70. Dictionary. *Commerce.*
https://www.dictionary.com/browse/commerce

71. Dictionary. *Commerce.*
https://www.dictionary.com/browse/commerce

72. Online Etymology Dictionary. *Com-.*
https://www.etymonline.com/word/com-

73. Online Etymology Dictionary. *Commerce.*
https://www.etymonline.com/word/commerce

74. Online Etymology Dictionary. *Commerce.*
https://www.etymonline.com/word/commerce

75. Dictionary. *Trafficking.*
https://www.dictionary.com/browse/trafficking

76. Dictionary. *Trafficking.*
https://www.dictionary.com/browse/trafficking

77. The Law Dictionary. *What Is Trafficking.*
https://thelawdictionary.org/trafficking/

78. Bible Gateway. *Romans 6:23.*
https://www.biblegateway.com/passage/?
search=Romans+6:23&version=KJV

79. The Free Dictionary. *Screw.*
https://www.thefreedictionary.com/screw

80. Dictionary. *Screw.* https://www.dictionary.com/browse/screw

81. Dictionary. *Coitus.* https://www.dictionary.com/browse/coitus

82. You Tube. *The Golden Web Part 1.*

https://www.youtube.com/watch?v=5PgX8l9AgzE

83. Online Etymology Dictionary. *Trader.*
https://www.etymonline.com/word/

84. Dictionary. *Trader.* https://www.dictionary.com/browse/trader

85. Dictionary. *Traitor.* https://www.dictionary.com/browse/traitor

86. Dictionary. *Stock.* https://www.dictionary.com/browse/stock

87. Dictionary. *Livestock.*
https://www.dictionary.com/browse/livestock

88. Dictionary. *Stock.* https://www.dictionary.com/browse/stock

89. Online Etymology Dictionary. *Stock.*
https://www.etymonline.com/word/stock

90. Online Etymology Dictionary. *Trunk.*
https://www.etymonline.com/word/trunk

91. Dictionary. *Trunk.* https://www.dictionary.com/browse/trunk

92. Dictionary. *Trunk.* https://www.dictionary.com/browse/trunk

93. Dictionary. *Mortgage.*
https://www.dictionary.com/browse/mortgage

94. Lexico. *Mortgage.*
https://www.lexico.com/en/definition/mortgage

95. Online Etymology Dictionary. *Mortgage.*
https://www.etymonline.com/word/mortgage

96. Online Etymology Dictionary. *Mortgage.*
https://www.etymonline.com/word/mortgage

97. Online Etymology Dictionary. *Pledge.*
https://www.etymonline.com/word/pledge

98. Online Etymology Dictionary. *Pledge.*
https://www.etymonline.com/word/pledge

99. Dictionary. *Pledge.* https://www.dictionary.com/browse/pledge

100. Dictionary. *Corpse.* https://www.dictionary.com/browse/corpse

101. Online Etymology Dictionary. *Sin.*
https://www.etymonline.com/word/sin

102. Bible Gateway. *Romans 6:23.*
https://www.biblegateway.com/passage/?
search=Romans+6:23&version=KJV

103. Online Etymology Dictionary. *Tender.*
https://www.etymonline.com/word/tender

104. The Free Dictionary. *Tenant.* https://legal-
dictionary.thefreedictionary.com/tenant

105. The Free Dictionary. *Tenant.* https://legal-
dictionary.thefreedictionary.com/tenant

Chapter 6

1. Online Etymology Dictionary. *Gospel.*
https://www.etymonline.com/word/gospel

2. Bible Gateway. *John 8:12.*
https://www.biblegateway.com/passage/?
search=John+8:12&version=ESV

3. Bible Gateway. *John 9:5.* https://www.biblegateway.com/passage/?
search=John+9:5&version=ESV

4. Bible Gateway. *John 8:12.*
https://www.biblegateway.com/passage/?
search=John+8:12&version=ESV

5. Bible Gateway. *Mark 13:26.*
https://www.biblegateway.com/passage/?
search=Mark+13:26&version=ESV

6. Bible Gateway. *John 19:5.*
https://www.biblegateway.com/passage/?
search=John+19:5&version=ESV

7. Online Etymology Dictionary. *Crown.*
https://www.etymonline.com/word/crown

8. Dictionary. *Corona.* https://www.dictionary.com/browse/corona

9. Wikipedia. *Orion's Belt.*
https://en.wikipedia.org/wiki/Orion's_Belt

10. Earth Sky. *Sirius is Dog Star and Brightest Star.*
https://earthsky.org/brightest-stars/sirius-the-brightest-star

11. Biblioteca Pleyades. *The Pagan Origins of Jesus Christ and Christianity.* http://www.bibliotecapleyades.net/biblianazar/esp_biblianazar_33.htm

12. Online Etymology Dictionary. *Lucifer.* https://www.etymonline.com/word/Lucifer

13. Online Etymology Dictionary. *Lucifer.* https://www.etymonline.com/word/Lucifer

14. Flowers, Stephen. *Fire & Ice: The History, Structure, and Rituals of Germany's Most Influential Modern Magical Order: The Brotherhood of Saturn.* Llewellyn Publications. St. Paul, MN. 1994.

15. French Linguistics. *Je.* http://www.french-linguistics.co.uk/dictionary/je.html

16. Numen - The Latin Lexicon. *Sus.* https://latinlexicon.org/definition.php?p1=1015706

17. Bab. *Je Suis.* https://en.bab.la/dictionary/french-english/je-suis

18. Your Dictionary. *I-Am.* https://www.yourdictionary.com/i-am

19. Abarim Publications. *Christ Meaning.* http://www.abarim-publications.com/Meaning/Christ.html#.WWp8XlGQzIW

20. Online Etymology Dictionary. *Messiah.* https://www.etymonline.com/word/Messiah

21. Abarim Publications. *Christ Meaning.* http://www.abarim-publications.com/Meaning/Christ.html#.XVLjmXt7lPb

22. Carey, George W. and Perry, Inez P. *God-Man: The Word Made Flesh.* The Chemistry of Life Co. Los Angeles, California. 1920.

23. Online Etymology Dictionary. *Occult.* https://www.etymonline.com/word/occult

24. Mystery Babylon. *The Christmas Connection.* http://mystery-babylon.org/index.html

25. The Free Dictionary. *Mass.* https://www.thefreedictionary.com/mass

26. Online Etymology Dictionary. *Mass.* https://www.etymonline.com/word/mass

27. Online Etymology Dictionary. *Christ.*
https://www.etymonline.com/word/Christ

28. Dictionary. *What Is the X in Xmas?*
https://blog.dictionary.com/xmas-christogram/

29. Lat Dict. *Mas.* http://www.latin-dictionary.net/search/latin/mas

30. Simple To Remember. *The History of Christmas.*
https://www.simpletoremember.com/vitals/Christmas_TheRealStory
.htm

31. The Tech. *DNA Basics.* http://genetics.thetech.org/ask/ask456

32. Dictionary. *Chroma.* https://www.dictionary.com/browse/chroma

33. Dictionary. *Soma.* https://www.dictionary.com/browse/soma

34. Dictionary. *Hue.* https://www.dictionary.com/browse/hue

35. Online Etymology Dictionary. *Eucharist.*
https://www.etymonline.com/word/Eucharist

36. Lexico. *Eucharist.*
https://www.lexico.com/en/definition/eucharist

37. Online Etymology Dictionary. *Manna.*
https://www.etymonline.com/word/manna

38. Online Etymology Dictionary. *Saint.*
https://www.etymonline.com/word/saint

39. Online Etymology Dictionary. *Saint.*
https://www.etymonline.com/word/saint

40. Online Etymology Dictionary. *House.*
https://www.etymonline.com/word/house

41. Dictionary. *Harvest.* https://www.dictionary.com/browse/harvest

42. Online Etymology Dictionary. *Harvest.*
https://www.etymonline.com/word/harvest

43. Online Etymology Dictionary. *Ripe.*
https://www.etymonline.com/word/ripe

44. Online Etymology Dictionary. *Ascension.*
https://www.etymonline.com/word/ascension

45. Springfield Springfield. *Jupiter Ascending (2015) Movie Script.*

https://www.springfieldspringfield.co.uk/movie_script.php?
movie=jupiter-ascending

46. Freemasons Freemasonry. *The Sacred Pentagram.*
http://www.freemasons-
freemasonry.com/pentagram_freemasonry.html

47. Amazing Discoveries. *Paganism and Catholicism: Christmas.*
https://amazingdiscoveries.org/S-
deception_Catholic_pagan_Christmas_feasts

48. Dictionary. *Devil.* https://www.dictionary.com/browse/devil

49. Online Etymology Dictionary. *Nick.*
https://www.etymonline.com/word/Nick

50. Online Etymology Dictionary. *Saint.*
https://www.etymonline.com/word/saint

51. Dictionary. *Holly.* https://www.dictionary.com/browse/holly

52. Glosbe. *Sancta Sedes.* https://glosbe.com/la/en/Sancta%20Sedes

53. Online Etymology Dictionary. *Saint.*
https://www.etymonline.com/word/saint

54. Dicios. *Holly.* http://en.dicios.com/enno/holly

55. Online Etymology Dictionary. *Christ.*
https://www.etymonline.com/word/Christ

56. Merriam Webster. *Claustrum.* https://www.merriam-
webster.com/dictionary/claustrum

57. Dictionary. *Claw.* https://www.dictionary.com/browse/claw

58. Dictionary. *Clause.* https://www.dictionary.com/browse/clause

59. Carey, George W. and Perry, Inez P. *God-Man: The Word Made
Flesh.* The Chemistry of Life Co. Los Angeles, California. 1920.

60. Bible Gateway. *Matthew 6:22.*
https://www.biblegateway.com/passage/?
search=Matthew+6:22&version=ESV

61. Online Etymology Dictionary. *Easter.*
https://www.etymonline.com/word/Easter

62. Dictionary. *Easter.* https://www.dictionary.com/browse/easter

63. Gnostic Warrior. *What is the meaning of Easter?*
https://gnosticwarrior.com/easter.html

64. Last Trumpet Ministries. *The Pagan Origin of Easter.*
http://www.lasttrumpetministries.org/tracts/tract1.html

65. Last Trumpet Ministries. *The Pagan Origin of Easter.*
http://www.lasttrumpetministries.org/tracts/tract1.html

Twenty Solutions to Free Mankind

1. Ouaknin, Marc-Alain. *Mysteries of the Alphabet.* Abbeville Press Publishers. New York, NY. 1999.

2. Jewish Encyclopedia. *Dual.*
http://www.jewishencyclopedia.com/articles/5339-dual

3. Ouaknin, Marc-Alain. *Mysteries of the Alphabet.* Abbeville Press Publishers. New York, NY. 1999.

4. Ouaknin, Marc-Alain. *Mysteries of the Alphabet.* Abbeville Press Publishers. New York, NY. 1999.

5. Online Etymology Dictionary. *Primal.*
https://www.etymonline.com/word/primal

6. Online Etymology Dictionary. *Alpha.*
https://www.etymonline.com/word/alpha

7. Online Etymology Dictionary. *Descend.*
https://www.etymonline.com/word/descend

8. Bible Gateway. *John 6:41.*
https://www.biblegateway.com/passage/?search=John+6%3A41&version=NKJV

9. Ouaknin, Marc-Alain. *Mysteries of the Alphabet.* Abbeville Press Publishers. New York, NY. 1999.

10. Ouaknin, Marc-Alain. *Mysteries of the Alphabet.* Abbeville Press Publishers. New York, NY. 1999.

11. Ouaknin, Marc-Alain. *Mysteries of the Alphabet.* Abbeville Press Publishers. New York, NY. 1999.

12. Online Etymology Dictionary. *Nun.*
https://www.etymonline.com/word/nun

13. Latin Lexicon. *Definition of Sus.* https://latinlexicon.org/definition.php?p1=1015706

14. Forrest, Isidora M. *Isis Magic.* Abiegnus House. Portland, Oregon. 2013.

15. Carey, George W. and Perry, Inez P. *God-Man: The Word Made Flesh.* The Chemistry of Life Co. Los Angeles, California. 1920.

16. Learner's Dictionary. *Trinity.* http://learnersdictionary.com/definition/trinity

17. Dictionary. *Change.* https://www.dictionary.com/browse/change

18. Merriam Webster. *Change.* https://www.merriam-webster.com/dictionary/change

Index

About the Author

2019

Pao Chang is the author and founder of EsotericKnowledge.me, an empowering blog that teaches people about esoteric knowledge, genuine spirituality, word magic, legalese, freedom, sovereignty, and law. He loves to explore the mystery of alternative medicine, quantum mechanics, spirituality, consciousness, sacred words, sacred geometry, occult knowledge, and God's Law (Natural Law).